**Selected Plays by Cuban Playwright
Abel González Melo**

Selected Plays by Cuban Playwright Abel González Melo

Chamaco (Kiddo)
Nevada
Weathered
Outside the Game
Tell Me the Whole Thing Again
Abyss

Translated by
WILLIAM GREGORY

methuen | drama
LONDON · NEW YORK · OXFORD · NEW DELHI · SYDNEY

METHUEN DRAMA
Bloomsbury Publishing Plc
50 Bedford Square, London, WC1B 3DP, UK
1385 Broadway, New York, NY 10018, USA
29 Earlsfort Terrace, Dublin 2, Ireland

BLOOMSBURY, METHUEN DRAMA and the Methuen Drama logo are trademarks of
Bloomsbury Publishing Plc

First published in Great Britain 2024

Copyright © Abel González Melo, 2024
English Translation © William Gregory, 2024

The authors have asserted their right under the Copyright, Designs and Patents Act, 1988, to be identified as authors of this work.

Cover illustration © Gita Govinda Kowlessur

All rights reserved. No part of this publication may be reproduced or transmitted in any form or by any means, electronic or mechanical, including photocopying, recording, or any information storage or retrieval system, without prior permission in writing from the publishers.

Bloomsbury Publishing Plc does not have any control over, or responsibility for, any third-party websites referred to or in this book. All internet addresses given in this book were correct at the time of going to press. The author and publisher regret any inconvenience caused if addresses have changed or sites have ceased to exist, but can accept no responsibility for any such changes.

All rights whatsoever in this play are strictly reserved and application for performance etc. should be made before rehearsals to Bloomsbury Publishing Plc of 50 Bedford Square, London, WC1B 3DP, UK. No performance may be given unless a licence has been obtained. No rights in incidental music or songs contained in the Translation are hereby granted and performance rights for any performance/presentation whatsoever must be obtained from the respective copyright owners.

A catalogue record for this book is available from the British Library.

A catalog record for this book is available from the Library of Congress.

ISBN: HB: 978-1-3504-5379-1
PB: 978-1-3504-5378-4
ePDF: 978-1-3504-5381-4
eBook: 978-1-3504-5380-7

Series: Methuen Drama Play Collections

Typeset by Newgen KnowledgeWorks Pvt. Ltd., Chennai, India
Printed and bound in Great Britain

To find out more about our authors and books visit www.bloomsbury.com and sign up for our newsletters.

Contents

Introduction by Ernesto Fundora 1
Author's Note by Abel González Melo 5
Translator's Note by William Gregory 7
Chamaco (Kiddo) 9
Nevada 57
Weathered 111
Outside the Game 173
Tell Me the Whole Thing Again 229
Abyss 279
Glossary 327
Author and Translator Bios 333

Introduction

A Stage the Size of the World

When theatre director Carlos Celdrán premiered Abel González Melo's *Chamaco* (*Kiddo*) in Havana in 2006, Cuban theatre was entering uncharted territory. Piece by piece, the play's 'ten chapters for performance' dismantled a range of elements that had become characteristic of Cuban playwriting.

Revising the widespread acceptance of realism – and its linear temporality – as a mode of construction, González Melo proposes a fragmented structure, narrating events through analeptic scenes ('flashbacks' to earlier points in the story), prolepsis ('flashing forward' to a point later in the plot), and the coexistence onstage of multiple spaces. In contrast to the traditional understanding of family as a heteronormative, patriarchal, fixed social structure, *Chamaco* presents a queer family with an absent mother and a *pater familias* who deviates from his conventional role. In its dialogue with a complex reality, *Chamaco* also displays onstage a gallery of themes never addressed in such a way before, in all their brutality and deprivation (rampant corruption, police extortion, male prostitution, trafficking, family disintegration, queer identities and the violence that secretly infiltrates the characters' lives, among others), depicting a very different cityscape of Havana. Having been produced almost all over the world, translated into twelve languages and published in several anthologies, *Chamaco* has already entered the Cuban theatrical canon, a status reserved for only the truly greatest plays. Therefore, opening this collection of Abel González Melo's *Selected Plays* with *Chamaco* not only acknowledges a seminal text of Cuban theatre history, but also offers an objective point of departure from which better to access the other five plays compiled in this volume.

Born in Havana in 1980, Abel González Melo studied Theatre in the Cuban capital's University of the Arts (ISA). He was a member of the generation of playwrights that started to publish and be produced towards the end of the 1990s and the beginning of the new millennium, after the crisis that resulted from the collapse of the Soviet Union and the subsequent debacle for the Cuban economy and daily life on the island. He would witness onstage the works of the great Cuban theatre-makers still active at that time, including Vicente and Raquel Revuelta, Roberto Blanco and Berta Martínez, along with productions by companies established in the 1980s like Teatro Buendía and DanzAbierta. As an audience member first, then as a professional, he would also experience the new dramatic languages forged in the aesthetics of theatre groups founded in the 1990s, such as Carlos Díaz's Teatro El Público, Nelda Castillo's El Ciervo Encantado, Carlos Celdrán's Argos Teatro and Raúl Martín's Teatro de la Luna, to name a few. In 2006 González Melo established himself in Madrid, where he continued his studies at the Complutense University, completing his PhD in Literary Studies in 2017 under the supervision of José Luis García Barrientos, one of the most prominent and influential contemporary theatre theorists.

An expert in – and devotee of – the classical authors of Western theatre, González Melo began early in his career to write in trilogies, just as the tragedians of classical Athens had done. But unlike those of his Greek predecessors, the plays in González

Melo's triptychs are not presented as a continuous narrative, nor are they thematically linked. Rather, they are connected by a common approach to a diverse collection of social, political or historical circumstances. As an avid reader of canonical Cuban playwrights such as Gertrudis Gómez de Avellaneda, Joaquín Lorenzo Luaces, Virgilio Piñera, José Triana, Abelardo Estorino, Antón Arrufat and Raquel Carrió, González Melo shared with them the desire to find a theatrical language that would support both coherent dramatic structures and an authentic understanding of the most pressing dilemmas of their time.

Fugas de invierno (*Winter Escapes*), his first trilogy, encompassed *Chamaco* (2004), *Nevada* (2005) and *Talco* (*Talc*, 2009). The plays centre around escape in its many forms – from reality, from a country, from life. Perhaps no other Cuban playwright has captured the secret dynamics of Havana, that many-faced city, like González Melo has, constructing his plots by opting to look at the centre from the margins. *Chamaco* and *Nevada* reveal a social fabric where all interactions are transactional. Money, sex, food, the body, anything goes as long as you can escape such a world; towards a life without misery and scarcity in *Chamaco*; towards Las Vegas and a promising future sketched in neon lights in *Nevada*. The author depicts a repressive reality through the very language, behaviours and codes that are used to disguise it. In both plays, marginality itself seems to have the power to trigger utopia, as borne out in their respective final scenes: one final act of heroism performed by an anti-hero in *Chamaco*, and a snowfall – a *nevada* in Spanish – that buries every desire, every spoken word, everything.

Intemperie (*Weathered*, 2016) and *Fuera del juego* (*Outside the Game*, 2018) revisit two key moments of Cuba's history. In *Intemperie*, the 1994 exodus – in which many Cubans left the island in almost anything that could float, hoping to reach the coasts of Florida – and a return twenty years later set the scene for a heartbreaking reflection on the meanings of family, parenthood and exile in a world where politics is all-destroying. *Fuera del juego*, meanwhile, is the third piece in a trilogy devoted to exploring the always-tense dialogue between Power, Poetry and Censorship across the three main periods of Cuban national history: Colonial, Republican and Revolutionary. The first play, *Cádiz en José Martí* (*Cadiz in José Martí*, 2020), follows the journey of Cuba's national hero on his arrival in Spain after being banished from the island by the colonial authorities for political reasons. *Bayamesa* (2019) – winner of the prestigious Casa de las Américas International Award in 2020 – explores the circumstances surrounding Cuban poet María Luisa Milanés' life and suicide in the early twentieth century. *Fuera del juego* completes the trilogy and centres around the Padilla Case of 1971.

Viewed together, these three plays exemplify a genre González Melo has coined as *ficción documental* (documentary fiction), a creative writing exercise where dramatic fiction arises from a rigorous exploration of the archive, revealing gaps the author can then fill through a fictional account of actions that *could have happened*, and where the collision of competing narratives in search of the truth – that of the archive, and that of the fiction – becomes the driver for theatrical performance. By accessing such major historical events through the perspectives of individual subjectivity, the plays invite the audience into scenic spaces where they can consider the consequences of maintaining intellectual integrity in a political and social order that privileges precisely the opposite. In private, marginal spaces, the power of individual imagination becomes the centre from which all perspectives emerge, a sort of Vitruvian Man transferred to a stage the size of the world. Facing the impossibility of knowing what really happened, González Melo stages competing memories by moving the action back and forth along the temporal axis, like a hand plane removing layer after layer in an effort to uncover the truth – not a historical truth, nor a scientific truth, but a theatrical one: a truth that might lead to an understanding of fiction as a strategy, where theatre can make use of those places where the archive offers only silence.

González Melo has also benefitted from working alongside actors and directors, in addition to serving as an accomplished theatre director himself. These opportunities have allowed him to experience playwriting from the very stages he writes for. In something of an homage to theatre itself, *Vuelve a contármelo todo* (*Tell Me the Whole Thing Again*, 2015) and *Abismo* (*Abyss*, 2022), respectively, reimagine William Shakespeare's *Macbeth* and Arthur Miller's *The Crucible* not as versions, nor as rereadings, but as explorations of the potency of their respective original conflicts, relocated to the contemporary world in all its beauty, acceleration and drive for self-destruction. Here, two theatre companies serve as microcosms from which to explore the turbulent relationship between insatiable desire and its customary outcomes, ranging from the endless hunger for recognition and success to its impact in the light of recent protest movements related to gender and racial justice. Thus, the final two plays of this volume open sundry avenues for the dramatic imagination concerning the ethical dimensions of contemporary social debates.

Translating theatre also entails the construction of a language that will be *inhabited* onstage. William Gregory's translation of Abel González Melo's plays is attentive to the centrality the author gives to certain linguistic structures and expressions. In finding the right equivalencies to colloquial language and idioms, his careful work as a theatre translator allows these plays to speak to English-speaking audiences with all the vitality and distinctiveness with which they were originally conceived in the playwright's vibrant Spanish. This edition of González Melo's *Selected Plays* illustrates how playwriting can locate spaces from which to capture gestures, behaviours, strategies and words that challenge the social and political order and its narratives of victory, equality and prosperity.

The protagonists of these plays are often individuals looking within from the edges. There may be room for a final heroic act in a boy from the countryside who sells himself, traffics and kills. It may snow in Havana, the flurries falling over a city claimed by corruption and darkness. The most intimate, domestic discussions can shed light on a silenced past. Echoes of Shakespeare's and Miller's masterpieces can lure age-old themes of plotting, rivalry and thirst for power into new spaces. González Melo offers both a radical approach to reality and a very particular way of articulating it onstage. Through words in which it is difficult not to recognize our own desires and failures, these *Selected Plays* quietly unveil for their audience a subtle assertion: in the constant search for human fulfilment, faced with our own incompleteness, perhaps theatre offers an unending possibility: that of filling the emptiness we all bear within ourselves.

Ernesto Fundora
University of Jamestown
May 2024

Author's Note

To Traverse Desire

I am deeply moved to be writing a few words introducing this book to an English-speaking readership. First, because this project has arisen from a two-decade collaboration with my translator and friend, William Gregory. Second, because being connected to the English language has been essential to my training and career as a playwright in the UK and the US. And third, because this selection of plays is being published by Bloomsbury, a press in whose titles I have read the works of so many authors I admire.

William and I first met at London's Royal Court Theatre, thanks to that 'fairy godmother' to so many, Elyse Dodgson. That summer of 2005 is also powerfully etched on my memory because of the extraordinary artists who facilitated the work of the International Residency there: Harold Pinter, Tom Stoppard, Caryl Churchill, Stephen Jeffreys, David Hare, Winsome Pinnock, Tanika Gupta and Simon Stephens, as well as the generous companionship of Indhu Rubasingham as the director of my play, *Nevada*.

Since then, fate has had it that William should translate six of my plays, for projects as varied as they have been stimulating. Six plays which, brought together in this volume, might almost seem chosen on purpose, as they offer a broad panorama of my work, both thematically and stylistically, while at the same time representing three important stages of my journey as a playwright.

Havana's nocturnal margins at the beginning of the twenty-first century, the map of strange creatures inhabiting them and the ethical crisis permeating our nation: *Chamaco* and *Nevada*. The clash with Power, the injustice and failure of the political system, and reviewing the past in order to shed some light on the present: *Weathered* and *Outside the Game*. The mystery of theatre and its play of mirrors, the inescapable need to negotiate with tradition and the canon, the brilliance and the darkness of our profession: *Tell Me the Whole Thing Again* and *Abyss*.

I started writing in my teens. The Berlin Wall had fallen and the Soviet project that had kept Cuba afloat was disappearing with it. The comfort of my childhood gave way to massive economic and civic instability, even as the Communist government insisted that the US was still our mortal enemy. Hunger, blackouts and collapse, both material and human, began to take over. Cubans were confined to the Island as everything around us was politicized to the extreme. Sex became both a refuge and a source of pain. I wrote *Chamaco* following the unexpected, violent death of my father: what could I do with all the things we had never said to each other? Then, life in Europe, the fear of the unknown, uncertainty and nostalgia afforded me a healthy distance from which to view the Island and write about it. Drama, tempered by humour and irony, was my escape valve, a way of overcoming the barbarity and desolation.

The stories and language of my playwriting are born from that pain, from that fracturing, from those shadows, from those absences. Rewriting history with the freedom of documentary fiction: being censored in my own country and recognizing myself in the skin of other writers who suffered censorship and exile. I love, and greatly enjoy, playing with the artifice of theatre itself: blurring narrative and drama, disrupting timelines, having multiple actions occur simultaneously in space, finding structures that respond uniquely to each dramaturgical journey.

If there is one thing I seek, it is to make contact with the specific and avoid the general and the obvious. To embrace semi-darkness, hidden urges, ambiguity and whispers. As my mother would say, 'to traverse desire'.

William has found a delicate, ferocious way to embody this truthfully in the beautiful language that is English. More than translating them, he has meticulously rewritten these characters and universes, given them renewed meaning and found them a new home. We invite you to step inside.

Abel González Melo
February 2024
Translated by William Gregory

Translator's Note

A Travelogue

I write this during a stint as Interim Literary Associate at the Royal Court Theatre. This seems fitting, as it was the Royal Court that brought me into contact with Abel's work for the first time. Throughout the early 2000s, under the leadership of the late Elyse Dodgson, then director of the theatre's international projects, the Royal Court invited a cohort of global playwrights to London every summer to work on a new play. Following the first of what would be several new-writing projects in Cuba, a country that was particularly close to Elyse's heart, Abel was invited to take part in the residency of 2005. I was assigned as his translator. *Nevada* was the play that resulted from this collaboration.

My abiding memory of that time is the newness of it all. I had only recently begun translating. The setting of the Royal Court and the brilliance of those around me were imposing. Abel and I were strangers, and I was still feeling my way as a translator. Revisiting *Nevada* almost twenty years later and Abel having rewritten it comprehensively, I see the play and my own work on it in a different light. The text published here is a complete revision of both the play and the translation.

Following the work on *Nevada*, Elyse sent me one of Abel's earlier plays, *Chamaco*, to read. I was won over immediately. It was one of the rare times when I pressed the Royal Court to commission a full translation. Although the English version was never produced at the Royal Court, in 2016, HOME in Manchester programmed it for its then-annual *VIVA!* festival of Latin American art and performance. Under the auspices of the World Stages project, which saw international theatremakers take up residencies in venues across the UK, Abel came to Manchester for the production and was commissioned by HOME to write a new play, *Weathered*.

In the intervening time, both my and Abel's practice had developed and matured. By then, Abel was a prolific playwright whose work had been widely produced and translated. I, meanwhile, had amassed tens of translations for the Royal Court and elsewhere. Abel was shifting from the stories of contemporary Cuba to wider themes. *Outside the Game*, inspired by the title of a book of poems by the play's hero, Heberto Padilla, was a reimagining of one of Latin America's most infamous cases of literary censure, far removed in both time and tone from the underbelly of the Havana night depicted in his earlier works, but no less desirous of peeling away the surface of Cuban society and examining what lay beneath.

Abel's works for Arca Images in Miami, the final two plays in this volume, represented yet another shift. Here, Abel imagines the inner workings of theatre itself, the machinations of those seeking power and the challenges faced by those who already have it. Connoisseurs of dialect will also notice a shift in the voice of the translations here. Written for a US company, they adopt a more transatlantic language.

Bringing these six translations together and working so closely with Abel on them, in rehearsal rooms, over email and Zoom, and on the page as we prepared to submit the manuscripts for this volume, have been a retracing of my journey with him as a playwright. I know we both feel gratitude to our dear Elyse for bringing us together. I write with gratitude to Abel for the privilege of travelling with him through so many worlds of imagination and for all I have learned in them.

William Gregory
January 2024

Chamaco
(Kiddo)

A Report in Ten Chapters
(for Performance)

Chamaco premiered at the Teatro Nacional de Cuba, Havana, on 25 May 2006, produced by Argos Teatro, directed by Carlos Celdrán, with the following cast: Fidel Betancourt, Caleb Casas, Yailín Coppola, Pancho García, Fernando Hechavarría, José Luis Hidalgo, Ulises Peña, Laura Ramos and Daysi Sánchez.

It won the 2005 Spanish Embassy in Cuba Playwriting Award and the 2006 Villanueva Theatre Critics' Award.

This English translation was commissioned by the English Stage Company at the Royal Court Theatre.

It premiered in English at HOME, Manchester, on 21 April 2016, directed by Walter Meierjohann, with the following cast: David Fleeshman, Jason Furnival, David Judge, Jacqueline Pilton, Jamie Samuel, Robin Simpson, Kenny Thompson and Katie West.

For Ariel Díaz Cid

Chapters of the Report

I. Debris

II. A Spy in the House of Love

III. The Moral World

IV. Rents

V. Happy in the Short Term

VI. Tomorrow Is Another Day

VII. Attempts

VIII. Fathers and Sons

IX. Raid

X. Vanishing Point

Persons Involved

Protagonists

Kárel Darín, *a young man*
Alejandro Depás, *a judge*
Miguel Depás, *his son*
Silvia Depás, *his sister*

Witnesses and Snoopers

Roberta López, *warden of a garden square*
Felipe Alejo, *Kárel's uncle*
La Paco, *a flower-seller*
Saúl Alter, *a policeman*

The action takes place in Havana, between Monday 23 and Thursday 26 December, any recent year.

Chapter I

Debris

Outdoors, if so desired. The first minutes of the first hours of Christmas Day. Parque Central, a green square in Old Havana. In the corners, fountains. In the centre, the statue of the hero. Any hero; not ours. We'll not see ours for a while.

A young man's body lies prostrate on the ground.

Roberta López *stopped sweeping some time ago. She crossed the street to the snack bar, La Revoltosa, hoping they'd close up late and give her time to warm up there. But the cashier had already left: for dinner, perhaps, late; or for an early breakfast in the warmth of his family. Then she walked past the high glass doors of the cinema, looked in, and observed her reflected image. She wanted to trust someone, opt for something. But the cars all passed the square without stopping. And the body was still there. She would dictate all this later, for the final write-up of the report, in an exhaustive and organized fashion.*

She has returned to the square and remains still. The broom beside the litterbin.

Along the pavement passes **La Paco**, *a girl, almost, who sells flowers. She carries a basket and, in it, little bouquets wrapped in cocoons of the finest glass. Despite the cold, she wears only a satin miniskirt and organdie blouse, both very tight. A hat with reindeer horns. She stops at the corner.*

Roberta (*approaches slowly. Stares at her*)   You're a man.

La Paco   You're an old woman.

Roberta (*she doesn't want to offend her – offend 'him', she thinks*)   Oh, no, I –

La Paco   Wizened old hag.

Roberta   Watch it ... I'm the warden on this square.

La Paco *does not look at her. She whistles.*

Roberta   I'm guarding the statue of the hero.

La Paco   Big deal.

Roberta   Not that there's ever any trouble; it's so well lit.

La Paco   Fantastic.

Roberta   No, not really. It's not fantastic. Or a 'big deal'. Not to me. Not to me, at least. It passes the time.

The wind filtering through the branches weighs heavier.

Roberta   The things you see.

La Paco   Statue, streetlamps, trees, benches and lots of things besides, right?

Roberta   You're waiting for someone.

Total silence.

You're up to something.

La Paco   Go back to your place, woman, please. You're practically pushing me into the road. I'll get run over.

Roberta   Young lady, there have not been any cars come past here for a good while. I mean, young *man*, there have not been –

La Paco   Listen, I've had enough of this. What do you want me to do? I sell flowers. I'm not giving you one; the diners at El Floridita give me a dollar for them sometimes. Anything else you want to know? I'm waiting for my husband. He's a policeman; have you heard of those?

Roberta   The police better not come here.

La Paco (*she hates repeating herself. She tries to explain. She doesn't see much point, but she explains*)   Well, he is coming; of course he's coming. So go find a bench and have a sleep. Merry Christmas.

Roberta   I shall have nightmares from watching that boy lying there for so long.

La Paco (*observes*)   That's why I gave up drinking. They'll not find me lying in the middle of the street. It'll just be some drunk.

Roberta   No.

La Paco   Is he anything to do with you?

Roberta   No.

La Paco   Word to the wise, then: forget it.

Roberta   I've been walking around for ages trying to forget it ... Ever since I was a girl I've been scared of blood.

La Paco   He's bleeding?

Roberta *points; she retreats to a lamppost on the corner and clings to it.* **La Paco** *approaches the body, crouches, goes to touch it and sees the pool of blood. She covers her face. Puts the basket on the ground.*

La Paco (*returns to where* **Roberta** *is*)   He's a child.

Roberta   A child.

La Paco   And he's dead.

Roberta   No, no.

La Paco (*shakes her*)   Yes, yes, he's dead. His mouth's open, his eyes are rolled back and he's not moving. (*Returns to the body.*) I can still feel the skin warm on his face. Oh, God, so pretty. And it wasn't Sunday, or Monday. It was just a while ago, he died just a while ago … Fighting; it must have been a fight. Sick little squabbles. Play-fights, 'til someone ends up dead … I look after myself, I know this game and I look after myself. That's where I always go: by that block, opposite the cinema. Flirt with whichever guy's there, let him tease me a bit, sweeten me up. They like me, I know they do. Tough guys in their tight shirts. Chat for a bit, then press myself up against them behind the columns. But that's where it ends: no phone numbers, no second dates … Saves trouble. They're dangerous. You see them with their chains, their tattooed shoulders, and you don't imagine it. I've been doing the rounds here for years, I've lived through horrors, but I've never, on my mother's life, I've never seen a man look so peaceful. Not a word. Just the breath of a cigarette beside his lips. Gives me chills. Turns my stomach … Oh, his stomach … God in Heaven, what can his name be? Come here, woman, give me a hand.

Roberta *does not move from the lamppost: frozen there, she watches everything. With great effort* **La Paco** *turns the body face-up. She rummages in his trousers but finds nothing. She searches his coat. Finds an I.D. card in his pocket.*

La Paco (*sighs. Reads*)   Miguel Depás. What a sweet name to die like this, covered in blood, on Christmas Eve.

A motorcycle parks on the corner. **Saúl Alter** *alights from it. He's not wearing a uniform; he tends not to. He stops beside* **Roberta**. *Straight away he spots* **La Paco** *and approaches her.*

Saúl   What does 'corner' mean to you, woman? (*Sees the body.*) What's up with him? (*The blood.*) Fuck … (*Crouches.*)

La Paco   The old woman showed me. His name's Miguel –

Saúl   You touched him?

La Paco   I got close.

Saúl   Why did you touch him?

La Paco   Oh, Saúl, I just did, all right? Anyone would've. He's been killed; that's what matters. He was lying there, next to the baggage who looks after the square. Place looks like a desert now but maybe two hours ago … I'm freezing to death.

Saúl *removes his coat and puts it on her. Hugs her.* **La Paco** *sobs.* **Saúl** *strokes her long, red hair.*

Roberta *approaches.*

La Paco (*to* **Saúl**)   Have you eaten yet? I'll stay for a bit if you like.

Saúl (*opens his wallet and gives her a banknote*)   Take a taxi, go on.

La Paco *puts the banknote away, gives* **Saúl** *a kiss on the cheek, takes her basket of flowers. Looks at* **Roberta**. *Looks at* **Miguel**'*s body and places a flower on his chest. Leaves.*

Roberta I'd never seen him before.

Saúl The killer or the victim?

Roberta It was nearly snowing; I thought he was going to freeze.

Some parts of the square, in darkness until now, light up weakly and open the way for **Roberta**'s *story.*

Chapter II

A Spy in the House of Love

Our hero sits on a bench playing chess.

Loneliness that edges close to fear. 11:35 p.m. on Tuesday, 24 December. Very cold, just as winter tends to be in any decent city, like this one.

Roberta López *sweeps.* **Kárel Darín** *moves the pieces around the board. A white light reflects in their faces and dies down immediately.*

Roberta   There's nothing doing now, child … The snack bar's closing; look: La Revoltosa. I'd run over there if I had three pesos, ask Punche to sell me a drink. But there's nothing falling into my stomach, not unless I swallow my own spit or breathe in and gulp down the air. Not so much as a microbe. I've never seen this dustbin so empty before; it's like a reptile cat's been chasing after the leftover bits of pizza and hot-dog. Nothing on at the pictures since eleven, and there was me planning on watching the midnight show of that film. What's it called? … *American Beauty* … You already saw it, did you? Is it really any good? Punche wanted me to see it last night; said I'd like it. But I had a packet of churros instead. He did go on! Said he'd lend me two pesos if I wanted. Not on your life; he'd try and touch me up afterwards. And today, no cinema, no churros, not a drop to drink or a mouthful of coffee to warm me up. Just the broom, the ground, the wind squeaking through the bay trees like a door that never closes, and the cold coming up through my skirt … You'll freeze in that pullover.

A lad appears. He goes to cross the street but looks at **Kárel***, who looks up. The lad approaches.*

Miguel   My sister's got a boyfriend looks like you.

Smiles and moves away. **Kárel** *looks back to the chessboard. At this moment he wants the lad to return; no one has been past for at least fifteen minutes.* **Miguel** *returns. He should have crossed the street, disappeared and run the few blocks that separate him from his home, but he returns.*

Kárel   You playing?

Miguel   Hard, though.

Kárel   How much you got?

Miguel   Dunno. Seven dollars.

Kárel   Give you a game for five.

Miguel   Not played in a while. Anyway, it's cold.

Kárel   I'm cold. You've got at least three coats on.

Miguel   One thick one.

Kárel   All right.

Miguel   Whites. I'm lucky with whites.

Kárel   White girls, too?

The second smile. **Miguel** *sits. They set up the game.* **Kárel** *has been playing chess since he was fifteen and now he's twenty-one and eleven months. He learnt two weeks after arriving in the city.* **Miguel** *has known chess all his life; his father has been teaching him since primary school. The game seems dynamic. They play and talk.*

Kárel   Watch that queen; don't leave her alone.

Miguel   I'll leave her if I like. She can look after herself.

Kárel   With that knight prowling 'round all the time? Best leave him in one place, I say; put him down and there he stays. Doesn't kick up a fuss. Doesn't even neigh.

Miguel   Your knight's dumb; mine's got a big mouth.

Kárel   Not any more it hasn't.

Miguel   You shouldn't move so quick.

Kárel   Weren't you the prince of the whites?

Miguel   Yes, prince of the blacks.

Kárel   Your girl must be mixed, then.

Miguel   Let me know when you see her.

Kárel   'Cause you do like girls, don't you?

Miguel   D'you like losing so many pawns?

Kárel   Pawns don't matter. No one ever tell you that?

Miguel   And castles don't either?

Kárel   Castles do, yeah.

Miguel   Down falls a castle.

Kárel   Down falls a castle.

Miguel   Really late. Dawn soon.

Kárel   I'll throw the match for a smoke.

Miguel   Shit, man …

Kárel   I won't throw the match for a smoke.

He prefers strong ones, but **Miguel** *smokes menthols.* **Kárel** *felt a little nauseous the last time he tried a menthol cigarette, and if he feels a little nauseous he won't* *feel good, and if he doesn't feel good – we should explain – he might do something careless.*

Kárel Lights make me sick.

Miguel Take it.

Kárel Forget it.

Miguel *insists despite* **Kárel***'s refusals; only because he insists, our boy may acquire a trace of heroism the moment he accepts. He lights the cigarette and smokes.*

Kárel So why you going 'round with so much cash in your pocket?

Miguel Not that much.

Kárel Someone might mug you.

Miguel Who'd do that?

Kárel Just saying. Someone could turn nasty.

Miguel People aren't that evil.

Kárel They turn evil, all of a sudden. Look. (*Pulls a face to scare him.*)

Miguel (*smiles*) Seen scarier things.

Kárel What you gonna do with the money if you beat me?

Miguel Save it up.

Kárel Get married to your little mixed girl? Rent somewhere? Aren't you from Havana?

Miguel Yeah, I'm from here.

Kárel But you don't like your house.

Miguel Do you like yours?

Kárel I'm starving; I'm buying a pizza if I win. One of the nice ones.

Miguel If I let you beat me.

They resume the game.

Kárel What were you saying about your sister?

Miguel When did I mention my sister?

Kárel Said I looked like her boyfriend.

Miguel Don't be stupid.

Kárel She pretty?

Miguel Shut up and play.

Kárel She's not pretty.

Miguel Yeah.

Kárel I like visiting a pretty girl now and then. It's fun, going in the evenings after the gym, taking a taxi if she lives on the other side of the tunnel, turning up with an orchid. All of that if you have money to pay for the gym, pay for the taxi and pay for the flowers, of course. I could. When I make enough money I'm gonna do it with three girls at a time, or five … Play on. Chess is all mechanics, really. D'you know about mechanics?

Miguel Let me think.

Kárel You're taking a minute to move a bishop. Move it here, I reckon.

Miguel Shhh. Better the castle.

Kárel Down falls a second castle and the queen's left exposed.

Miguel I'm threatening your king.

Kárel And I eat up the knight that's threatening it.

Miguel I come back with the bishop.

Kárel And the queen drops dead. Check.

Miguel I take this knight; freaking me out.

Kárel And I take the bishop. Check mate. How much did we say?

The wind freezes one of **Miguel**'s *ears.*

Miguel *tuts.*

Kárel How much did we say?

Miguel (*watches in silence. He knocks over his white king. He rises*) Some other night. I'm in a rush.

Kárel The money.

Miguel What?

Kárel The five dollars. Get your wallet out and give me the five dollars.

Miguel Let's leave it there; I'll see you 'round one night.

Kárel (*rises*) Are you out of your mind? Give me the money.

Roberta (*a few steps away, rummages in the rubbish bin*) Don't kick up a fuss, child; it's Christmas Eve. Give me the money and I'll give it to him … (*Sings.*) 'If I had a peso I'd buy myself a good night and a beautiful day …'

Miguel *makes a half-turn and hurries to leave.*

Kárel (*holds him from behind*) I said 'give me it', you bastard.

Miguel Get the fuck off me; I haven't got –

Kárel (*squeezes the back of his neck. In a whisper*) Pay me. I beat you, you piece of shit; give me the money and fuck off.

Miguel I haven't got any.

Kárel What?

Miguel Look in my pocket; I can't fucking breathe.

Kárel What? What?

Roberta *doesn't sweep; she observes. They fight.* **Miguel** *punches furiously. For a few seconds they cling to each other. Some chess pieces fall to the ground.* **Kárel** *begins to weaken; he feels his back pocket. I think this morning he left his knife on the table in his room; it's lucky he doesn't have it; a knife with an eight-centimetre blade that he uses to peel oranges. I think, but I'm wrong. He does have it; he takes it out. He plunges it into* **Miguel**'s *stomach. Once. Twice. It looks like an embrace.* **Miguel** *begins to fall slowly; I cannot describe the sound that he emits.* **Kárel** *looks at his own hands and immediately rubs them against his pullover. We see now that the chessboard is made of card, because our hero folds it up and puts it into one of his jeans pockets, beside the knife, as well as the chess pieces in a small woollen bag. He looks once more at* **Miguel**'s *body and flees.*

Roberta (*approaches. She moves her foot close to* **Miguel**'s *chest. She leans over and checks his pockets but finds no money. She sighs*) You're going to freeze, you're going to freeze …

The blood flows.

Not a single car passes.

Chapter III

The Moral World

The dining room appears, simply but not distastefully furnished. The dark wooden table has two small catches on its sides so panels can be added to make the table bigger should many guests come to dinner. But **Silvia** *cuts a solitary figure at one end of the table. It is set for three, with ceramic plates and a complete set of cutlery, a half-covered pot that will contain steaming black beans, persistent smoke that does not leave the pot all at once but rather seeps out rhythmically and monotonously, lending the Depás family's Christmas Eve a certain warmth.*

Alejandro Depás *returns from the bathroom. He's been washing his hands and face, and dries them off with a flannel.*

Silvia   Maybe he won't make it. He'll be off with some girlfriend.

Alejandro *enters the kitchen.*

Silvia   It's nearly twelve and he's not here. I suggest we eat and leave some for him for breakfast. You had a snack this afternoon, didn't you? I got back early from the hospital. I went to Cuatro Caminos market. Got a taxi there from 5th and 82nd Street. It was about four o'clock. The meat was more expensive, of course, with it being the end of the year, and half green; I insisted to the man and he brought out a chunk of pork leg for thirty-five pesos a pound. That's what I've cooked. He gave me a good piece and half a tub of fat to fry the fritters in. But fritters don't fry well in lard, do they. Try them anyway if you like but I know they won't be any good. I didn't fold them up properly anyway; I got tired of rolling that rolling pin; I'm not patient like Mum … And then the rice has got burnt bits; the gas suddenly went up. The beans were the last thing. Oh, and the salad: it's only carrot; they looked so lovely on the counter … (*Opens the pot and loses her gaze in the dark broth. Seven, eight seconds. She sits back down.*) Tell me when to dish up.

Alejandro (*beside the door to the street*)   Dish up and eat if you're hungry.

Silvia   No, no, I'll wait for you.

Alejandro   Eat.

Silvia   I'll get the rest of the things. (*Rises and exits.*)

Alejandro *could take a bath. Perhaps* **Miguel** *might return during this hiatus. Perhaps not.* **Silvia** *could advise* **Alejandro** *to take a bath, and that would give* **Miguel** *more time, but she's too busy in the kitchen: she opens the pressure-cooker, stirs the rice, mixes the burnt bits and the white grains with a fork because she likes the bitter taste the metal leaves. Perhaps none of this will be visible. She returns to the table and places the pot on a tea towel, a very light noise that makes the father look at her.*

Alejandro Sometime I think if you got married we'd get on better. Yes. You'd live far away, on the beach, and we'd visit each other from time to time. Or call each other on the phone, check everything's OK. Those occasional calls that give you a bit of comfort, like in the films, simple calls that fill your Sundays with joy and convince you that marriage, your own house and the distance are really doing you good.

Silvia Sometimes I think if you got married again –

Alejandro Don't even say it.

Silvia (*a dryness, a false desire*) I'd love to taste your wife's cooking.

She goes back out.

Alejandro Did you have enough money? (*Louder.*) I said, 'did you have enough money'?

Silvia (*off*) I bought everything.

Alejandro But you wanted apples.

Silvia I put them away in the fridge. I'm going to surprise Miguel.

Alejandro He's never going to get here, is he.

Silvia (*returns with the dish of fritters. She sits with it on her legs*) It's quite natural, Dad. You went on at him but he didn't want to be at home tonight. You insisted and I thought maybe you'd succeed; maybe something would make him want to stay in; I don't know, finish at the bar and come home early; not at eight or nine, I didn't think that; that's why I cooked late, took my time. I thought maybe he'd come at half past ten. Eleven. Half eleven. That lock's been silent ever since you came in; it gives me the shivers … It's Christmas Day already; he'll be out there downing glasses of rum with some friend. He's got exams in two weeks. It'll be New Year before you see him studying in his room. Or even sleeping there.

Silvia *places the dish of fritters on the table. She goes to try one but changes her mind. She runs the index finger of her right hand along the edge of the thin transparent glass dish. She offers it to her father, who declines and sits down facing her.*

Silvia How was your day?

Alejandro It went; you know. Flew by.

For the second time **Silvia** *could suggest that her father take a bath, she could light the boiler or put a jug of water on the stove. She does none of this. She did take a bath earlier, before chopping the carrots, and in the kitchen she didn't sweat because it really is very cold. So cold that a current of freezing air comes in through the window that looks out onto the patio.*

The voice of **Roberta López** *is heard singing a dense melody.*

Alejandro Who's that singing?

Silvia   Some neighbour.

Alejandro   How sad.

Silvia   It's a long way off. It's frightening.

Alejandro   I've heard it before.

Silvia   Of course. We've heard it forever.

Alejandro   Was it your mother used to sing that?

Silvia   I don't think so. I think I heard it in a film.

Alejandro   That'll be it.

The song ceases.

How much was everything, then?

Silvia   Everything?

Alejandro   The food, I mean.

Silvia *has memorized how much everything cost. She always does.*

Silvia   I don't know; about three hundred pesos, wasn't it? A little bit more. Let's see … Two hundred and forty-five for the meat. Twelve for the carrots. Fifteen for the onions and the potatoes for roasting.

Alejandro   Oh, I brought a bottle of cider. It's there, in the briefcase.

Silvia   We already had rice in the house and I didn't buy oil, so altogether it was … Fourteen pesos for two pounds of yucca. Two eggs and a pat of butter. I'm missing something. And then six dollars for the apples. About five hundred altogether, if you work it out.

Alejandro   My salary for the month.

Silvia   Mine.

Alejandro   I'll put the bottle in to cool.

He goes to the room and returns straight away with the bottle of cider; he does not stop in the dining room; he goes through into the kitchen. He opens the refrigerator, sees the apples and thinks of **Miguel**.

Alejandro   I popped into the Church of the Angel on my way up the avenue; see if I could hear a bit of the Midnight Mass at least. There was still a while to go before it started, of course. I suddenly fancied it, I don't know why.

Silvia   I go in and have a look if I'm not tired. Sit down; talk to myself. But I don't usually have time, or I don't feel like it. What with work and Miguel …

Alejandro   I asked him to be here. Now he'll turn up at all hours and the food'll be ruined.

Silvia I'll dish up as soon as you want.

Alejandro Aren't you worried?

Silvia Only a little bit. He can take care of himself, Dad. He's twenty-two years old.

Alejandro They want it all at that age.

Silvia They want it all at *your* age. I don't care if he does go out. I'm sure he's not in any danger; he'll be having a whale of a time. You often come home late. People don't get shot in this city, you know.

The idea of death is a block in **Alejandro**'s *mind.*

Silvia Come and taste the rice with me. We'll cover up a big chunk of meat for him. He can eat it when he gets in.

The father picks up his coat from on top of an armchair. The report confirms that this coat is coffee-coloured, like the eyes of **Kárel Darín**.

Silvia You're not going out looking for him …

Alejandro *hurries towards the door to the street and disappears.* **Silvia** *insists on the sound of a spoon against the side of the pot of rice.*

The beans stop smoking.

Chapter IV

Rents

A lamp sheds light on a bare wall. The walls of the rest of the room were painted many years ago, doubtless with one of those oil varnishes designed for wood that, used on bricks, accentuate the appearance of dirt. So, to give them a lick of paint, one would have to scrape the surfaces with a wire brush or a spatula.

There are no windows. An entrance door, one upstage and another on the right that gives access to the adjoining bedroom, perfectly visible at this moment, where **Kárel Darín** *sleeps almost every night.*

The key jams in the lock. It is removed and put back in again. Finally **Kárel** *enters, bare-chested; he closes the door with his foot and heads for his room. He carries his keys and the woollen bag in his left hand and, in his right, his pullover, folded up. Once inside his room, he secures the door with the bolt. He unfolds the pullover, slightly bloodstained.*

Felipe Alejo *enters through the upstage door, half asleep. Too many drinks, perhaps. He comes in from his room. An old Santa Claus hat. Satin pyjamas. He goes to the wall. He stops still in the light of the lamp.*

Felipe   That's you, isn't it! You came back. And me wishing all night you'd gone forever. Or, no, that you'd come back. I mean, that you'd get lost.

Kárel *cannot hear very well given that the door separates them. He hears the murmuring but is not interested. He takes out the chessboard and places it on a small table. He places the pieces onto them, very slowly. He puts them in their exact place and thinks deeply. Then he will remove his shoes and his jeans.* **Felipe** *continues.*

Felipe   Christmas Eve is shit. Any other night you'd feel more like eating and having a laugh. I can't even chew a pork scratching with these gnashers of mine falling apart. And there's no one to find me a nice tender piece of meat or a fillet of fish or a little chicken breast to cook, not unless I go out and buy it myself. Been out clowning around, have you? Taking a turn with some little girl who sleeps with you for three dollars. Where do you find the money, eh? You'd do better to hang onto it. Keep your arse tight and don't let it go. You already owe me two months, Darín; you'll owe me three months on the 31st and I'm not waiting 'til your birthday, just to have you to tell me you want a new tee-shirt, a pair of trainers, running shoes; you'll beg me, for Epiphany: 'I need them, Uncle, for work.' I can hear you already, like every December, like every time you're broke. I can hear you already, I see it coming: prettier, more attentive than ever, better-mannered, running to buy the bread in the mornings, jumping the queue for the newspaper, and I give in, I indulge you, and I start looking at you and I look at you and I look at you again and you even let me touch you. But it won't be like that this year. I don't want you disappearing off and then finally coming back, begging me like I'm an idiot, which I am: I listen to you, I feel badly and I let it happen, night after night after night. Those people you bring 'round here who I don't know … You don't even introduce me to your friends. I turn a blind eye, all in exchange for a brush, a little caress, one afternoon a week, one afternoon a month, one afternoon a year. On your knees; I want to see you on your knees! And even then I won't feel sorry for you. You don't feel sorry for me. You don't pity me. You hold out your hand and I know you'd rather put it somewhere else, in some unknown place, a thousand miles from this house. Well go! If you're never gonna pay me, go! (*Approaches* **Kárel***'s door and bangs on it.*) Darín! Darín! You're not asleep! Open up! Darín! You've just come in. I know you have. Some nights I only have ears for you. (*Silence.*) See? I'm talking quietly. Come out, please. I want to wish you Merry Christmas.

Kárel *is in his underpants, without socks. He bundles up the bloodstained clothes and approaches the door. He sees the knife that has fallen on the floor. He picks it up, cleans it with the clothes and puts it on the table, beside the chessboard. He puts the clothing away in a wardrobe. His hands retain traces of the blood that spattered him and has now dried, completely dried. He spits on his fingers and rubs his hands with them; this action coincides with* **Felipe***'s final words, during which* **Kárel** *untidies the bed sheets even more and shouts:*

Kárel   What is it …? (*He approaches the door, opens it, covers himself with his arms and yawns.*) What's going on?

Felipe   You haven't had time to fall asleep.

Kárel   I was out cold.

Felipe   I'm not stupid … I know exactly what your key-ring sounds like. It's not next-door's or the one from the house on the corner.

Kárel *tuts and goes to close the door.*

Felipe   No, don't close the door. I wanted to wish you Merry Christmas.

Kárel   You should wash your mouth out after you drink a bottle of rum. (*Tries again to close the door.*)

Felipe (*holds him*)   Put a jumper on; celebrate with me. Or stay naked if you want. I can't, you see; I'd start coughing. (*Coughs.*) I've been so alone waiting for Christmas, no energy, freezing to death, not a drop of heat. I've needed you so much, Darín. (*Hugs him.*)

Kárel *sighs.* **Felipe** *has often hugged him like this. He shouts, holds him, prevents him from closing the door and hugs him. That's why he accepts it. It's not pleasant – in fact* **Kárel** *detests the gesture – but he puts up with it. He raises his hands and sighs again.*

Kárel   I'm tired, man. Go to bed now. Tomorrow's another day.

Felipe (*sobs, but stays pressed to* **Kárel***'s chest*)   A day the same as today. You'll come back late.

Kárel I'll come back early and I'll go to bed, to sleep, like I would do now if you'd let me.

Felipe Liar. You know you're lying to me and you know I know. You come in at all hours, you think I'm asleep but really I don't even close my eyes.

Kárel *finally pushes him away. He goes to the sink and fills a glass of water. He drinks.*

Felipe But you've no time for anything any more. That wasn't the deal, Darín; it wasn't what we agreed.

Kárel I don't make trouble. I don't knock on your door because I'm not crazy. Leave me in peace; go on: go to bed; we'll talk when you're feeling better.

Felipe I'll never feel better than now. I've hardly touched a drop: half a glass of old wine to calm me down and clear my head. You eat here and you have your fun out there. You wash here; you take the water from my cistern to clean the grime off you and wash your ears. When you turned up at this house your fingernails were black and I cut them so you wouldn't look like a beggar.

Kárel Drop it now; go on.

Goes to return to his room but **Felipe** *stands in front of the door.*

Felipe You don't go back in there if I don't feel like it.

Kárel Easy; you don't want any trouble.

Felipe 'Easy, easy!' You don't frighten me.

Kárel (*tries to squeeze into the room*) Let me get past, old man.

Felipe *puts on the pressure.* **Kárel** *turns, paces and looks at the floor. With his left fist he punches his right palm very gently. He hums a tune.*

Felipe You'll never know how much I love you. I let you come into this house, sleep in that room; I hoped you'd forget that dump you were living in forever, where you cut your hands on the shovel and the earth. Yes, I said to myself, the man had finally arrived. And I wash your clothes and I cook your food and I nurse you when you're ill.

Kárel And you charge me for all of it.

Felipe I charge you but I do it.

Kárel I've heard this so many times … And my head's gonna fucking burst; it's a holiday; I went out on the street to try and make some money.

Felipe But you spend your whole life out there, on the other side of that door! In the sunshine, in the moonlight, hot or cold; you don't care if you come home dry or drenched. If you try so hard to make money, why do you never succeed? Put it on the table, one note on top of the other. It's hard? Yes, I know it's hard. The street is hard.

But even if you've no money, you're still twenty years old. Pay me any way you can, you ungrateful little shit.

Kárel *pushes him to the floor. He goes into his room and closes the door. He sits on the bed.*

Felipe   Open up or I'll scream! Look: I'm screaming! (*Bangs on the door.*) I'm screaming! I'm screaming!

Kárel *covers his ears. He rises. He moves quickly. There is no way he could calm down now. He could not behave like a hero now. He could neither go to bed nor go out; sleep nor turn the other cheek. He begins to dress and* **Felipe**'s *screams continue. Another pair of jeans. Another thin tee-shirt even though he knows it's cold. There's no time to place the chess pieces in the bag; he leaves the game set up, on the board. He picks up the knife and puts it away in his pocket, beside his wallet. He goes out. He closes his bedroom door. He opens the door to the street and disappears into the night. It is after 1:00 a.m.*

Felipe *pursues him with his eyes. He is speechless for a second.*

Felipe   Come back, Darín! I've calmed down now! Come on! Come back! Come and have dinner with me!

He drags himself to the threshold and beats his head furiously against the door.

Chapter V

Happy in the Short Term

The Louvre Arcade stretches out, opposite Parque Central and beside the Grand Theatre. It strikes a French tone of faded glamour, with bars lit up and fine patisserie, where all through the night one can eat a croissant or drink a café au lait of middling quality.

Kárel, *however, prefers the opacity of the opposite pavement, where the twinkling lights of the Louvre reach by extension. Intermittent lights pursue his footsteps. He thinks he'll not return to his uncle's house. He thinks immediately that he has to return; there's no alternative. He looks at the ground and looks straight ahead. He fears the closeness of Parque Central, the blood, the knife. Cold and emptiness.*

Alejandro *has left his house and passed the India Fountain. In the instant that* **Kárel** *passes in front of the bookshop, he is smoking against a column.* **Kárel** *stops slowly, turns back, looks at him and puts his hands in his jeans pockets.* **Alejandro** *notices.* **Kárel** *approaches the column and leans on it. The sole of his left shoe against the wall.*

Kárel   Strong?

Alejandro   Lights. (*Offers him the packet.*)

Kárel   No way. Make me ill.

Alejandro *looks at him lingeringly.* **Kárel** *folds his arms.*

Alejandro   Cold, isn't it.

Kárel   Bit. (*Yawns. Stretches.*)

Alejandro   Hungry or tired?

Kárel   Woken up now.

Alejandro (*takes some coins from his pocket and gives them to him*)   Go to La Revoltosa. Buy yourself a pizza.

Kárel   No chance. It's nearly two in the morning. They closed early today.

Alejandro (*puts the money into his hand*)   Try over in the Louvre, then; they're better there. And bring me one.

Kárel   Is there enough?

Alejandro   You'll tell me if there isn't, kiddo.

Kárel *runs across and disappears from view. The report mentions the persistence of the lights from the other pavement. The sound of an ambulance or a faraway police* *patrol.* **Alejandro** *turns his head but doesn't move from his position. The lad returns with two pizzas.*

Alejandro That was quick, wasn't it?

Kárel Waiter wanted to see what was going on in the square.

Alejandro In the square?

Kárel I dunno. Not even been near there.

Alejandro (*bites and begins to eat*) Are there people there?

Kárel Must be a fight. Some whore. (*Bites.*) Tastes good. Hot, at least. Not eaten since noon.

Alejandro How was your Christmas Eve?

Kárel Fine, thanks.

Alejandro And your folks?

Kárel (*chews and talks*) I love cheese. (*Moves away. Looks over at the square. Comes back to* **Alejandro**.) You ate at home.

Alejandro *shakes his head.*

Kárel So this is your Christmas Eve dinner.

Alejandro Spending it with you; you see.

Kárel (*laughs*) Fuck off. It's already Christmas Day.

Alejandro Then we're practically having breakfast.

La Paco *passes them, fleetingly.*

Kárel I fancy that girl.

Alejandro It's a boy.

Kárel Does the same things as a girl, though.

Alejandro And you get hard just thinking about it.

Kárel Wanna feel?

Another police siren.

Alejandro I think the police are near the cinema.

Kárel Minding their own.

Alejandro I like getting close to criminality sometimes. I should stay away, but I get close.

Kárel You work 'round here?

Alejandro 'Round the corner.

Kárel   In La Revoltosa?

They laugh again.

Alejandro   In the courts.

Kárel   Prosecutor?

Alejandro   Lawyer, judge, prosecutor; what difference does it make?

Kárel   Hard work.

Alejandro   You listen. Look closely at their faces. Make a more or less just decision.

Kárel   And you don't mess up?

Alejandro   I'm sure I mess up constantly.

Kárel   Give your verdict with a knife against your neck.

Alejandro   No. It's a job like any other.

Kárel   I've heard so many stories! They say there was a famous musician who was a judge. Day before the trial he was killed by the same man he was gonna send down. He was a mafia guy from the old days.

Alejandro   You live in fear.

Kárel   Not really. Not you either, shouldn't think.

Alejandro   Oh, I do.

Third siren. **Alejandro** *moves away from the column and walks along looking at the square. They have finished eating.*

Kárel   Even so, you call me over; you talk to me.

Alejandro   I didn't call you over. You came up and asked me for a light. No, you asked me for a cigarette.

Kárel   And then you asked me.

Alejandro   Do you want another question?

Kárel   Many as you want if you take me back to yours.

Alejandro   Not now.

Kárel   We'll have a good time.

Alejandro   I know, but not now.

Kárel   Tomorrow, day after. Up to you.

Alejandro   Need a bed, do you?

A gust of wind blows through the columns.

Kárel I need money. Blue, green, red, money, any kind. I owe three months' rent. It's cold; everyone's at home. You're the only guy here and you gave me an 'in'. I don't want you getting away. Can't go back without any money. (*Moves away a little. Turns back.*) What d'you say?

Alejandro (*looks at him. Opens his wallet again and takes out two dollars*) Take this for tonight. It's not much but it'll do for now.

Kárel (*takes them*) Let's go somewhere; you can suck me off.

Alejandro Careful …

Kárel Come on.

Alejandro Tomorrow.

Kárel Tomorrow, tomorrow … Now. You know you won't turn up tomorrow. You're just giving me the slip.

Alejandro What if I'm not? What if I do turn up?

Kárel *tuts.*

Alejandro Go on; I promise. I'll be here, trust me. What do you say?

Kárel What time? I've got something at eight but I'll be quick.

Alejandro Half past nine. No, half past ten.

Kárel Where?

Alejandro Right here.

Kárel Too many people here before twelve.

Alejandro In the Park of Lies, then. Opposite the Church of the Angel, near where the number 15 stops.

Kárel (*smiles*) I hope you're not lying to me.

Alejandro It's a date. (*Pinches him.*) Right, let's see what's happened over there.

Kárel Hey, what if it rains?

Alejandro I have an umbrella.

Kárel *smiles and stays beside the column with his arms folded.* **Alejandro** *advances towards the square.*

Saúl *comes along the street on his motorbike. He turns it off and alights.*

Saúl Do you know who that is going 'round the corner?

Kárel He just gave me a light.

Saúl Follow him; arrange to meet him somewhere.

Kárel No, no. He's cool.

Saúl Exactly.

Kárel I'm off to sleep. (*Tries to leave.*)

Saúl (*grabs him by the back of the neck, with some violence*) Come here. You're not going anywhere yet. Listen to me. You've never seen him before? He comes along this pavement every day. Stops beside a column and starts smoking. Looking for lads. Gives them a few pesos and makes them crouch down naked in some rented house. And you know where he works? He told you, didn't he? They're rotten, these streets. As well as queer crap like that, he shits his judgements out of his arse.

Kárel I don't know anything about it; get the fuck off me.

Saúl Ah, you don't know anything, poor baby. (*Tough.*) Well, you soon will. That guy always comes alone. But he's got a family: a daughter, a son … No one in this town earns enough money to spend it on rent-boys every night. Where does he get it from? (*Squeezes.*)

Kárel (*breaks free*) Get off! Get off me!

Saúl (*grabs him again*) Find out.

Kárel I'm not finding out; I don't want to.

Saúl (*into his ear*) I'll leave you alone 'til January; how about that? Free 'til January: not one I.D. check, not a single night in the cells. Good business. Go after him; you know what to do. You're pretty and he still hasn't had you inside him. He'll follow you. He'll want you to besiege him. (*Touches one of his buttocks.*)

Kárel (*breaks away, worked up*) Bastard!

Saúl (*grabs him. Drags him to him*) You like that?

Kárel (*breaks away again*) You're a bastard!

Saúl The bastard is whoever just killed that kid in the square. Have you not been 'round there?

Kárel Dunno anything about it.

Saúl If you say so … Don't forget. You get me something and I'll leave you in peace. Now get lost. (*Gets on his motorbike.*) I'll be back around three. Make yourself scarce. (*Pulls off and disappears.*)

The lights from the Louvre Arcade cover **Kárel**'s *face with coloured stains.*

Chapter VI

Tomorrow Is Another Day

Dawn in the Depás house; they have not slept. The light of the Christmas sun filters through the window that looks out onto the patio: all of the light comes from upstage. Thus, almost in silhouette, the image of **Alejandro** *can be distinguished leaning on the table, completely still, with his face hidden in his arms. And suddenly, when the brightness becomes a little more intense, the figure of* **Silvia** *emerges, standing at the threshold, with two apples, one in each hand.*

Silvia   My name is Silvia Depás and I'm twenty-nine years old. At seventeen I started studying Medicine. At twenty I interrupted my studies to have an operation: I had myopia. It didn't take long to recover; the pain wore off in no time, luckily. I already knew life was the most important thing, but after six years of training I knew it even more. I liked volleyball but never played. I liked the theatre but never had time to go. Morning, evening, afternoon and night in the bathroom or the kitchen with huge tomes and textbooks, getting to grips with respiration. What causes it, and what causes it to stop. I qualified as a doctor and spent another four years training to be a surgeon. The smell of the operating theatre encrusting in my nose. Slicing with a scalpel; first rubber, then skin. The stench didn't sicken me. Blood didn't scare me. I opened, I extracted, I sewed. Bodies, switched off, inert; not a single protest, not a murmur. And then the relief. Knowing there was a miracle in my hands, in my skill for sewing things up and laying gauzes just so. And the man lived. Almost ten years of it! Any longer and I'd swear I'd grown old ... Comforted, happy now and then, flattered by a gift, but a silly girl just the same. Fearless. Building a crystal island. So much time on that shit but nothing prepared me for seeing my own brother dead! Because, maybe you do imagine these things happening, but to other people, to other brothers; never to you. A brick won't land on you as you're walking down the street; you won't drown in a swimming pool. It's so far removed ... So far away I can see it, touch it, feel it beside me! God! Rip my hands off; they couldn't hold onto him! A brother. It's easy to say. But how can I give these apples to my brother now?

She collapses, defeated, into a chair. The father looks up. He does not touch her. The daughter cries. He barely moves. He does not blink.

Alejandro   Breathe. Swallow. It's a habit with you. You cried yesterday, too. I was on the landing and I stopped. You thought I hadn't heard you both; you thought I'd just popped into the dining room, but all the time I was listening.

An angle of the dining room, from the side where **Silvia** *is, lights up from out front; thus, it stands out against the backlighting of the rest of the room.* **Silvia** *sighs; she stops crying.* **Miguel** *enters in shorts and flip-flops; he comes from his room. He stretches.* **Silvia** *smiles at him. They kiss. It is daybreak, the previous day.*

Silvia   I made coffee.

Miguel   My guts ache.

Silvia   You'll have eaten too late last night, like always. Coming in at all hours.

Miguel   Give it a rest, Silvi. Give me a break. I've been sick.

Silvia   Are you feeling better now?

Miguel   Yeah, it's just a hangover.

Silvia   I can bring you something from the hospital.

Miguel   Don't bother. Shouldn't think I'll be home tonight.

Silvia   I'm doing roast pork and potatoes.

Miguel   I fancy an apple.

Silvia   Oh, they're quite cheap at La Revoltosa.

Miguel   Yeah, right. Can't even get two for a dollar.

Silvia   So save up.

Miguel   So help me to.

Silvia   Do things properly, Migue. I don't know … Dump all those girlfriends you've got all over the place.

Miguel   Fuck, Silvia, you're just like Dad. I sometimes think this'd work better if there were more of us living here.

Silvia   Three's already a crowd.

Miguel   Especially when one of them's like him.

Silvia   It's not his fault.

Miguel   No, it's mine.

Silvia   He's demanding; he's like any other father.

Miguel   Where do you get your money from?

Silvia   From working, day and night.

Miguel   I prefer the night.

Silvia   And I prefer the day; I get tired at night. I do the shift anyway but I fall asleep.

Miguel   Not when you're operating.

Silvia   Depends on the operation.

They laugh.

Miguel   I'm leaving home.

Silvia   What?

Miguel Escaping. I'm not coming back.

Silvia What are you talking about, Migue?

Miguel I dreamt it.

Silvia What do you mean, 'you dreamt it'? You don't dream things like that. You just don't do them.

Miguel I wake up every morning with a headache.

Silvia Take a tablet, but don't get so angry about it.

Miguel I'm not angry but Dad just keeps going on. Look how little time I try to spend here; how late I come in so I don't bump into him … He doesn't understand. He's always understood you.

Silvia You're not being serious, are you?

Miguel *shrugs his shoulders.*

Silvia Has he said something to you? (*A silence.*) He's said something to you.

Miguel I won't put up with it next time. With him shouting. Getting worked up and shrieking. He'll hit me one of these days, like I'm a kid. And I swear I won't let him get away with it, Silvia; I swear. What more can I do? Tell me. I study all day; I work my shift at the bar. I'm not doing bad at school. Isn't that what matters? I thought about dropping out, getting a job doing something I like, not just the bar. But what? If you haven't got a degree they want you to speak English. Or I could get a job in a hotel if I bribed someone a hundred, two hundred dollars. I don't speak English; what can I do?

Silvia No one's asking you to leave school.

Miguel But Dad says I'm worthless.

Silvia He's never said that.

Miguel He says it, Silvia; not in so many words, but he says it. He wanted me to be a judge like him, or a doctor like you … That takes time, and quiet, and peace so you can live and study, and calm so you don't have the pressure on your shoulders all the time. He's put some money away, he's got his bank account; I don't always ask him but some days I put my hand in my pocket and all I feel is my thigh.

For a second, **Silvia** *imagines a peaceful life. A tear. Two.*

Miguel (*strokes her shoulders*) Hey, hey … Don't cry. I don't like it when you cry.

He makes her stand up. Hugs her.

Silvia I'm going up to get changed.

Miguel Why don't you ask that guy from the pictures 'round for dinner tonight?

Silvia (*smiles*) You saw me?

Miguel Yeah, but I didn't tell you.

Silvia What were you doing 'round there?

Miguel Picking up a girlfriend.

Silvia Another one! I can't have any secrets.

Miguel Exactly, so bring him 'round. Maybe Dad'll like him.

Silvia I'm not insane. (*Goes to the kitchen. Off.*) Are you hungry yet?

Miguel (*sings*) 'I have black tears …'

Silvia (*comes out*) I've put the butter on the table and there's bread in the larder. (*Gives him a kiss on the forehead.*) Do try, Miguel; come home, even if it is late.

Miguel It'd only be for you. Maybe I'll bump into that guy who takes you out for walks; give him a piece of my mind.

Silvia Very funny! I'm going to get changed.

Miguel *laughs.*

The light from the front goes down quickly and the backlight picks out the silhouettes of **Silvia** *and* **Alejandro** *once more.*

Alejandro All of his words were there. They're nailed into me; I can still hear them. I'm not crying. I won't shed a single tear!

Silvia You want me to feel uncomfortable. You want me to give in and accept it. But no. I won't touch him even if you ask me to. You dress him if you want, comb his hair, pay someone to do it for you. I can't look at him.

Alejandro (*a blow of terror*) And those two holes in his stomach!

The father groans for an instant, sharply. **Silvia** *cannot bear it; she goes to hug him. He contains himself.*

Alejandro I'll get washed and go out. I'll just stand close to the door. I don't think I'll go in. I'll watch the faces from the doorway. I can't face being asked stupid questions. And that policeman's bound to go on.

Silvia I'll go with you.

Alejandro Better not.

He goes into the bathroom. The brightness fades on **Silvia**; *her eyes are red.*

Water is heard falling in the shower.

Chapter VII

Attempts

Christmas morning sheds little light on **Felipe Alejo***'s house. The same filth. The same distribution of space, with* **Kárel***'s room visible.*

The report specifies that at 10:24 a.m. Inspector **Saúl Alter** *asked the following question:*

Saúl   Are you and Karel Darín related, Sir?

The report also states that **Felipe** *hesitates. He nibbles the nails of his left hand and replies*:

Felipe   I'm his uncle.

Saúl   His real uncle? You don't have the same surnames.

Felipe   No reason we should. I was married to his father's sister, dead now.

Saúl   The sister or the father?

Felipe   Both.

Saúl   Have you always lived here in the city?

Felipe   Here.

Saúl   And Kárel Darín is from the country.

Felipe   He was born in the country but he lives in the city now.

Saúl   You say last night he threw you against the sideboard and gave you those bruises.

Felipe   I didn't feel safe, so I called the police. I didn't think you'd come so quickly. With it being Christmas.

Saúl   People do kill at Christmas, too.

Felipe *nods.*

Saúl   So, specifically, you're accusing him of beating you up?

Felipe   And for lying and other bad things.

Saúl   What things?

Felipe   Maybe I can't say exactly, but I know he does them.

Saúl   And how long's this been going on?

Felipe   A long time.

Saúl   Weeks?

Felipe Months.

Saúl So why wait 'til now to report him?

Felipe You must understand it's difficult for me. I didn't want to get a relative into trouble; a loved one.

Saúl But you want him charged now?

Felipe He accosts me.

Saúl In what sense?

Felipe Asks me for money; says he wants to go out.

Saúl Go out?

Felipe Dancing, drinking, screwing around. He'll be twenty-two soon.

Saúl That's what lads do at that age.

Felipe He does it in spades. It's not healthy. He'll fall ill one of these days or come home one morning with his face smashed in.

Saúl Where is he right now?

Felipe Do you know? More than I do. I worry; I can't help worrying.

Saúl Does he sleep here every night?

Felipe When he's not hanging 'round park benches.

Saúl Where?

Felipe The only place kids like him are interested in these days. That square, of course: Parque Central. They gamble there; bet on anything. Cards, chess. They bet and they lose. And when they lose, they get into fights.

Saúl Has he told you that?

Felipe He keeps some parts of his private life hidden. And I don't insist. He frightens me. You've seen how angry he gets.

Saúl Did he eat here on Christmas Eve?

Felipe I asked him but he didn't want to.

Saúl Do you charge him to sleep in this house, Sir?

Felipe Please! He's my nephew.

Saúl I thought, perhaps … It's so difficult out there.

Felipe You're telling me.

Saúl Sir, do you have anything else against Kárel Darín?

Felipe It's the last days of the year and I know what kind of company he keeps. That's why I wait up. He thinks I'm asleep but I watch for him to get back. The night before last he said he was going to the cinema and I stayed awake. It would have been half past eleven when he opened the door.

Light from the door to the street that reaches **Darín**'s *room.* **Kárel** *and* **Silvia** *enter. Almost midnight on 23 December.*

Silvia   This place always looks such a hovel.

Kárel   Yours and mine. Don't you like it?

Silvia   I like you.

She hugs him. He squeezes her and kisses her. They enter the bedroom. **Kárel** *closes the door and sits on the bed. He pulls her to him. They roll over the mattress.*

Silvia   I think my brother was in the cinema.

Kárel   You should've called him over. I'd have asked for your hand in marriage.

Silvia   I'm not insane.

Kárel   Do you believe in me?

Silvia (*sings*)   'Let me believe in you …'

Kárel   Quiet; you'll wake my uncle.

Silvia   If you knew my father …

Kárel   You're not a child.

Silvia   But I live with them both. When a woman lives with two men, she gets jealous, obsessive, frightened.

Kárel   Depends on the woman.

Silvia   Depends on the men.

Kárel   And what d'you think of this man?

Silvia   I've already tried you out. And I've already told you.

Kárel   Tough girl.

They look at each other. It seems an eternity but barely a few seconds pass. **Kárel** *twiddles* **Silvia**'s *hair. They play.*

Kárel (*a melody*)   'Martina, little cockroach, prettiest by far.'

Silvia (*a whisper*)   'Knowing I'm not pretty, I thank you even more.'

Kárel   'Martina, little cockroach, will you be my wife?'

She could follow the game and imagine that life is a children's story. She could dream of being happy beside some lad or other; not an arrogant doctor, but a guy without a profession who lives in a tumbledown house. But she doesn't know. She never knows.

Silvia   I'll tell you tomorrow.

Kárel   Tomorrow's another day.

Silvia   Is that good or bad?

Kárel   We could spend Christmas Eve together. I don't normally bother, but …

Silvia   I'm going to be at home.

Kárel   Will I see you?

Silvia   Leave it 'til Wednesday.

Kárel   I will leave it; I will leave it if you want.

Silvia   Around half past seven, or eight o'clock. I might have to rush off; I'm on duty that day.

Kárel   In the Park of Lies?

Silvia   All right.

Kárel   I hope you're not lying.

Silvia   Idiot. I'll be there.

They separate.

Oh, Kárel, I forgot … (*Opens her bag and takes out two little boxes.*) The pills you asked me for. Do you think you can get a good price for them? People take them with alcohol. They say it makes them 'fly'.

Kárel   I've got the dregs of a bottle of rum.

Silvia   Oh, not on your life! And don't you go trying it either … It's up to them if they're used to it … Swear to me you won't.

Kárel (*raises his hands*)   I swear.

Silvia   This is for you, too. (*Takes out a photo.*)

Kárel   Really?

Silvia   That way I'll be here even when I'm not.

Kárel   Write on the back for me?

Silvia   I will on Wednesday.

Kárel   I've got too much on on Wednesday. (*He rises and goes to the table. He lifts up the glass that covers it and slides the photo under. The game of chess, set up on top of the table, does not even wobble.*) Next to mine.

Silvia   It's late.

Kárel   Wait, I'll come with you.

Silvia   You're not planning on wandering the streets all night?

Kárel   That's how you met me.

Silvia   But it's wild out there, Kárel.

Kárel   I'm not afraid of the wolf. (*Hugs her.*)

The room falls into darkness.

Felipe   They wrapped themselves around each other and switched off the light.

Saúl   How could you see it all so clearly?

Felipe (*points to* **Kárel***'s bedroom door*)   There's a hole in it. It's hardly noticeable. I made it so I could watch him.

Saúl   You watch him at night?

Felipe   When he has girls in there.

Saúl   You watch him or the girls?

Felipe   The girls, of course. What do you think? I'm not some old queer.

Saúl   I'm sorry ... Do you have a photo of your nephew?

Felipe   In there.

Saúl   Key?

Felipe   He keeps it. He always locks the door. But don't worry; you can break the door down. I'm tired of putting up with his cheek. Go on; knock it down!

Saúl *approaches the door. He knocks. He bangs it with his shoulder. The wood resists. He takes a run up and returns. The lock yields. They enter the room.*

Felipe   I've not been able to come in since he's been sleeping here. He wouldn't let me. Look at that chess game. Do you think Darín has any head for chess? (*Gently lifts the glass that covers the table and takes out a photo.*) Look at him.

Saúl (*takes the photo*)   Exactly. This is Kárel Darín.

Felipe   You've seen him?

Saúl   No, no.

Felipe (*takes out another photo*)   And this is the girl I was telling you about. Together beneath the glass. Since he doesn't have any frames ...

Saúl (*takes it and looks*)   Could you bring me a drop of water?

Felipe   Of course.

Felipe *exits.* **Saúl** *puts the photos away in his pocket. He searches the wardrobes avidly. He notices the bundle of bloodstained clothes. He separates them out. He bundles them back together and returns them to the wardrobe, which he closes straight away.* **Felipe** *returns.*

Felipe   Anything of interest?

Saúl   Nothing incriminating. (*Drinks the water.*)

46   Chamaco (Kiddo)

Felipe   You can't have looked properly. That chessboard could be a clue.

Saúl   Well, does he play chess?

Felipe   Just saying, that's all.

They leave the room.

Are there any more questions?

Saúl   No.

Felipe   One last one, like in all interrogations.

Saúl   Why do you call him Darín and not Kárel?

Felipe   That was his father's surname. I like him always to remember. He was a real man.

Saúl   I'll be in touch.

Felipe   Of course.

*The only lamp in **Felipe Alejo**'s sitting room suddenly goes out.*

Chapter VIII

Fathers and Sons

Any man other than **Alejandro Depás** *would have stayed at home. He would ruminate on his pain with his daughter and try to sleep. A cup of lime-flower tea and a pile of pills after coming home from the cemetery.*

He seems strong, however: serene and calm when the report focuses on him walking through the Park of Lies, barely half a block from the Paseo del Prado, at 10:40 p.m. on 25 December. He goes to sit on the bench closest to the number 15 bus-stop but sees that it is occupied, on its right-hand end, by an old woman who rummages through several plastic bags. Slowly he approaches the left-hand end and sits.

The bench is large. A metre and a half separate **Roberta López** *from* **Alejandro Depás**. *The intermittent light of a lighthouse illuminates them.*

Roberta   Does coffee not keep you awake?

Alejandro   Huh?

Roberta   It does me. I have to be awake all night so I brew two pots and pour them into this bottle. Not pure coffee, of course: half of it's ground-up peas. I've come to prefer it with time.

She pours him a plastic cup and offers it to him.

For God's sake, take it. If you give me a peso, so much the better, but it doesn't matter if …

Alejandro *searches in his pocket and takes out a coin.*

Roberta   No, no …

He insists and takes the cup.

Well … Don't think I always make coffee. I can't be doing it every night. If you only knew: I need a drink from this bottle even more than I need those sweets from the cinema … Is it nice? I do make lovely coffee. I can't help it. I do it without trying. It can never taste bad with sugar in it.

He hands her the cup.

It's only nice here for a little while. People come to the bus-stop early on and buy coffee from me. Then they go away. The bus comes by and of course they go off and sleep on a mattress. Better a mattress than these wooden bars! Or the stone benches in Parque Central.

Parque Central. The stone bench. **Alejandro** *shakes.*

Roberta   Yes, it is cold; you're shivering with cold. I could keep you company all night … No, no, don't worry; I'm filthy, I know. Besides, there's no point me staying here. If I go up the Paseo del Prado and stop near the cinema I can at least keep an eye on the statue of the hero. It's better lit. Maybe someone'll come past with a peso to spend on a little cup of coffee, suddenly stop under a streetlamp thinking it's safe, not think twice about it.

Alejandro *follows* **Roberta***'s eyes. She notices that* **Kárel** *is approaching along the opposite pavement. She puts the bottle and the cups away in the bags and rises.*

Roberta   If that coffee hasn't woken you up, you'd best go off and sleep.

She disappears. **Alejandro** *wants to follow her but* **Kárel** *arrives. The same clothes as in the early hours of the morning. He has not been home. God knows what he has been doing for all of Christmas Day.*

Kárel   What did that old woman want?

Alejandro   She gave me some coffee.

Kárel   They say coffee's bad for you.

Alejandro (*happy and dense in his idea of badness*)   You're a bit late.

Kárel   You won't believe me if I tell you I was here a while ago.

Alejandro   For your seven o'clock?

Kárel   A girl. Thought it might be fun, that's all. She was with her family on Christmas Eve: her dad and her brother; so we didn't eat together. We arranged to meet today but she stood me up. Stupid, getting your hopes up with women.

Alejandro   It could've been anything. Things come up. Complications. You don't know what's happened; you've no idea … She'll be somewhere in the city, sorting her life out, millions of little everyday problems turning into monsters … You think you've got the world in front of you and you don't see the precipice. It's madness. (*He presses his eyes with his hands; he cannot contain the weeping.*)

Kárel   What's up? (*Gives him a pat on the back.*)

Alejandro *cries without hysterics, bitterly.*

Kárel   Oh … You're in a bad way, man. Shall I buy you a drink? A beer? Shall I get something for you?

Alejandro (*dries his face with his arms*)   No, no.

Kárel (*takes out his handkerchief*)   Clean yourself up.

With the open handkerchief **Alejandro** *covers his face again. He cries.*

Kárel   No, shit … We're gonna have a good time. Hey, hey … What is it?

Alejandro *takes out a bottle.*

Kárel   That's pretty good.

Alejandro   Any rum'll do.

Kárel It's cold; do us good.

Alejandro You burn to death as soon as you drink this.

They drink directly from the bottle. **Kárel** *rubs his bare arms.*

Alejandro Do you want to put my coat on?

Kárel Nah, nah, I'll be all right.

Lighthouse. Smell of salt water. One swig of the bottle; another.

Alejandro (*slowly*) I like this park. You sit down and you can see the sea even if it's dark ... All the calm in the world, the smell of the waves if you get close, the sound of the water against the rocks. Go over to the Malecón: walk along the seawall if you fancy ... And on the horizon, the air and the water, the same colour, like cobalt. With no line; there's barely a line dividing them at this time of night. The lighthouse doesn't let up and then, suddenly, the shadows. It's hell itself!

The lighthouse seems to slow down. Or maybe it's the story.

I loved my son ... What did you say your name was?

Kárel Kárel. Kárel Darín.

Alejandro Well, I say Kárel, kiddo, and I say Miguel. The same age, I imagine; the same idea of the world. Maybe, look, maybe he didn't know it ... But I worshipped him ... He was talking to his sister yesterday and I heard it all from the staircase. I didn't interrupt. I could've done but I didn't interrupt. I waited for Silvia to go into her room.

Kárel Silvia ...

Alejandro And then I went downstairs.

In the depths of the park a fragment of the Depás dining room appears. Deformed, incomplete, cracked, like **Alejandro**'s *mind.*

Miguel *in shorts and flip-flops. He eats a piece of bread with butter. Christmas Eve morning, again.*

Alejandro (*enters*) Are you not going to school today? (*He goes into the kitchen. From there.*) The holiday's tomorrow.

Miguel *does not answer.* **Alejandro** *pours himself a glass of milk. He takes bread from the larder. He goes to the table.*

Alejandro Lost your tongue? (*As he eats.*) Your sister's going to buy the meat for tonight; she's bound to have onions and potatoes to carry. You could help her if you're not going to school.

Miguel (*thumps the table with his hand*) I am going to school. Course I'm going! I'm going right now! (*Rises and walks.*)

Alejandro Don't raise your voice to me.

Miguel Oh, I shouldn't raise my voice to you when you spend your whole life shouting.

Alejandro Sit down, Miguel.

Miguel I've gotta get dressed.

Alejandro If you got back earlier, if you came home when the bar closes –

Miguel What? What would change?

Alejandro I'd start believing you.

Miguel Don't give me the same speech as last night.

Alejandro Then don't ask me for money.

Miguel So you can hoard it, is it? It'll end up going mouldy.

Alejandro I pay for everything in this house, Miguel. The electricity, the gas, the water –

Miguel I gave Silvia fifty pesos last month for the phone. And I found the plumber to fix the bath.

Alejandro (*claps. Stands up*) Just what I've taught you all your life. Don't turn 'round without covering your back. You don't eat and shit in the same place.

Miguel Years ago, Dad, I sat down and told you straight. I was still small and maybe you didn't believe me. Or thought I'd grow out of it. I told you: I want to live on my own. And you laughed. You had it all: a house to rule over however you liked, a daughter about to graduate in Medicine and a great job in the courts … You had it all and you laughed. I was a kid and you thought it was a phase. But I understood all right.

Alejandro Understood what?

Miguel That Mum was getting in your way.

Alejandro What the hell – ?

Miguel No, no. You loved her. I'm sure you loved her. Went to pick her up in the car, took her out for walks. (*Touches his head with his index finger.*) Weekends at the beach, afternoons at the zoo, all together, they're all here … I haven't forgotten. Hug her, kiss her, give her a white rose. And you get home late. You're often at court 'til God-knows-what time … Really late, sometimes: after midnight.

Alejandro There's always paperwork to do, forms, signatures –

Miguel Stop; you don't have to justify yourself. You're the judge. I'm not judging you.

Alejandro But I hear your voice and I can tell where you're going; I don't want to think it but I nearly –

Miguel And Mum kept quiet. Putting up with things like a dog. Held her tongue. Kept quiet. Food ready, hot water for your bath … She never said a thing. How many years where you married? About twenty, was it? Eighteen, at least … Multiplied by three hundred working days a year. I don't think she ever asked you. You tell me, but I don't think she ever did. (*A gesture with his fingers.*) She didn't even have this much doubt. Didn't interfere; spared you a heap of trouble. Didn't interfere; gave you your freedom; defended *your* freedom. I had a happy childhood, too, thanks to her, her silence, her patience … Whatever you did, as long as it was outside the house, it didn't so much as cross her mind. (*Very close to the father.*) And you did things at night, didn't you? Sure you did. You still do.

Alejandro *slaps him in the face.*

Miguel (*his voice is about to break but there's not a single tear*) And despite all that, I … I still look up to you, Dad. (*Exits.*)

The angle of the Depás house disappears.

Alejandro He was killed last night in the square. In Parque Central. I was with you, remember? And I felt something strange, until we said goodbye and I went to see. Fucking siren! He was killed and I can't get my head around it: why, who it was, what it means. He was killed, and I couldn't tell him that, yes, he was right: I'm not a father; I am a piece of shit … But even so I did love him … With all my shitty heart I fucking loved him, I love him … And things could've changed, been better; we could have lived apart if that was for the best … I knew all that but I didn't tell him. I hit him and kept my mouth shut.

Silence.

And that bastard's loose out there, waiting for some other stupid kid in some other square, at the fair, at the cinema … The policeman didn't bother; he didn't look for any more signs. They work on inertia. It's horrific!

Kárel *does not say a word.*

Alejandro I'd love to have his killer in front of me in the courtroom, to ask him … (*Strokes* **Kárel***'s hair.*) What could I ask him, kiddo? What the hell could I ask him? (*He cries.*)

The waves of the sea crash intensely against the reef.

Chapter IX

Raid

A corner of the Paseo del Prado. The sea cannot be seen, but it can still be heard. Bay trees rustling. Almost midnight on 25 December.

Kárel *smokes, seated on a wall. Smoke in his mouth; smoke in his head.*

La Paco *hurries by. She carries her flower basket.*

La Paco (*picks him out in the darkness*)   Kárel? (*Approaches.*) It's so deserted here … Like everyone's been swallowed by the cold. I've sold three flowers in La Magdalena and I've been on the street since two in the afternoon. If you don't go up to Parque Central you don't get anything … Are you staying? No doubt you're waiting for someone. A fine spot for a date this is! I'm hardly selling anything; look. Not even paying attention to the men. Gives me chills, walking 'round on my own. That policeman keeps an eye on me; it's nice having him there, keeping me out of danger, but he's always watching me! Driving 'round and 'round. He'll turn up any minute. D'you know the one I'm talking about? I do like him, for a while, eating with him, letting him give me a squeeze … But I get tired of him eventually … Not in bed, but there's something heavy about policemen, even if they don't wear a uniform. You always think they're hiding something. If only they'd give you a guarantee, living together or having a baby … (*Laughs.*) Not that we can have a baby, of course. Fear, insecurity. This town that never gets any better. Just last night, in the square, that boy who was killed … Did you hear? There's still blood on the ground.

The branches on the trees beat relentlessly.

(*She takes out a cigarette*)   You got a light?

Kárel *offers her a lighter.* **La Paco** *lights up and smokes.*

La Paco   A girl could wake up dead on a street corner somewhere.

They are lit up by a motorcycle headlamp. **Kárel** *covers his face.*

La Paco   I think that's him coming now. See you later.

Goes to escape but bumps into **Saúl**.

Saúl   Weren't you supposed to be at La Magdalena?

La Paco   It's as empty as my fridge at home. I'm off to El Floridita; see if I have any luck there.

Saúl   Who was that talking to you?

La Paco   A boy. Come on, leave him alone; don't pester him.

Saúl   What boy?

La Paco Just a boy; don't be silly. (*Kisses him.*) Pick me up in a while.

Saúl *pinches her on the buttock.* **La Paco** *runs off.*

Saúl (*advances*) So, a boy … Kárel Darín.

Kárel *comes down from the wall.*

Saúl I was at your house this morning.

Kárel Where?

Saúl Your uncle called the station. I decided to pay him a visit.

Kárel Why?

Saúl He says you make trouble for him, says you're out in the street 'til all hours. Uncles' things. You smashed his face against the sideboard.

Kárel Are you mad? We get on fine.

Saúl But you didn't have a family dinner last night. You didn't sleep there either.

Kárel I've got a girlfriend; I went to her house.

Saúl Girlfriend or boyfriend?

Kárel What's your problem?

Saúl Don't act tough with me. That guy I told you about; what've you got on him?

Kárel I don't know anything about a guy.

Saúl (*grabs him by the neck*) The guy by the columns, the judge. Have you found anything out? I'm sure you've turned your trick with him already. And he paid you, didn't he? How much did he pay you?

Kárel Get off.

Saúl (*into his ear*) Maybe you gave him a discount. Seeing as you killed his son.

Kárel What the fuck you talking about?

Saúl If a job's worth doing, it's worth doing well.

Kárel I haven't done anything.

Saúl (*drags him over to the motorbike. Turns on the lights. Takes a photo out from his pocket*) Know who this girl is?

Kárel What is this? Why've you got that photo?

Saúl (*squeezes him*) What's her name?

Kárel Silvia.

Saúl Silvia Depás. Ring any bells? You know whose sister she is? (*Screws up the photo.*)

Kárel   Get off; get off me!

Saúl   Miguel Depás's. Who's Miguel Depás? He's the little kid you killed! Son of Alejandro Depás, the old queen who pays you to take him up the shitter!

Kárel   That's a lie! I didn't kill him!

Saúl   With a knife! I know you did; you stabbed him with a flick-knife!

Kárel   Haven't got a flick-knife.

Saúl   A pen-knife, a kitchen-knife! The doctors'll say. They'll know everything by the day after tomorrow at the latest. Your prints are on his clothes! The warden doesn't know you, or she's protecting you, but she said you were playing chess … Idiot! (*Throws him to the ground. Kicks him.*) Even to kill someone you've got to have some brains!

Kárel *could get up – he has some strength – but he remains collapsed in the middle of the pavement. He listens. Listens. Listens.*

Saúl   I saw your jumper covered in blood in your wardrobe but I put it back. Your uncle wanted to report you but I held him off; told him to wait. A deal's a deal. But you come here, you tell me nothing about that guy, you don't give me the slightest detail, not the tiniest way in.

Clumsily **Kárel** *tries to take out the knife.* **Saúl** *sees this and wrestles it from his hand.*

Saúl   What were you planning on doing with this? (*Kicks him even more.*)
Talk! Talk!

Kárel *raises his hands. He is going to talk. He is going to say something.*

One imagines that the hero always has something to say in the end. To keep his flame burning. 'For my emancipation', thinks **Kárel**, *remembering the books on the History of the Motherland. But he remains silent.*

Saúl *throws the knife at* **Kárel**; *it clinks against the asphalt.*

Saúl   You make me sick!

Spits and disappears on the motorbike.

Kárel Darín *is a body gasping for breath in a corner of the city.*

Chapter X

Vanishing Point

Alejandro Depás *does not look elegant. It is mid-morning on 26 December. The report has neglected until this moment to mention that this is a man who, despite entering his later years, retains all of the charms of youth.*

He is lit by a light from above.

Alejandro I swear I had nothing against him. I met him two days ago. In the Louvre Arcade, by the columns. The same night my son was killed. I liked him and I asked him to come back. I was heartbroken but I waited for him anyway, very close by, a few blocks away, on a bench in the Park of Lies, just where the number 15 stops. We drank together. Some rum or other. He didn't talk much that night. But he did listen a lot. I talked to him and it was like having Miguel in front of me. He listened to the things I'd kept quiet the previous morning and he didn't reply or ask questions. So many important words, saying them like that to a stranger! I think his silence made him look beautiful to me. He seemed different to the other lads you see on the streets in this city. The same age as Miguel. Oh, God. The same look in his eyes. (*A suffocation.*) We saw each other very early today. He came to the house – I never do that! – he came to my house because Silvia was on duty. I'd just buried my son and I was thinking about some boy! But it was the same thing. I know it's hard to understand but, when I saw him in the doorway, Miguel and Kárel were the same person. He must've had a bad night. He was bruised, beaten up … Bags under his eyes. 'So tired', I thought. He drank half a can of beer. We rolled around on the bed. He seemed so eager for it! One kiss. Two. And when we'd finished, he whispered into my ear: 'I don't want any money.' He picked up his trousers and took out a knife. 'So horrible', he said, like it had been his first time. And then, right next to his Adam's apple, he stabbed himself in the neck.

He remains still. Perhaps very still.

The light ends.

Nevada

**A Thermic Scale for Actors
in Thirteen Moments on a Single Day**

Nevada and this English translation were originally commissioned and developed by the English Stage Company as part of the 2005 Royal Court Theatre International Residency.

It premiered in Spanish at Teatro El Sótano, Havana, on 8 January 2010, produced by the Rita Montaner Company, directed by Fernando Quiñones, with the following cast: Loretta Estévez, Esteban León, Dayron Moreno, Rafa Quesada, Rogel Rodríguez and Giselle Sobrino.

For Giselle Sobrino,
my first Lucía

For Lucre Estévez,
Miriam Muñoz
and Rolando Estévez,
at the Teatro Icarón
and in the city of Matanzas

Moments on the Scale

I. Falling Flakes
II. Cloth and Humidity
III. Casting a Boat out to Sea
IV. Vaporetto
V. Up North
VI. Glacial
VII. Pirates
VIII. Heat Wave
IX. Working Out
X. Thaw
XI. Temperate Boulevard
XII. Take Me Sailing
XIII. Snowmen

Characters

Lucía Ferrer, *17*
Osmel Ferrer, *her brother, 15*
Magda Puentes, *their mother, 48*
Rosnay Durán, *25*
Frank Lobato, *46*
Higinio Mariñas, *68*

All the action takes place in Havana, from the middle of the night to the middle of the night, one Thursday and Friday in January.

I
Falling Flakes

In the centre of the city there is no one like her. In her red dress, **Lucía** *advances along the avenue in shadows and silence. Her approaching footsteps leave a trail of snow on the street. Just as she seems about to say something, the light goes out.*

In the darkness, somewhat distorted, we hear a children's choir, singing merrily: 'Little paper boat, my faithful friend, take me sailing on the open sea. I long to know ...' At this moment, the music stops and the sound of the Havana night floods everything.

At every point on the scale, even when the changes of temperature inside and outside the characters are most abrupt, there will be occasional, light, persistent snow.

II

Cloth and Humidity

5:30 a.m. Outside the Payret Cinema. Its façade, with filthy walls and high, opaque glass doors. **Higinio**, *seated on a small bench, listens to a radio.* **Magda** *arrives and looks around. She's distressed, exhausted, tired of walking around and sick of the darkness of the night. She's about to set off again, but instead approaches the old man.*

Magda   Have you seen a young girl dressed in red?

Higinio   Red?

Magda   Yes. A bright red dress.

Higinio *turns down the volume on the radio.*

Higinio   Yesterday, I think –

Magda   No, tonight. She was wearing it tonight.

Higinio   All the young girls like red.

Magda   This dress is different. You'd remember if she'd been here. She has been here. She always comes here, I know she does. Red doesn't suit her. The skirt's too tight for her. It barely reaches her knees. And she doesn't fill the top. It comes right up to her neck, looks like she's about to be strangled.

Higinio   Now you mention it …

Magda   What?

Higinio   Maybe the police took her.

Magda   The police were going 'round?

Higinio   Lots of patrol cars out until midnight. Started drifting off about one.

Magda   She's not the sort to get arrested.

Higinio   They pop up out of the blue, throw a bunch of people into a van and drive away. To clear out the corner, they say. Seeing as it's always so full.

Magda   It's empty now.

The corner is empty, a deserted junction, nothing more.

Higinio   That's hardly surprising … Sun'll be up soon … Something of yours, is she?

Magda   Something of mine.

Higinio   Your daughter?

II Cloth and Humidity

Magda　My daughter.

Higinio　Why're you looking for her this time of night?

Magda　I've been out looking for her for a while.

Higinio　Came out early, did she? Didn't tell you where she was going?

Magda　She never does. But I know where she goes.

Higinio　So now you're here.

Magda　This corner, then the next, then the pavement over the road …

Higinio　There was a lad killed in the park opposite, the night before last.

Magda　Killed?

Higinio　It happens. Out of the blue, just like that, on any given day, some youngster leaves his house early, doesn't come back, and next morning they find him dead with two stab wounds in his belly.

Magda　Do you enjoy talking about death?

Higinio　I respect it.

Magda　Makes me feel sick.

Higinio　Think I'm making it up?

Magda　People don't get killed in this city.

Higinio　All sorts goes on in that park.

Magda　I never go through it. I walk 'round the side.

Higinio　The youngsters go in there, gambling. Betting on their games. And when they lose, fights break out. That's what happened. The police can't admit people gamble for money, so they made up a story. Said he was killed over some whore.

Magda　Whore?

Higinio　I saw the blood. I was sitting here and they went past with him on the stretcher. Covered in a sheet, but dripping.

Magda　Oh, stop it! Stop talking like that, it makes my skin crawl.

Higinio　Oozing with it.

Magda　Maybe Lucía's at home now.

Higinio　Red drops.

Magda　Lucía's dress …

Higinio　Did it have blood on it?

Magda　What?

Higinio Your daughter's dress. I thought it was blood-red. Or red with blood.

Magda She knows how to keep herself clean.

Higinio Still, the streets are dirty.

Magda She can look after herself.

Higinio So why come looking for her?

Magda Because I feel like it.

She disappears.

III

Casting a Boat out to Sea

6:00 a.m. precisely. Very close to the door to the cinema, **Rosnay** *smokes beside a column, looking insistently from side to side along the street. He hasn't slept and he's not tired: the habit of loving the night.*

If no one talks to **Higinio***, he strikes up a conversation himself. There's nothing he likes more than dawn breaking with someone standing there on his patch.*

Higinio Didn't the police put you in their van last night?

Rosnay (*looks at him, surprised, for a few seconds*) No.

Higinio I could've sworn they did. Didn't they catch you with that blond girl in pigtails and put you in the van? Wasn't that you?

Rosnay Did no one ever tell you old men shouldn't ask so many questions?

Higinio Why not?

Rosnay Case they get in the neck.

Higinio Listen, don't take umbrage with me. If it was you –

Rosnay I'm telling you it wasn't.

Rosnay *moves away from the column and walks along the pavement. He sizes up the remains of the daybreak cheer: a cat climbing into the dustbin.* **Higinio** *follows him.*

Rosnay Are you following me?

Higinio Got a cigarette you can give me?

Rosnay Will you piss off if I do?

Higinio I can't go anywhere until seven. Not 'til sunrise, when the administrator comes. She opens her office and I sign the sheet. Sign the sheet and write down my hours. Seven p.m. to seven a.m. I sign to say I've been here all night, so they can pay me. Of course, they pay me a pittance. Doesn't stretch to anything. And if I decide to go to the market, well, what can I tell you? Bleeds me dry. Just for formality's sake, signing. Just so I know I've done some work, that I'm not a parasite, that I earn my bread. Don't want to be an old man on a measly pension. Not that there's much difference between a pension and a salary. Anyway, I wait and I sign, because it's the right thing to do, so I have my own source of income, so I don't get in the way of our system, in the way of our society, as it says in *Das Kapital*. Have you read *Das Kapital*?

Rosnay God spare me!

Higinio   Just as well. That doesn't worry you: signing or not signing. You've got your own business to care about. But this is my business: night-time at the cinema. Sometimes the young men ask to bring their girls in here. Let off a bit of steam. I turn a blind eye … For a few pesos, you know. Doesn't do anyone any harm. The cinema's empty, they go in and do what they need to do … And the hundred and twenty pesos I earn, I need them too. If I don't sign, the administrator won't know that I really have been sitting here on this little bench, with the radio to my ear, listening to a baseball game or the weather report –

Rosnay   Did you hear the weather report?

Higinio   Give me that cigarette?

Rosnay *takes out a pack and gives* **Higinio** *a cigarette.* **Higinio** *gestures to ask for a light.* **Rosnay** *lights the cigarette for him with his lighter.*

Rosnay   Did you hear if it's gonna rain?

Higinio   I couldn't hear too well, couldn't tune the station in.

Rosnay   It better not rain, not in fucking January.

Higinio   What are you up to?

Rosnay   Waiting for my girlfriend.

Higinio   Is your girlfriend the blonde one? It's just, I see you with her as often as I see you with that little mixed girl.

Rosnay (*smiles*)   Keep saying that and you'll get me in trouble.

Higinio   You've got the right idea. Making money out of women. Heck, we all have to make money somehow!

Rosnay *looks, astonished, at* **Higinio**. *He focusses on the eyes of the old man and looks for some reason to laugh again. One of those silly laughs one breaks into spontaneously. But he finds nothing.*

Lucía *appears behind his back, surprising him with a pinch.*

Lucía   Weren't we meeting on the other corner?

Rosnay   You got mixed up yesterday, too. What's wrong with you?

Lucía   All right, I'm here now.

Higinio *moves away and goes back to his little bench.*

Lucía   What was the old man saying to you?

Rosnay   Asking me for a light. Poor bloke, hasn't got a pot to piss in. Looks after the cinema all night.

Lucía   I see him here every time I go past. Wrapped up in a raggedy bedspread.

Rosnay   I'm freezing to death. Come here. (*Hugs her.*)

His top has no sleeves. It's almost freezing, but he prefers going sleeveless.

How did your night go?

Lucía   It went.

Rosnay   But how?

Lucía   Did you speak to that friend of Kiko's in the end?

Rosnay   Yeah, I spoke to him. It was a miracle, Luli, it really was. The last chance. When Kiko told me, I thought he'd want the place fully furnished, but no ... It's just as good to him as it is, half-empty. He's coming 'round in a couple of hours.

Lucía   And he's got all the money? 'Nay, this is too good to be true.

Lucía *loves how lucky she is.*

Rosnay   Only, he also wants ... to see you for the night.

Lucía   And what did you tell him?

Rosnay   I said we'd work something out.

Lucía   Oh, Rosnay ...

Actually, she hates how unlucky she is.

Rosnay   Luli, listen: we'll be on that boat this time tomorrow. We need the money.

Lucía   You don't know what could happen between now and tomorrow.

Rosnay   Yes, I do. I'll get the cash off him, then I'll pay the coastguard and the fee for the boat ride. You just have to be a good little girl for a while, be nice to him –

Lucía   Not today, 'Nay. Not today.

Rosnay   It's today or not at all. Don't say 'not today'.

Lucía   I've got so much to sort out at home.

Rosnay   Then sort it out quickly. You always do things quickly.

Lucía   This is crazy.

Rosnay *kisses her, pressing her against the wall.*

Lucía   I love it when you taste of cigarettes.

Rosnay   And I love it when I bite you, like this. And like this ...

Lucía   You're not slobbering all over my neck.

Rosnay   Oh yes I am.

Lucía   How old is this guy?

Rosnay   Twenty-five.

Lucía (*laughs*) Like you? You must be mad, asking me to sleep with a twenty-five-year-old. You'd rather cut out your own tongue.

Rosnay Doesn't scare me.

Lucía OK, I'll do it.

Rosnay He's not the dangerous one. You are.

Lucía No. You are.

They kiss and in this instant they are two good kids.

Rosnay He's forty-something. Won't take you long.

Lucía I really don't feel like it. I'm bored of always doing the same thing … Is it always gonna be like this? Even if we leave, is it gonna be like this?

Rosnay Until you leave me.

Lucía Come off it. I'm not leaving you.

Rosnay Then it won't always be like this. I mean, I don't know … It's a good little deal today, Luli. Don't fuck it up.

Lucía How would I fuck it up?

Rosnay By disappearing all day and not turning up.

Lucía When have I ever not turned up?

Rosnay Only takes one day.

Lucía Well, it won't be today.

Rosnay It can't be today.

Lucía Yesterday I thought I wouldn't go with you. I thought I'd tell you I'd decided to stay here. Tell you, just to see what you'd do. But then straight away I realized that'd be stupid.

Rosnay Not leaving?

Lucía No. Telling you. Telling you I didn't wanna leave.

Rosnay Why?

Lucía 'Cause you'd leave anyway.

Rosnay Don't be daft.

Lucía Wouldn't you leave anyway?

Rosnay *says nothing.*

Lucía It's like an obsession. Like a fashion. Ever since you heard Aldito had made it there in one piece, on a boat, that he was with his family now, you got the idea into your head … Why am I following you?

Rosnay *still says nothing.*

Lucía I could kill you.

Rosnay I dare you.

Lucía Bite you 'til you bleed to death.

Rosnay Go on, then.

Lucía Could you handle that?

Rosnay Depends where you bite me.

Lucía This finger, see? And your elbow, and your ear … (*Nibbles at him.*)

Rosnay Not bleeding yet.

Lucía Haven't bitten you properly yet.

Rosnay I'll wait, then.

Lucía Idiot.

Rosnay Call me at midday and I'll tell you what I've arranged with him. Here's his number. (*Hands her a scrap of paper.*)

Lucía What are we doing tonight, you and me?

Rosnay I'll tell you at noon.

Lucía What are we doing, 'Nay?

Rosnay We'll get a bus as far as Cojímar. And then the boat, all right?

Lucía It's scary.

Rosnay What's scary?

Lucía Will it be safe? Have you made sure? You talk like that, so relaxed, and it makes me so uncertain … But at the same time you seem so convinced.

Rosnay You won't believe it when we're in Miami.

Lucía They say it's gonna start raining after midday.

Rosnay It won't even spit.

Lucía What if it's choppy? I heard the worst thing's when the sea's choppy. On the TV they're always saying the sea's really rough on the north coast, dangerous for small boats. I've heard it so many times, I've got it memorized.

Rosnay Come here when the cinema closes. Half past twelve … Better still, one o'clock. Bring everything with you.

Lucía What if I don't come?

Rosnay You're not gonna get scared now, are you?

Lucía *sighs.*

Rosnay What?

Lucía *shakes her head.*

Rosnay You told your mum yet?

Lucía *shakes her head again.*

Rosnay You are going to, aren't you?

Lucía I love you, 'Nay.

Rosnay Yes, Luli, I know you love me. And I love you. You're the one I'm leaving with, no one else. Come on, off you go. Stop thinking about it.

She looks at him. They've been looking at each other all along but now she looks at him properly.

Lucía Maybe I'll have a sleep. I'm dead on my feet.

She blows him a kiss and disappears.

Rosnay *stays beside the column. He has no more business here but he stays. God knows why.*

IV

Vaporetto

The living-dining room in **Magda**'s *house at 6:30 a.m. The dawn light begins to filter through the windows, rescuing the colours in the faded room. Resting her head on the table,* **Magda** *sweats, the kind of sweat that keeps you from sleeping properly even on winter mornings. She looks asleep, but is so anxious that she's merely lying in wait.*

Lucía *enters, sees her, and tries to make as little sound as possible. She tiptoes towards her room. Just as she is about to go in, the mother speaks.*

Magda   Why do you insist on wearing my clothes?

Lucía   I'm shattered. I'm going to sleep.

Magda   Not until you tell me why you went out in my red dress.

Lucía   It's my dress, you gave me it last week. I remember. I went to the shop and brought you some chocolate Crunch, your favourite, I got you it just because, because I felt like getting you something. You were so pleased, you gave me the dress.

Magda   I didn't think you'd take it.

Lucía   I didn't at first but you insisted.

Magda   I insist every day that you don't spend all night gallivanting out there and you never take any notice. But suddenly I insist on giving you my best party dress and you don't think twice about taking it.

Lucía   I didn't have any other clean clothes.

Magda   Why don't you do some laundry?

Lucía   I'll do it later, after I've slept a bit.

Magda   I hope you haven't got it dirty.

Lucía   It doesn't fit you, Mum.

Magda   I started exercising yesterday, I'm sure it'll fit me now.

Lucía   I went out late last night, I thought you were at the hospital.

Magda   And you took advantage. Well, no, it wasn't my shift. You knew fine well it wasn't my shift. I went for a wander, I shan't tell you where I went, I don't have to tell you. When I got back and opened the drawer and saw you'd taken my red dress … Not that it suits you, anyway. Stand up straight. Let me see you. Turn around. Oh, no, it doesn't fit you. It's too loose 'round the hips and too tight 'round the knees. Doesn't do anything for your legs. Well, you never did have good legs.

Lucía   I just left the belt off.

Magda No, the belt's not the problem. The belt used to do something for me, but you can't expect it to work miracles … Please. The dress doesn't suit you and that's an end to it.

Lucía I'll take it off, then.

Magda Hang on a second.

Lucía Don't you want me to take it off?

Magda I want you to sit down. Just for a minute.

Lucía *sits down.*

Magda Aren't you going to school today?

Lucía Do you want me to do the laundry or go to school?

Magda Do the laundry, then go to school.

Lucía Fine.

Magda It's not fine. You say it in that tone and I know you won't go. I already did my studying, Lucía. I work myself to the bone, every other day.

Lucía I work every day.

Magda Not in a hospital! You don't spend all night fretting about some old man who needs his injection or treating some burn victim or cleaning up some sick person's shit. You sleep here all day, then at night you're outdoors 'til all hours. That's why you're dead on your feet in the morning and don't want to go to school or do the laundry or the ironing or the cooking. You always disappear off.

Lucía I come back.

Magda That's the worst thing.

Lucía Me going out?

Magda You coming back.

My mother would say, at this point, that there's nothing more to say. Which is why **Lucía***'s first instinct is to get up and go to her room, leaving her mother screaming or saying nothing, who knows.* **Magda** *knows her so well that she barely gives her time to react, to move. Deep down, like all mothers, she worships her.*

Magda I went out looking for you.

Lucía When?

Magda I couldn't stand it and I went out looking for you.

Lucía Why were you collapsed on the table when I came in?

Magda I miss you so much, Lucía …

She hugs her. Groans.

When I opened my eyes this morning I thought I should forgive you for never doing the things I expect of you ... Even for always doing the opposite.

Lucía   What is this?

Magda   Yes. You act like you live on your own.

Lucía   You go out, too.

Magda   It's not the same.

Lucía   You go out on the street, too. You live your life.

Magda   Don't talk back to me.

Lucía   I never ask you questions.

Magda   Stop it! I never say a word to you either!

Lucía   And then suddenly today ... Why did you go out looking for me? There was no need, I was coming back. What do you need, money?

Magda   Why do you always think it's money?

Lucía   Ask me for something else, then. Ask me for a kiss, for example.

Magda   That's just what I wanted, I wanted you to give me a kiss. A kiss, here on my nose, like when you were a girl.

Lucía *thinks how it wasn't on her nose but on her chin where she used to kiss her.*

Magda   Every time you open that door and go outside, I have this feeling I'm going to lose you forever. It's such a big city.

Lucía   And this is such a tiny house.

Magda   We could move.

Lucía   Oh, Mum, how could we move?

Magda   There are ads in the paper. People wanting to split their houses up, divide them into two. People looking to share.

Lucía   Hardly anyone wants to share.

Magda   Just was well your brother went to military school.

Lucía   I think he'd be better here with us.

Magda   I love him being there. Far away from home. Well protected. Better fed.

Lucía   I really need to go to bed. We'll talk later.

Magda   I'm going to the hospital in a while.

Lucía   When you get back tomorrow, I'll have all your clothes washed, dried and folded up in the wardrobe.

Magda I wanted to ask you … Well, I had a bit of money left over and I bought that cooking oil they'd had come in at the shop. But the shopkeeper gave me a filthy look. We haven't bought any milk from him for a week. It's the ration for children up to age seven. Evaporated milk this month, not in cans because people fiddle them. It came in cartons … Can you imagine having a nice milky coffee, or a glass of cold milk for breakfast, or rice pudding, or caramel curds for afters?

All that **Lucía** *can think about is that Russian cartoon with a little boy who got lost in a village called Curdled Milk, or something like that. And then she thinks immediately of a snowfall of milk.*

Lucía I can't give you any, Mum. I don't have any spare right now.

Magda My stomach hurts. It's my gastritis, I know it is. I can't sleep a wink with this ulcer.

Lucía I haven't, Mum.

Magda I thought maybe you'd help me out. What with me not getting paid 'til next month … If only I had something to sell …

Lucía Is there no milk left at all?

Magda There's a bit in the bottle.

Lucía Well then.

Magda I'm dying, Lucía.

Lucía What d'you mean, 'dying'?

Magda I'm going to sell my engagement ring.

Lucía What?

Magda That way I won't have to depend on you. I saw one in the shop, one of those where they sell old things on commission. It cost eight hundred pesos and it was only silver. Mine's gold, and it's got a diamond. It'll be worth more. A thousand, at least.

Lucía Don't you dare. Dad gave you that.

Magda You said yourself we don't have enough money.

Lucía But we will tomorrow, or at the weekend. Have you lost your mind? Trading Dad in for some milk? Dad's memory, the only memory you have, for a glass of milk?

Magda It's gold I'm trading for the milk, not your father.

Lucía Do what you want.

Magda That is what I want: not to die.

Lucía How much do you need?

Magda Four cartons. A hundred pesos.

Lucía *sighs, opens her handbag, takes out some banknotes and holds them out.*

Lucía   Buy ten.

Magda   Don't you need that money for something?

Lucía *tuts.*

Magda   You'd best not go to school. You've terrible bags under your eyes. I'll do the laundry if you like, you have a rest.

Lucía   Don't worry about it.

Magda   Are you going out tonight?

Lucía *does not respond; she heads for her room.*

Magda   Will you be home early?

Lucía *goes into her room.*

Magda   For something to eat, I mean. So I know whether to leave you any food.

Silence.

Will you be coming home?

V

Up North

*A nearly empty room in **Rosnay**'s apartment, 10:00 a.m. Until yesterday night there were boxes in one corner and piles of clothing, but someone took care of taking everything away. Seated on a mattress, **Rosnay** and **Frank** are having a few beers.*

Frank   I really do like your place. Could be a pleasure to live here if you forget all the dross out on the street and the Black dudes playing dominos. If you got the roof fixed up. Stop it collapsing.

Rosnay   Nothing's collapsing here.

Frank   There's no problem with ownership, you say? Look: if some funny business turns up and they take it off me …

Rosnay   It's all legal. Jorgito's organising the handover, he'll make it look like a straight swap. He's a lawyer, he knows how it all works. Anything to do with home ownership, he's your man. Listen: if he could sort me out to keep this place when my mum went Up North, he can do anything.

Frank   Isn't it fantastic how we always call the States 'Up North' … It's cold Up North, things are better up there, the candy comes wrapped in shiny paper …

*Talking about his mother isn't one of **Rosnay**'s favourite things, but here he makes things clear:*

Rosnay   Mum's getting on fine. Nothing out of this world, but things are working out. She sends money sometimes.

Frank   And you save it up.

Rosnay   That, and what I earn out there.

Frank   You're a good-looking man. Must have girls queuing up to do business for you… Kiko told me all about it.

Rosnay   Kiko's got a big mouth.

Frank   Maybe you need a little chain 'round your neck. Complete the look.

Rosnay   Men don't wear chains.

Frank   But they do have long hair?

Rosnay   I do. And I make use of it.

Frank   You should know.

Rosnay   And you should know about chains. I spend my money on other things.

Frank   Where is it your mum lives?

Rosnay   Nevada.

Frank   Nevada's in Las Vegas.

Rosnay   Las Vegas is in Nevada. They say it's the only place in the world where the working girls don't get any grief from the police. They just let 'em get on with it.

Frank   I'm sure they take their share. Whoring costs money everywhere.

Rosnay   Well, I love Nevada!

Frank   And I love your little Lucía. She's not even twenty yet, is she?

He'd rather not talk about this either and replies quickly:

Rosnay   Seventeen.

Frank   I've had my eye on her ever since I first saw you with her.

Rosnay   You're a stubborn bastard. All those whores in Monte and Cienfuegos and you pay all your attention to a little girl who just hangs around El Capitolio and the Payret Cinema.

Frank   You've squared it with her?

Rosnay   All sorted.

Frank   You're the one who doesn't like the idea.

Rosnay   I like the idea of getting the hell out of this country.

Frank   Never crossed my mind to do that.

Rosnay   That's 'cause you've got a nice set-up here.

Frank   So have you.

Rosnay   Do me a favour! The fridge was empty when they came to buy it. Nothing in there. I've been eating bread and croquettes on the corner near El Capitolio for the last month.

Frank   You're not the bread-and-croquettes type.

In another time, when he used to go out in his Pull & Bear shirts and acid-wash jeans, when he was a young kid who walked the streets around El Capitolio, when no one knew him and he'd go with a different foreigner every night to a hotel room, when he made money to take to his mother at weekends, he wouldn't have mentioned the bread and croquettes to anyone, even though he did eat them. But now he doesn't care.

Rosnay   I am sometimes. Where's the money?

Frank *takes a roll of notes out of his pocket and holds them out to* **Rosnay**, *who counts them.*

Rosnay   It's not all here.

Frank   No.

Rosnay   What about the rest?

Frank   I'll give it to her.

Rosnay   To Lucía? Why?

Frank   I think it's a good deal. Especially for you.

Rosnay   Half the money's missing.

Frank   So is half the deal.

Rosnay *smiles.*

Frank   You scared, you old beast?

Rosnay   No.

Frank   You're scared to death.

Rosnay   I know how deals get cut, Frank. And it's not by force. Best be polite, otherwise things just get nasty. Ask Kiko. He's known me for ages.

Frank   From hanging 'round El Capitolio.

Rosnay   Sometimes that's the best way for two men to get to know each other.

Frank   Except Kiko does the woman's job half the time.

Rosnay   Don't go there … First, you say you'll pay me. Second, I believe you.

Frank   And third, I cough up.

Rosnay   Lucía'll call you this evening. You can come here. It's no trouble. You can't play any music: I already sold the tape deck. But there's hot water in the bathroom. And this part of Old Havana doesn't get power cuts.

Frank   Better than a hotel. Be quite luxurious once I've fixed it up. Shame if it rains today and water starts dripping through when I've got your girl with me … What with them forecasting bad weather.

Rosnay   It won't rain, you'll see. And the roof doesn't leak that much. (*Gives him a key.*) Here. I'll be here 'til seven.

Frank   And I'll be here with your girlfriend just before nine.

Rosnay   Use my bed.

VI

Glacial

The brightly lit living-dining room in **Magda**'s *house. 11:00 a.m. The brightness of the winter sun floods the house.* **Osmel** *opens the front door and comes in. He wears military uniform and carries a rucksack.*

Osmel   Mum!

He puts the rucksack on the table and lies face-up on the floor. He stretches out his hands and feet.

Mum!

Lucía *opens her bedroom door. Her hair is unkempt.*

Lucía   What's wrong with you?

Osmel   Did I wake you up? (*Gets up.*) Is Mum not here?

Lucía   She just left for the hospital. She's on shift 'til tomorrow morning. Is something wrong?

They kiss just as they always have, as if it were any normal day, even though it's no such thing for either of them.

Osmel   No.

Lucía   What about military school?

Osmel   I'm not cut out for the forces, Luli.

Lucía   Are you hungry?

Osmel   Make me something.

Lucía   There's bread. And Mum bought milk.

Osmel   Bread and butter.

Lucía *goes to the kitchen. She talks from there.*

Lucía   Are you on leave? You don't get leave today. Or is it because it's Thursday?

Osmel   They threw me out.

Lucía (*comes to the kitchen door*)   Very funny.

Osmel   It's true. They threw me out.

Lucía   But you're still wearing the uniform.

Osmel   I've got this, too.

Places a gun on the table.

Lucía (*comes over with the bread for her brother*)   You took a gun?

Osmel   I felt like keeping it. I piled all my stuff on the bed and covered it in a sheet. Except the gun. I'm gonna sell it to a mate.

Lucía   Sell a gun? Do you think you're in a Western?

Osmel   It was easy. I just had to take it.

Lucía   What have you got in your head, Osmel? It's a pistol, not a pea-plant. They'll realize you took it. Don't they keep count of them? Didn't they search you when you left? You're taking it back.

Osmel   I'm not going back there. Anyway, I like it … I learnt to shoot yesterday.

Lucía   You are. You're taking it back there.

Osmel   I said 'no'.

Lucía   What do you mean, they 'threw you out'?

Osmel   Oh, Luli, they just threw me out. They threw. Me. Out. In capitals. Does it need that much explanation?

Lucía   But you were doing so well.

Osmel   Well, I suddenly did badly.

Lucía   Why?

Osmel   'Why' what?

Lucía   I don't understand.

Osmel   What is there to understand?

Lucía   You come here, you say they threw you out and you're not going back … And there's no reason?

Osmel   No, there isn't.

Lucía   There's nothing I can help you with?

Osmel   Like what?

Lucía   I don't know.

Osmel   Mum's the worst thing.

Lucía   Mum's unbearable lately.

Osmel   You have to go to the school on Monday.

Lucía   Monday?

Osmel   You can go, can't you?

Lucía   Mum'll go.

Osmel No, not her. You go.

Lucía What did you do? It's so weird that they threw you out and left you like this.

Osmel They're throwing tonnes of people out. There's miles of marching, loads of exercise, the food's bad.

Lucía They say the food there's the best in the world.

Osmel Fish once a week, on Wednesdays. That's the best day.

Lucía It's still weird, though … You must have done something for them to throw you out. And when they did throw you out … you must have tried to convince them to let you stay. This doesn't happen every day. It's pretty hard to get thrown out of a school in this country! You've not even been there a year.

Osmel OK, just don't think about it.

Lucía How can I not think about it?

Osmel Forget it.

Lucía 'Forget it'? You, here, alone in the house with Mum?

Osmel 'Alone'? Why? What about you?

Lucía I'm not the problem. You are.

Osmel I'll get it in the neck from Mum when she gets home. I don't need you to start, Luli.

Osmel *woke up before dawn. He thought he was going to be thrown out, that he already had been. He must have thought this was the story he'd tell at home and to the neighbours, even though he never goes outside and has no one to give explanations to. But for himself. For himself, he believed he'd been thrown out. And then in his life, and in his mind, there was no space to think anything else.*

Lucía Eat your bread.

Osmel I'm not hungry.

Lucía Something's wrong with you. You just said –

Osmel I'm fine.

She strokes him.

That tickles.

Lucía You'll have to go to a boarding school in the countryside.

Osmel I'd rather be dead.

Lucía You're only fifteen and you're already this much of a pain. I pity your wife when you get married.

Osmel I'm not getting married.

Lucía So what are you gonna do: piss about your whole life?

Osmel Why don't you get married?

Lucía I'm too young.

Osmel Then I'm a baby.

They laugh.

I thought you'd be out. Mum's always complaining you come home really late. She says you sometimes don't come home at all.

Lucía I'm doing the laundry. Have you got any dirty clothes?

Osmel What do you do at night?

Lucía I keep my mouth shut and sleep.

Osmel I mean when you're out.

Lucía I make money.

Osmel For yourself?

Lucía For everyone in this house. I thought once you became a colonel and had a respectable salary –

Osmel You could make money in the daytime.

Lucía But I know how to do it at night.

Osmel Oh.

Lucía *puts the bread in his hands. He starts to eat.*

Osmel Are you going to school in the end?

Lucía I can't, Osmel.

Osmel You're gonna miss a whole week, like in December?

Lucía It's not a whole week.

Osmel So you can go, then.

Mine was a shorter journey, but still I put it to my sister this way:

Lucía I could. It's just … I'm leaving.

Osmel Where you going?

Lucía I'm leaving. And I'm not coming back.

Osmel Leaving home?

Lucía Leaving Cuba.

Osmel What?

Lucía I've made my mind up.

Osmel Pull the other one, Luli. You've never wanted to leave.

Lucía I should be in Miami this time tomorrow.

Osmel Up North? Don't take the piss!

Lucía I want you to come too in a year's time.

Osmel But, Luli … You need passports and stamps –

Lucía No, I don't.

Osmel What about tickets? And money?

Lucía A boat.

Osmel A boat?

Lucía Yes, a boat. Thousands of people go on boats. You just don't know it because they don't show it on TV.

Osmel Those boats never make the crossing. It's a fairy tale. People get stuck alone in the middle of the sea and starve to death. What do you mean by a 'boat', anyway? Some sort of raft? Who put that idea into your head?

Lucía We're both going. Me and Rosnay.

Osmel Rosnay?

Lucía You don't know him.

Osmel You're leaving 'cause of him?

Lucía No, I'm leaving just because.

Osmel Yeah, but you love him. It's a bit much, you suddenly leaving like this, without so much as a by-your-leave, for some bloke …

Lucía *knows that it's a bit much to suddenly leave like this, without so much as a by-your-leave, for some bloke.*

Osmel Does he love you? … Get a grip, Luli. Don't do anything stupid … What is this? Disappearing off with some random person.

Lucía He's not a random person. I like him, Osmel. I like Rosnay. He's a guy I really like. Maybe it's less about leaving, more about not losing him.

Osmel Please! How do you know if he wants to live with you? What will you do over there with him? Are you out of your mind? How will you live?

Lucía The same way everyone lives. We'll work. I work here, and look: the strap's broken on my sandal and I can't afford to get it fixed. I gave Mum the last dollars I had so she could buy milk.

Osmel That's got nothing to do with it. Get a needle and sew the strap back on yourself. Then go out tomorrow and sort yourself out some cash. Right? You always sort yourself out, don't you?

Lucía Not always.

Osmel I can find some way to make money. My mate's gonna give me eighty dollars for the gun. His dad works at customs.

Lucía Stop talking about the gun.

Osmel OK.

Lucía Mum's been a nurse for thirty years and how much does she earn? You can't live off a salary.

Osmel At the military school they say you can.

Lucía Maybe they can. But not you or me.

For the second time this morning, **Lucía** *feels this is the end of the conversation. The sun is getting stronger and has heated up all the walls of the house. To keep herself from suffocating, she thinks about her mother's milk, about the snowfall of milk, about the Russian cartoons, about the lost boy, and says:*

Rosnay's got family in Nevada. They've been there for years and they're doing fine.

Osmel Nevada?

Lucía It's a nice name. I like the sound of it.

Osmel Nevada.

Lucía Once I've got a bit of money I'll send you some and you can come with us.

Osmel And you think you'll find work there when you're so young? Don't you need qualifications? Or to speak English, at least? No way, I don't wanna leave.

Lucía You'll want to when you see the photos. There's jelly and yoghurt – flavoured yoghurt, of course. And they sell chocolate in great big bars ... And if it's called Nevada, it can't be as hot as here. It means 'Snowfall'.

Osmel Maybe it doesn't even snow there.

Lucía It must snow sometimes.

Osmel Or you'll be dreaming of snowmen.

Lucía And I'll freeze.

A happy silence.

Osmel And we'll leave Mum here in Cuba?

Lucía Oh, for a while, yes ... Then, later, you tell me.

Osmel It's so sudden, so … You're not giving me time to … Can't I ask you to stay?

Lucía You're such a drama queen … I'm not dying … But I can't stay here. Maybe if I was Mum's age –

Osmel It's really bad, you leaving. This Rosnay –

Lucía You'll like him.

Osmel Am I gonna meet him?

Lucía In Nevada.

It is such a faraway landscape.

Osmel Isn't it scary? Aren't you scared?

Lucía I'm scared to death of staying here.

Osmel I'd have a panic attack if I left now. Running away … I still can't believe you're going like that, on a boat, without Mum knowing.

Lucía It's best she doesn't know.

Osmel Yeah, it is best she doesn't know, but all the same, Luli … I'd do anything to make you stay.

Lucía I'm worried about your school.

Osmel Can't you stay?

Lucía Why don't we go out for a pizza together?

Osmel *kisses her on the forehead and smiles. She sobs. He holds her.*

Osmel Don't cry. Come on. Breathe.

Lucía And that gun there on the table.

Osmel It's just a stupid gun. I just took it, just because. Who cares? When I left the lieutenant's office I realized it didn't matter what I said. I'd never fit in there anyway. All the discipline, all the getting up before dawn, all those men together … I just wanted to run away and take something with me. Now the gun's mine and I can sell it.

Lucía Does it fire blanks?

Osmel These guns don't use blanks, Luli. It's loaded with real bullets. The kind that go 'bang', and make everything stop.

Lucía *shudders.*

Osmel (*laughs*) No, idiot, of course they're blanks. I just can't tell my mate that.

Lucía I've never seen anyone with a gun in their house. I heard once they could put you in prison. It's against the law to bear arms in Cuba … Didn't you know that?

Osmel Yes, I know.

Lucía So why?

Osmel It's just a game. It's no big deal.

Lucía Prison isn't a game, Osmel. I'd rather die than have a gun in my hand. Why don't you put it away, right now? Put it somewhere Mum won't see it, go on. Look: in that drawer in the dresser no one ever opens.

He takes it to the drawer and puts it away.

Osmel In plain sight like that?

Lucía It's not in plain sight.

Osmel Shall we go out?

Lucía Will you go on Monday and take it back?

Osmel If you come with me.

VII

Pirates

A bedroom in **Rosnay**'s *house, dimly lit by a bare bulb. He lies on the bed, naked, making paper boats.*

Magda *switched her shifts at the hospital. A nurse has little difficulty in doing this. She didn't want anything special, nor did she need the day for admin or visits. She spent all afternoon doing jigsaw puzzles, which left her exhausted, even sweatier, despairing, and anxious. As soon as she arrived at* **Rosnay**'s *place, she went into the bathroom and took a shower; he wouldn't have touched her otherwise. Or maybe he would have; she thinks he would touch her anyway and that she only showered because she wanted too, because she's overheated.*

Now, at 5:00 p.m., **Magda** *sits beside* **Rosnay** *and caresses him.*

Magda   You're like a little boy.

Rosnay   I like boats.

Magda   It's no fun if they're made of paper. I'd love to go for a boat ride. Not in some old raft or little rowing boat, though. A real boat, a ship, like pirates used to have.

Rosnay   There are no pirates any more.

Magda   Maybe I could put a hook on your hand and turn you into a pirate. My pirate. (*Ruffles his hair.*)

Rosnay (*laughs*)   You're mad.

Magda   I've never felt better.

Rosnay   You say that now. You'll forget tomorrow. We always forget.

Magda   You know I won't.

She takes some banknotes from her handbag and hands them to him. He puts them away in his wallet.

Rosnay   I was wondering last night why you keep coming here.

Magda   Don't think so much.

Rosnay   Why not?

Magda   Do you want a drink?

Rosnay   No.

Magda   I brought some beers but they're warm.

Rosnay   They came and took the fridge just this morning.

Magda I've never known anyone move house in such a strange way. Most people pile everything onto a van at once and go, but you're doing it all so slowly … It's like you're scared, like you're not sure. It is a lovely place. I'd never leave it.

Rosnay I'm not moving apartments.

Magda What do you mean? You've already sold everything.

Rosnay I'm moving countries.

Magda That's a good one.

Rosnay I'm going to Miami. Then on to Nevada.

Magda You're dreaming, aren't you?

Rosnay Daydreaming.

Magda They never give visas to anyone. You're twenty-five years old. They won't make an exception for you. They'll say you're a potential immigrant or maybe a terrorist. Cuba's on the black list.

Rosnay My wallet's my visa.

Magda What about your passport?

Rosnay Forget it.

Magda *goes back into the bathroom.* **Rosnay** *arranges the boats beside the bed. She returns.*

Magda I thought I could come 'round and cook something nice for you tomorrow when I leave the hospital. We can do it early if you like. You might be busy at night … Anyway, I mentioned having dinner together last week –

Rosnay Tomorrow when you leave the hospital the only thing I'll be able to do is remember you.

Magda Drinking beer on the corner near El Capitolio.

Rosnay Eating a McDonald's.

Magda That joke's really working out for you.

Rosnay Just like everything else, hopefully.

Magda Are you being serious?

Rosnay Very.

Magda You can't leave.

Rosnay I don't wanna stay.

Magda Who are you going with?

Rosnay I'm going on my own. Same way I came into the world.

Magda   What about your ticket?

Rosnay   I just told you: I've got money.

Magda   You haven't got a ticket.

Rosnay   So?

Magda   Money can only get you so far. You're not leaving.

Rosnay (*smiles*)   You're very sure of yourself.

Magda   You can't leave, Rosnay.

Rosnay   Course I can.

Magda   No, you can't.

Rosnay   Relax. You're getting worked up. I don't like people getting worked up.

Magda   'Relax'! 'Relax'! What are you thinking?

Rosnay   What the fuck are *you* thinking?

Magda   I'm thinking you should listen to me. I haven't been coming here, bringing you food, washing your clothes and cleaning your house, just so that one fine day you can –

Rosnay   This isn't your house.

Magda   I've looked after it like it's mine, and more. Every week, every day. Much more. Every peso that goes into my pocket ends up on your table.

Rosnay   Will you be quiet?

Magda   A woman like me!

Rosnay   Calm down.

Magda   A woman like me doesn't need this! I'm forty years old.

Rosnay   You're almost fifty.

Magda   But I still feel whole!

Rosnay   Well, get lost, then! Leave, if you feel so whole! What are you doing here? What are you waiting for? Go on!

Magda   Don't be cruel. I always come here.

Rosnay   And then you leave.

Magda   Caress you.

Rosnay   And then you leave.

Magda   Pay you.

Rosnay   And then you leave! You always leave!

Magda   I call you. I come back.

Rosnay   That's the deal. No one gets involved. No one gets hurt. Why are you shouting?

Magda   I don't need this place, or this mattress, or this bathroom … It's trash, all of it! I have my own house!

Rosnay   And I'm selling mine and using the money to leave.

Magda (*hugs him very tightly. Groans*)   I need you, Rosnay. I still need you.

Rosnay   Now you're gonna cry.

Magda   Because it's driving me mad.

Rosnay   You're making a scene.

Magda   Stay, please.

Rosnay   You're not my mother.

Magda   If your mother were alive, do you think she'd do everything I do for you? The day I met you, when I called you over and you were talking with your friends on the corner of the boulevard and I asked you to go as far as the park with me, that day, after we talked and you held me tight and bit me all over, I knew there were strange things inside your head, like a yearning to leap, like a rage … Of course, you needed a mother's love. And that's what I've tried to be for you. If my son didn't have me I'm sure he'd go off the rails, he'd look for –

Rosnay   Don't talk about my mum! What do you know about her?

Magda   What you've told me: that she's dead. That she never –

Rosnay   I went with you that night because you were gonna give me three dollars and I was getting the money together to buy a jersey, or some trainers, or I don't remember what … And in that rented house I chewed on your tits because you paid me two dollars more. What, you think I like you coming here and making you cum like a fifteen-year-old girl?

Magda *breaks away from him, sits on the bed and tries to calm herself. She is a fifteen-year-old girl who wears a red dress and walks along the boulevard and enjoys herself looking in the windows. She has a good little girl's dreams, she has her doll's house.*

Magda   I was thinking of moving as well. Exchanging the house and separating from my daughter. We'll be better off living apart.

Rosnay   Suit yourself.

Magda   I thought, maybe, since I was going to be on my own … You might want to come and see me at my place. A little house in El Vedado or Miramar.

Rosnay   You could never afford that.

Magda   What if I can? What if I can afford it?

Rosnay   I don't care.

Magda   You've seemed strange to me ever since you started making boats. Make a little space for me. I might find a way, some miracle. It might be nice.

Rosnay   It's worked fine like this but now it's over. End of story.

Magda   If you're leaving, why are you rubbing my face in it?

Rosnay   So you can start thinking where else to get a servicing from.

A heavy silence.

Magda   I wanted to give you this.

She removes her engagement ring and puts it into **Rosnay**'s *hand.*

Rosnay   You buy it from a shop?

Magda   No, it's mine.

Rosnay   Looks like it's from one of those commission shops.

Magda   It's got my initials on it.

Rosnay   Let's see … (*Looks at it carefully.*) I don't like it. Maybe it looks good on a woman but I don't like it.

Magda   Stay here, please.

Rosnay   Keep your ring.

Magda   You have it. Sell it. Just don't leave.

She hugs him tightly. He sighs.

Are you going to leave?

Rosnay (*pushes her away*)   Finish getting dressed. I'll be late.

Magda   I'll come with you.

Rosnay   Just as far as the corner, though.

Magda   If you like.

The mobile sounds. **Rosnay** *picks it up from the bedside table. And reads the message.*

Magda   Who was it?

Rosnay   A pirate.

VIII

Heat Wave

The same room at 8:30 p.m., even more untidy and darker than before. **Lucía** *and* **Frank** *are now on the bed, rolling around and laughing.*

Frank   I do like you.

Lucía   I'm nothing out of this world.

Frank   Still, I do like you. Touching you like this. Stroking you … You know this bed really well, don't you?

Lucía   Why ask if you know the answer?

Frank   He's crazy to leave you alone here.

Lucía   Who is?

Frank   That Rosnay. He's good for nothing. Circling outside the cinema looking for whores to take to the park. Or men.

For **Lucía** *there are some things that are best to run away from, things that are best not talked about.*

Lucía   He's not into men. And he doesn't go with whores. Why do you think everyone's either a poof or a prostitute?

But **Frank** *enjoys pressing the point.*

Frank   That Kiko swings both ways and Rosnay's mates with him. Maybe he lets Kiko suck him off now and then.

Lucía   What do I care about Kiko?

Frank   He goes with you.

Lucía   I'm his girlfriend.

Frank *bursts out laughing.* **Lucía** *tries to get up.*

Frank   Come here.

Lucía   Why don't you give me the money?

Frank (*joking*)   I already paid your boyfriend.

Lucía   No, he said you had to pay me.

Frank   To go Up North, is it? Oh, relax, I know you're both desperate to leave … He already told me.

Lucía   No one's told you anything. Give me the money.

Frank Sending you in to tame the lion while he stands outside the cage.

Lucía You don't roar. And this isn't a cage.

She gets up and begins to get dressed.

Frank We're locked in right now. You squealed like a pig when I put it inside you and none of the neighbours heard a thing. It's a quiet flat, this.

Lucía How old are you?

Frank How old do you think?

Lucía Because you're fat, I mean. You're not bad looking but you're fat.

Frank (*goes up to her and squeezes her up against him*) I may be fat, but I can set you on fire.

Lucía Twenty years ago, maybe. If you could see me on that bed with Rosnay …

Frank You're a tough cookie … You seem so soft … I could set you up in this house like a queen.

Lucía I don't want that.

Frank You're lonely. I can tell you're lonely.

Lucía Rosnay said you were friends.

Frank Rosnay's not anyone's friend. Look at yourself, here. And where's he?

Lucía None of my business.

Frank It is your business. He'll be fucking some old foreign woman. Or man. You know that and you let him … He's pulled the wool over your eyes. What the hell do women like you see in men like him?

Lucía Come on: give me the money. I've put up with you enough. Stay here with your nice new place and give me the cash.

Frank I gave all of it to him.

Lucía You gave him half and you're giving me the other half.

Frank I'm telling you: he took all of it.

Lucía Liar.

Frank Stay here a while.

Lucía (*launches herself at him*) Give me the money!

Frank (*throws her onto the bed and holds her down forcefully*) Come and get it, then. Come on.

Lucía (*tries to wriggle free*) I don't want to any more. Stop!

Frank I already paid. Now come on!

Lucía (*struggles*)   Stop! Stop it!

Frank   Calm down!

Lucía   Get off me! (*Bites him.*)

Frank   Ow, fuck … You bit me, filthy bitch!

She tries to break free but he grabs her by the hair and the head and throws her against the wall.

Dirty slut! (*Kicks her.*) Dirty, filthy whore!

Lucía *cannot get up.* **Frank** *kicks her over to the door.*

IX

Working Out

*Living-dining room in **Magda**'s house, 8:40 p.m.*

Osmel *is still wearing the trousers from his uniform. He does press-ups on the floor, frenetically and almost out of control. The doorbell rings. **Osmel** gets up and goes to open the door.*

Rosnay   This Lucía's place?

Osmel   Are you Rosnay?

Rosnay   Uh-huh.

Osmel   Come in.

Rosnay   She here?

Osmel   No. Come in.

Rosnay   I'll come back later.

Osmel   She might not, though.

Rosnay   I had a message from her.

Osmel   Maybe she will, then.

*I wouldn't have gone in, but **Rosnay** does.*

Osmel   Sit down.

Rosnay   You look sweaty.

Osmel   Press-ups.

*You wouldn't have sat down, but **Rosnay** does.*

Osmel   Mind if I carry on?

Rosnay   No, no.

Osmel *shouldn't have started doing press-ups again, but he does. And everything else also starts, with a useless sentence that **Rosnay** says:*

Rosnay   Press-ups aren't any use if you set your hands that far apart.

Osmel   Aren't they?

Rosnay   No. Waste of time.

Osmel *hates wasting his time, so he stops exercising. **Rosnay** gets down on the floor.*

Rosnay Better to set them this far apart. (*Does a press-up.*) See? Works the triceps more.

Osmel Let's see.

Feels **Rosnay**'s *triceps as he does more press-ups.*

Rosnay Strong, isn't it?

Osmel Nearly bursting.

Rosnay You get used to it.

Osmel You know a lot about press-ups.

Rosnay I go to the gym every afternoon. (*Gets up.*)

Osmel I wouldn't mind going to a gym.

Rosnay You Lucía's brother?

Osmel Uh-huh.

Rosnay Doing your military service.

Osmel No, military school. I'm still only fifteen.

Rosnay But you wear khaki anyway.

Osmel Did she tell you?

Rosnay She always talks about you.

Osmel She never talks about you.

Rosnay How come you know my name, then?

Osmel I know more than that.

Rosnay (*smiles*) You're nothing like her, kiddo.

Osmel She's more like Dad.

Rosnay You're more like your mum, then?

Osmel Did she say what time she'd be back?

Rosnay No, she sent me a message on my mobile. It's weird … She's never asked me 'round here before.

Osmel I sent it.

Rosnay What?

Osmel The message.

Rosnay …

Osmel The one on your mobile. I sent you it. I used Lucía's phone.

Rosnay Where is Lucía?

Osmel I don't know.

Rosnay So …?

Osmel I saw you together on Sunday. At the Saratoga Hotel, under the arcades. I was with some friends and I saw you together on the corner.

Rosnay And you messaged me now because …?

Osmel You're leaving Cuba.

Rosnay Yes, I am.

Osmel And Lucía's going with you.

Rosnay She already told you? Is there a problem?

Osmel No, no problem at all.

Rosnay This country's a piece of shit, kiddo.

Osmel I like it.

Rosnay And your underpants don't have holes in?

Osmel I don't wear any.

Rosnay Doesn't take much for you to get it up then.

Osmel When I feel like it.

Rosnay Well, I got tired of working for a whole month just to buy a pair of trainers and then having nothing left in my pocket. I'm used to wearing a watch. I had a plastic watch once, with a blue and orange strap. Loved it. A Swatch. Have you seen them? D'you know what I'm talking about? I always need a watch, stops me from wasting time. Then last week, I suddenly felt the need to exchange it. Took myself quite by surprise. I swapped it for this bracelet. I swapped it because I wanted to swap it, because I liked the bracelet. But I don't want one thing or the other, I want the watch *and* the bracelet. Both of them! At the same time! They shouldn't make you choose. No one can force you to choose. It's stupid. It's ridiculous. The bracelet doesn't fill my stomach, but I feel like wearing it!

Osmel *watches him. He once saw a Swatch in the window of the Ultra department store, a sphere with little fish swimming around in circles.*

Rosnay Up North, it won't be like that. Lucía thinks you could come too, later.

Osmel Lucía's a child. She doesn't know what she wants.

Rosnay (*laughs*) And you do? At fifteen years old?

Osmel You can know lots of things at fifteen.

Rosnay When I was your age I still lived in the countryside. You know what I used to do there? I used to fuck the goats. Didn't care about anything else.

Osmel I've never fucked a goat.

Rosnay Maybe you've got a little girlfriend for that.

Osmel I don't have a girlfriend.

Rosnay You don't know what kind of country you're living in at fifteen.

Osmel So why are you leaving?

Rosnay What's it got to do with you?

Osmel A lot.

Rosnay 'Cause I'm taking your sister?

Osmel Maybe Nevada's more of a shit-hole than here.

Rosnay Maybe.

Osmel You're twenty-five, ten years older than me, and you make money at night. You make money out of everything.

Rosnay Who told you that?

Osmel I know you do. You make money out of Lucía.

Rosnay Lucía's my girlfriend.

Osmel Do you like her?

Rosnay I think I'll go now.

Osmel Why do you?

Rosnay You ask a lot of questions, kiddo. Don't mess me about.

Osmel She's my sister.

Rosnay Yes, I like her. We run the business between us. She likes going out with me.

Osmel I've seen you in the streets on your own sometimes.

Rosnay And you've never said 'hello' to me.

Osmel I sneak out of school at night with a couple of friends. Go to the Payret Cinema, walk 'round El Capitolio.

Rosnay Dangerous.

Osmel Why don't you teach me?

Rosnay (*smiles*) Teach you what?

Osmel Don't laugh. Why don't you teach me?

Rosnay You're a child.

Osmel At the hotel, Lucía was holding you so close. It was hot ... Your tee-shirt was covered in sweat but she still held you close.

Rosnay So what?

Osmel Licked you all over.

Rosnay What is this, kiddo?

Osmel Why don't you take your top off?

Rosnay What the fuck – ?

Osmel I've got a porno mag in my room. I stole it from a guy at school.

Rosnay What are you talking about?

Osmel Why is Lucía leaving with you? What do you do for her?

Rosnay You're queer.

Osmel No.

Rosnay You're fucking queer!

Osmel Let me undo your flies ... It won't hurt ... I can tell Lucía –

Rosnay (*grabs him around the neck*) Tell her what?

Osmel Don't you want to leave Cuba?

Rosnay I am leaving.

Osmel Not if I don't feel like it. Touch me. Come on: touch me.

Rosnay You want me to touch you? Touch you, will I?

Punches him in the face and throws him against the wall.

Osmel Fuck ... (*Goes to the dresser, opens the drawer.*)

Rosnay (*grabs him by the hands*) Queer piece of shit! (*Beats him against the wall and throws him to the floor.*)

Osmel (*trying to get up*) Oh ...

Rosnay *spits at him and leaves.* **Osmel** *writhes on the floor.*

X

Thaw

Magda's house from the same angle, at 10:20 p.m. **Osmel** *lies on the sofa.* **Lucía** *opens the front door and comes in.*

Osmel Luli?

Something is wrong. In his voice, in the tone he used to say the last syllable of her name.

Lucía What happened to you?

Osmel I fell.

Lucía You fell?

Osmel I was doing exercises.

Lucía Come off it … You didn't fall. Did you get into a fight in the street? Did you get beaten up? Let's see … It's all swollen above your eye.

Osmel It's nothing. I'll take a pill and go sleep it off.

Lucía What happened, though, Osmel? What happened?

Osmel *tuts.*

Lucía You're gonna drive me mad.

Osmel Go and have a bath. You look really tired.

Lucía Tell me what happened.

Osmel That friend of yours.

Lucía Who?

Osmel He came looking for you.

Lucía What friend?

Osmel The one you meet at the Payret Cinema. The one you're leaving with.

Lucía Rosnay?

Osmel That's him.

Lucía Rosnay was here?

Osmel Was.

Lucía I don't understand.

Osmel He rang the bell, I opened the door and he came in.

Lucía   What did he come here for?

Osmel   First he said you'd sent him a message. Then I realized later he was lying.

Lucía   A message?

Osmel   You said you were leaving together tomorrow while it's still dark so I thought maybe –

Lucía   What did he do?

Osmel   Nothing.

Lucía   Osmel, what did he do?!

Osmel   I thought it was weird, him coming here like that. He'd never been to the house before … I was working out and he started correcting me. Touching my arms, telling me how to set my hands for doing press-ups … And then he started feeling me up.

Lucía   Feeling you up?

Osmel   He said you'd told him about me. Said he'd wanted to meet me for a long time.

Lucía   Meet you?

Osmel   Then he tried to …

Lucía   What?

Osmel   Tried to touch my arse.

Lucía   What?

Osmel   I'm not a queer, Luli.

Lucía   Rosnay? It can't be …

She knows it can't be, she's sure, she believes in him. What **Rosnay** *wants is to go to Nevada.*

Osmel   I told him I didn't want to. What could I say to him, Luli? What could I have said?

Lucía   What time did he come?

Osmel   Just after eight.

Lucía   That was when I was …

Lucía *is a clock marking every minute of the day.*

Osmel   He tried to force me. I got really angry and I hit him 'round the face. Then he went completely crazy and jumped on top of me and grabbed me 'round the neck. I tried to break free, Luli, but he held onto me, and I was screaming and he was on top of me … 'I'll fucking kill you', I said … And I wasn't joking. I wanted to kill him, stab him in the stomach ... I looked for the gun, but where did you put it, Luli, where did you put it?

She remembers it on the table.

Lucía   The gun ...

She remembers it in the drawer.

Osmel   I opened the drawer and it wasn't there.

She remembers it among the clothes.

Lucía   In your room. I took it to your room. I put it under the towels.

Osmel   But you didn't tell me! I could have shot him! Who is that guy, Luli? It's horrible! He's crazy. He's out of his mind! Tell me what else I could have done? He was holding my hands and I was hitting him with my elbows and my knees... But he's strong. He doesn't look it, he looks skinny, but he's strong. (*A silence.*) Now I've calmed down I think I could have done something else ... But all I could do at the time was scream and scream and scream!

Lucía *paces to-and-fro; she picks up her handbag. She doesn't need to but she thinks about her lipstick, her comb, her handkerchief ...*

Osmel   Don't leave now. Don't leave me on my own. Come here. Come on ... Sit with me for a bit.

She goes to the front door, opens it and disappears into the darkness.

XI

Temperate Boulevard

At 11:00 p.m. on a Thursday in January there is barely anyone still out on the streets of Havana. But **Magda**, *tired and bewildered, is trying to avoid going home.*

Magda   Can you sell me a dollar?

Frank *can.*

Frank   What for?

Magda   I want to buy an ice cream from the arcades at the Saratoga Hotel, and stand there remembering my honeymoon from 1982.

Frank   Let's both go, I'll buy you one.

Magda   Can you or not?

Frank   What's wrong with you?

Magda   Everything.

He looks through his wallet.

It's just, I want to go alone.

He sees the dollars.

Frank   Sorry, I thought I had some … Must have left my money at home.

Magda   Can you tell me what I can do in this city with twenty-five pesos?

Frank   Catch a shared cab back home.

Magda *tuts.*

Frank   What?

Magda   Nothing. I was just asking.

She disappears around a corner of the boulevard and he feels a pain in the pit of his stomach, from the beers, perhaps, which can hurt so much.

XII

Take Me Sailing

Outside the Payret Cinema, 12:15 a.m. **Lucía** *stands on the pavement, motionless.* **Higinio** *listens to the radio and approaches her.*

Higinio Are you going into the cinema? There's been nothing on for a while.

She does not answer. She moves away.

You're waiting for someone.

Not a word. The old man looks her up and down.

Weren't you wearing a red dress last night?

Lucía Please, Mister! Aren't you looking after the cinema? Go and sit in the doorway.

Higinio I am looking after it, yes. But sometimes my buttocks go to sleep and I need to have a little walk around. I've seen the film about ten times. I go into the darkness and hope to shut my eyes and have forty winks. But no: I'm like an owl! I get drawn into what's going on. Even if I do know Robert Duvall's going to shoot the blond woman every time.

Lucía *stares at him but does not remember who Robert Duvall is.*

Higinio Still, it's only pretend. You know it's only pretend, she gets up straight away and keeps on walking.

Lucía What film is that?

Higinio One of these … Come and see it tomorrow.

Lucía Tomorrow …

Higinio Are you … Are you a transvestite?

Lucía What?

Higinio No, I –

Lucía What's wrong with you?

Higinio I like those little dolls you have hanging from your handbag.

Lucía Can you not change the radio station?

Higinio Follows me everywhere, this music. They play it on the buses, my neighbour listens to it full blast –

Lucía I don't know … Try and find a baseball match. Or a weather report. Didn't they say it was gonna rain?

Higinio   Well, it didn't.

Lucía   Go to sleep, then.

Higinio   Too cold.

Lucía   It's heat I can't stand.

The old man yawns and stretches. He goes back to the door.

Lucía *stands alone on the pavement. So alone that I can see nothing else: just her image laid bare in the middle of the street. Her head spinning and her at the centre of a horde of passing trucks, police whistles, young men screaming. Or silence, complete darkness and just her and her anxiety illuminated.*

Rosnay *appears.*

Lucía   I thought you weren't coming.

Rosnay   Weren't we meeting in the park?

Lucía   I thought we said the cinema.

Rosnay (*smiles*)   You're making a lot of mistakes lately.

Lucía   And you never make any, is that it?

Rosnay   Oh, why so serious?

Lucía   Why did you go to the house?

Rosnay   What house?

Lucía   Why did you go to my house?

Rosnay   He told you?

Lucía   Told me what?

Rosnay   No, he didn't tell you.

Lucía   He's a child … Can't you see he's a child?

She takes the gun out from her handbag.

He brought this to the house but he's a child. (*Holds the gun up to her own temple.*)

Rosnay   What the fuck are you doing with a gun?

Lucía   What the fuck are you doing touching my brother? (*Aims at him.*)

Rosnay   Luli! Put that down!

He grabs her wrists and makes her lower the gun.

He's half-crazy. He asked me over to yours and –

Lucía   What do you mean, 'he asked you over'? He doesn't know you. How the hell could he have asked you over?

Rosnay He sent me a message … I don't know, Luli, but I went in and he started to –

Lucía What are you doing with my brother?

Rosnay Say whatever you like to me but I'm not a queer, Luli … What could I do? Tell me: what the fuck could I do? Did he say what happened? Did he tell you everything that happened?

Lucía I don't know what happened. But you're gonna tell me right now. You and I had arranged to meet here, so why would you turn up at my house, knowing I wouldn't be there? Knowing I was not going to be there!

Rosnay You were busy with your thing and I thought –

Lucía No, Rosnay, I was busy with *your* thing! I was with that guy of yours, with that fat bastard of yours. I was busy with *your* business! (*Aims the gun at him.*)

Rosnay Put that down. Put it down!

Lucía Stay there. Don't move.

Rosnay Why don't you give me the gun?

Lucía *closes her eyes for a second. He makes her lower the gun. They stand very close.*

Rosnay Look what I've got for you.

He takes her empty hand and puts the engagement ring on her finger.

It's pretty. I don't like it for me – it's very thin just here, see? – but it looks nice on your hand.

She freezes. She turns the ring round on her finger and considers it. She thinks, for the third time in one day, that this conversation ought not to continue. She knows, I'm telling her, that she ought not to say another word. But **Rosnay** *insists:*

That woman I told you about gave me it. That forty-year-old who cleans the house. She gives me things sometimes … Poor cow! I told her I was leaving and she went crazy. She gave me it. Now it's yours.

He goes to kiss her. She turns away.

So … Did Frank give you the money?

Lucía The money?

Rosnay Yeah, of course. Like I said: half the money.

Lucía You're joking. Right, Rosnay? This is a joke, isn't it?

Rosnay What happened?

Lucía You're playing me. What money?

Rosnay Hey –

XII Take Me Sailing

Lucía You're screwing me over.

Rosnay No, I'm asking you for the money. The money, the trip … Nevada … What is this? We're leaving in a few hours.

She aims the gun at him.

Put that down. Put it down!

They struggle. The gun falls. She is the first to pick it up.

Give it to me … Give it to me … That's it. Easy. (*He goes too close.*)

A shot is fired. He falls to the ground. A veil covers everything. The snow, whispered throughout the scale, begins to fall thickly.

Another shot. On **Higinio***'s radio, a presenter reports that the weather will be cold and dry, with no chance of rain.*

The choir of children, severely distorted, sings slowly: 'The sea was calm, calm was the sea … The sea was calm, calm was the sea …'

XIII

Snowmen

At 4:00 a.m., the morgue is pure white. The bodies of **Lucía** *and* **Rosnay**, *immobile and naked, are almost completely covered in snow.*

On either side, **Magda** *and* **Osmel**. *With two shovels they advance through the snow and uncover the bodies. Perhaps they sob through their whole conversation. Or perhaps there is no sobbing at all.*

Magda   Those policemen will be back … I'm a bit scared, you know? It's strange: I can't find the words … I'm a bit scared, thinking what kind of relationship Lucía can have had with someone like this. A man like this, covered in tattoos … And that gun! Why did she shoot him?

Osmel   Didn't you know him?

Magda *sighs and shakes her head.*

Magda   Did you? Think carefully, Osmel. Lucía always told you more than she did me … Just think back for a second … I know people say any old thing to the police but … Look at me. Had you ever seen him before?

Osmel *walks behind the bodies, looks at them again, sinks his feet into the ice over and over again. He stops behind his mother, who is seated.*

Osmel   Never.

The light goes out violently. The snow stops.

Weathered

A Photo in Shreds

Weathered and its English translation were originally commissioned and developed by HOME, Manchester, as part of World Stages 2016.

It premiered as a staged reading at HOME on 23 April 2016, directed by Cat Robey, with the following cast: Kate Coogan, David Judge, Jamie Samuel, Robin Simpson and Katie West.

The play was the winner of the 2021 City of Santa Clara Foundation National Playwriting Award.

In memory of my father

Shreds of the Photo

I. A Gentle Bobbing
II. Uncertainties
III. The Virtue of the Birds
IV. A Family Resemblance
V. Those Ghosts
VI. Old Stone
VII. Such a Big Place
VIII. Boiling Water
IX. Less Than a Week
X. Full Moon
XI. Some Flowers
XII. The Truth
XIII. A Bit of Calm
XIV. Accidents
XV. If You Weren't Here
XVI. A Little Shell Surrounded by Sand

Characters

David, *21*
Elvira, *27–28 and 49*
Josué, *21*
Sebastián, *21–22 and 43*
Celia, *20*

All of the action takes place in Havana, in two time periods: 1993–94 and 2015.

I

A Gentle Bobbing

2015. December. Night. The promenade by the sea.

Elvira   I'd forgotten this part of the harbour.

Celia   It's new.

Elvira   The church, though, and the hospital … That's all old stone.

Celia   Yes, hard stone. They've stood here, in the same position, in the same place, weathering the centuries. Too many.

Elvira   I was sitting on the bench waiting for you and I tried to pull a shell off of the rock. It's odd: it looked like it was on the surface, a little shell surrounded by sand … But it was wedged in there so tight that all I managed to do was break a nail; look.

Celia   Why did you do that? You'd have never got it off.

Elvira   I would have with a knife.

Celia   No, you wouldn't. We live with things wedged forever in this place.

Elvira   …

Celia   It's a joke; don't be so serious … Mind you, it's true … For example: do you think all that oil will ever disappear from the bay?

Elvira   It always was a pretty bay.

Celia   Yes. It is pretty.

Elvira   But dirty.

Celia   The oil's glued to the reef.

Elvira   Aren't those machines starting to dredge the sea bed?

Celia   I'll believe it when I see the water clean.

Elvira   The surf's up.

Celia   The best thing about the wind is it blows the smell of oil away.

Elvira   …

Celia   I like coming here at night, when it's windy. It only happens in winter, of course; bit of breeze to calm the infernal heat on this island. I like coming out onto this pier; it's like snatching some territory back from the sea … I come up to the barrier and look out at everything. Imagine losing myself on the water and watching the infinite open out in front of me, plunging into the darkness. Dream about what would happen if I managed to escape on top of this platform.

Elvira   They've fixed it to the sea bed with metal columns.

Celia No. They're flexible columns. They're on pontoons and they're tied to the seawall with ropes; see?

Elvira This whole huge pier?

Celia The whole thing.

Elvira We're floating?

Celia Can't you feel it bobbing?

Elvira …

Celia …

Elvira Yes, but I thought I was imagining it. It's so gentle.

Celia But you can feel it, right?

Elvira And the silence.

Celia …

Elvira Why would they have built a pier that isn't held down?

Celia Because of the cyclones, they say. So it doesn't break when there's a cyclone.

Elvira Makes sense.

Celia …

Elvira Shall we try and cut the ropes?

Celia Don't joke. Besides, the mouth of the bay is too narrow … If we did try to escape, the pier would get stuck.

Elvira Yes, it's an absurd dream.

Celia It's not absurd; it's stupid.

Elvira We have to trust our stupidities sometimes.

Celia …

Elvira I'm getting cold.

Celia Come to the house then?

Elvira Well. I'll have to stay somewhere.

Celia Do you smoke weed?

Elvira I will if you will.

Celia I'd buy some for you but I'm out of money.

Elvira …

Celia What did you say your name was?

Elvira Elvira.

Celia Have you seen? Everyone's left. We're all alone.

II

Uncertainties

2015. December. Night. **David**'s *house.*

Sebastián   Alone at last. I thought they'd never leave.

David   They think they're doing their duty by coming to the house; to me, to her …

Sebastián   As if your grandma could see them.

David   Maybe she can.

Sebastián   The neighbours really loved Aurora.

David   Yes, they did.

Sebastián   You don't need to tidy all that up; leave the table and have a lie down. I'll take care of this.

David   I can do it.

Sebastián   Come on; leave it.

David   It helps me to be doing something; moving. I'm all on edge, Sebas; I won't be able to sleep. It's like I've been set off. I can't stop. How about we go for a run?

Sebastián   …

David   …

Sebastián   No, don't cry … Easy. It's over now.

David   …

Sebastián   Easy …

David   …

Sebastián   It's all over now.

David   So many weeks hanging on …

Sebastián   At least she died without pain.

David   How can you be sure of that?

Sebastián   I was right beside her, David. Beside you and beside her. You saw her. You kissed her. You heard her final words. We kept her calm.

David   But just like this, on this day … Burying her before Christmas Eve …

Sebastián   …

David   Christmas was her favourite thing.

Sebastián She's at peace now.

David I don't know if I'll get used to being alone in this house.

Sebastián We can move into my place whenever you like.

David For good?

Sebastián For a change of scene, I mean.

David …

Sebastián We've nothing to lose by trying.

David I've always lived here.

Sebastián Whatever you prefer.

David …

Sebastián Just say the word. And we'll do it.

David It's good you could swap shifts and stay tonight.

Sebastián Perk of being the boss.

David I never say this to you, Sebas … But I'm always so grateful to you.

Sebastián You don't need to –

David No, it's true. I'm such an ungrateful person.

Sebastián No –

David If it weren't for you, bringing the medicine here, keeping up with the injections, the drips … There's no way to repay something like that.

Sebastián …

David All I ever do is cause you trouble.

Sebastián It's no trouble.

David …

Sebastián I'm happy to do anything for you.

David You've been here, with me. Putting up with Gran grimacing at you, that annoying way she treated you …

Sebastián Old people get jealous.

David Jealous?

Sebastián She was scared I'd hurt her only grandson.

David After all this time?

Sebastián Time doesn't wipe away fear.

David   Doesn't it?

Sebastián   It increases it.

David   …

Sebastián   …

David   Do you think … she knew?

Sebastián   You never told her.

David   No, we never told her.

Sebastián   But you can't keep secrets from grandmothers.

David   …

Sebastián   …

David   Feeling you near is the only thing that's kept me calm.

Sebastián   …

David   I wouldn't know what to do if you weren't here.

Sebastián   You're very strong.

David   I wasn't crying from sadness just now … You saw I didn't cry all day. When I signed the papers, when the cortège went into the cemetery, when I was standing at the grave … Even then I didn't feel like crying. I can see things from a distance in the open air; I can breathe; everything makes me less anxious … The hard thing was coming back to the house. Being left alone here.

Sebastián   You're not alone.

David   I'm with you. I know.

Sebastián   …

David   But I have to understand that you're not always here. You have things to do. You work. You have your life to live.

Sebastián   …

David   It's not your fault. But you're not inside me. I have to learn to live with that.

Sebastián   All you need right now is rest.

David   Don't treat me like I'm crazy!

Sebastián   …

David   Sorry … I'm sorry, Sebas, please.

Sebastián   …

David   I'm exhausted. I need to sleep.

Sebastián   Yes. Tomorrow's another day.

David   …

Sebastián   …

David   Just now, when you were walking the neighbour home …

Sebastián   What?

David   I think I had another hallucination.

Sebastián   …

David   Can you give me a pill?

Sebastián   You don't need one.

David   I thought I saw her here and I spoke to her.

Sebastián   Your grandma?

David   …

Sebastián   That's normal; she's just died.

David   No. My mother.

Sebastián   …

David   She was here.

Sebastián   Calm down.

David   She spoke to me.

Sebastián   …

David   It wasn't her, was it?

Sebastián   Your mother's dead.

III

The Virtue of the Birds

1993. December. Night. **Elvira**'s *house.*

Elvira   Is she dead?

Josué   I think she's asleep.

Elvira   You didn't notice?

Josué   I don't look in the cage every time I come into the house.

Elvira   She hasn't sung since yesterday.

Josué   She must be tired.

Elvira   Birds don't get tired of singing.

Josué   Oh, don't they?

Elvira   No. They live to sing.

Josué   …

Elvira   Oh, thank goodness: she's alive.

Josué   Have I done something to annoy you?

Elvira   No. Are you annoyed about something?

Josué   …

Elvira   …

Josué   Give me a kiss, at least. Prove you're not annoyed.

Elvira   Shall I heat the water up so you can have a wash?

Josué   There's not enough left in the tank for me to have a shower?

Elvira   There's not been any since this morning. I scooped up what was left with a bucket and put it in the kitchen. That's why I said to heat it up. It'll be freezing.

Josué   Will there be water tonight?

Elvira   Should be.

Josué   I'll wait 'til later, then.

Elvira   …

Josué   I'm gonna get changed.

Elvira   Those ideas you've been sharing in class for the past few weeks …

Josué   What ideas?

Elvira Walls have ears in that school, Josué. The rector found out about the debate you started in class. He called me to his office.

Josué What are you talking about?

Elvira That explanation of the public health crisis.

Josué What, it wasn't true?

Elvira Why did you have to quote those figures about doctors leaving the country?

Josué They're leaving in droves!

Elvira But it wasn't relevant.

Josué I was just expressing a point of view.

Elvira No, it was more than a point of view … It's not the first time you've talked about things that –

Josué That I shouldn't talk about in school?

Elvira You're studying Medicine in a government university, remember?

Josué It's a public university.

Elvira Yes. Thanks to a government that lets you study there without paying a cent.

Josué We're not having this discussion again.

Elvira And your wife – who, as well as being one of your lecturers, belongs to the Party – doesn't think it's appropriate –

Josué Doesn't think what's appropriate?

Elvira None of the rumours going around about you are good ones. Why is that?

Josué Well, if you will pay more attention to the gossips in the corridor than you do to your own husband …

Elvira They're not gossips in the corridor, Josué. Life has its protocols. You're going to be a doctor, aren't you? Well, stick to treating people and nothing else.

Josué How dare you talk to me like this?

Elvira Don't get involved in politics.

Josué …

Elvira All of those things you think … Of course you can think them; I'm not arguing with that. But couldn't you just keep them to yourself and keep your mouth shut?

Josué I don't think I'll be accused of anything just for my opinions.

Elvira Why didn't they publish your article in *University Life*?

Josué They said it was a bit strongly worded.

Elvira Just a bit?

Josué …

Elvira No, darling. It was beyond what was tolerable. You can't analyse statistics from that angle and expect to be published. They say it was full of errors of composition.

Josué Please, it wasn't the errors of composition that bothered them.

Elvira You have to learn to control this rebelliousness of yours. I refuse to live in a constant state of tension.

Josué And you think I like it?

Elvira How can I feel good, calm, peaceful, when you're an unstoppable whirlwind?

Josué We clearly can't have a conversation today, can we.

Elvira That won't be my fault.

Josué Seems Sebastián's the only one who understands me.

Elvira Yes, of course. That's why you're with him all the time.

Josué Yes, of course.

Elvira …

Josué Exactly why.

Elvira …

Josué I'm going to the bathroom; I'm pouring that bucket of water over myself and then I'm changing my clothes. We can go for a walk and talk about all this outside, without all the steam there is between these four walls. We'll walk over to the harbour, and have a calm conversation. OK?

Elvira …

Josué Good.

Elvira Wait.

Josué …

Elvira I'm pregnant.

IV

A Family Resemblance

2015. October. Midday. **Celia***'s house.*

Celia   I really want to get pregnant.

David   Didn't you want to leave the country?

Celia   Yeah, that too. They don't cancel each other out. It's the twenty-first century: half the island wants to leave. It's just that I want to get pregnant too. You got a problem with that?

David   Let's see; pass me that yellow envelope.

Celia   Lucky I found that box of photos in the wardrobe; Dad had it kept in a drawer.

David   They're getting all mouldy; see?

Celia   I never paid any attention to them, but when the teacher said we had to work with old photos, I suddenly remembered.

David   Especially the edges: they're in a real state.

Celia   Corners have nearly come off.

David   They still look good, though.

Celia   Photos did use to be good in the old days.

David   Photos that last, even when they've been shut away for decades.

Celia   Surviving the damp.

David   Photographic paper rots away these days; it peels off … Before, look how tough it was, like cardboard. And they were all matt.

Celia   I prefer gloss.

David   Glossy photos are vulgar.

Celia   No, they're not; they make the people in them look more alive.

David   Gloss does away with all the mystery. I hate gloss.

Celia   OK, fine.

David   …

Celia   …

David   There's lots of them.

Celia   We'll have to choose.

David I like these ones; look.

Celia Dad at the Medical School.

David …

Celia How are the two of you?

David Fine. You know. He's helping me so much with my grandma.

Celia Is she doing better?

David Sebas says she's stable and she could hold out like this for another few months. I don't see the point of her staying alive lying in a bed.

Celia Does she not recognize you?

David Yes, she recognizes me but it's not the same. Such a feisty woman, such a fighter … She's depressed, that's why she doesn't want to get up. Or can't.

Celia These things happen to the old.

David Can someone die of depression?

Celia …

David …

Celia Dad and I hardly ever talk.

David I've already told you what I think about that.

Celia Yes, I need to get closer to him, communicate more … But I try and I don't know how to reach him, I swear … He doesn't make the slightest effort to understand me. Last week – you remember? – I had to ask you to talk to him about renting out a room … This house is enormous, David. I know it's in a terrible state, but it's so central; if he'd let me rent out the rooms, we'd make a bit of money.

David You know your dad doesn't like that sort of thing.

Celia But we don't even need to apply for a licence: we could do it on the quiet and no one would even know.

David That's even worse.

Celia There are so many foreigners coming to the island, and the hotels are so expensive.

David So sit down and explain it to him.

Celia He spends all his time working at the hospital. He's one of the best psychiatrists in the country but his salary isn't enough to pay for anything, not even to fix up this house which is falling to pieces all around us.

David …

Celia If I get pregnant and leave here, at least I'll be able to dream of having a house of my own where I can make the decisions.

David Everything's much harder abroad.

Celia Plus, if I do leave, I won't have to explain myself to Dad any more.

David Stop acting like a child.

Celia It's easy for you: he gives you everything; he always understands you.

David That's not true.

Celia Yes, it is. He treats you like the son he never had.

David …

Celia …

David Come on: let's finish choosing these photos.

Celia Do you really fancy my dad?

David Where's that question come from all of a sudden?

Celia I respect you, David. And I love you. We're nearly the same age. You're a lot younger than Dad.

David …

Celia No, I'm not asking you to explain. I'm used to seeing you with him. We're family. But you must understand: I think it'd be more natural for you and me to be boyfriend and girlfriend.

David Celia!

Celia …

David …

Celia Yeah, let's finish choosing the photos.

David Don't talk that way about those things again, please.

Celia OK, fine.

David …

Celia …

David …

Celia Dad always was an interesting man.

David …

Celia Even now he's over forty, he still is … Look how handsome he was then.

David What year would this be?

Celia It doesn't say.

David That beach looks like Santa María.

Celia And this one; look: at night.

David That's Sebas too, isn't it?

Celia Who are those two standing next to him?

David All with their arms 'round each other.

Celia Look at her, standing between them; she looks gorgeous.

David With the sea in the background. Skinny but happy.

Celia The guy on the right looks a bit like you.

David No, he doesn't.

Celia It's unbelievable, the power of an old photo.

David Yes. Magnetic.

Celia …

David Like they're looking at us.

Celia …

David What does it say on the back?

Celia It's written in pen: 'To my brother Sebas, with the love and madness of these years, and for everything yet to come.'

David Who signed it?

Celia J.

David J?

Celia Yep. Autumn '93.

David Do you have any aunts or uncles?

Celia Not that I know of.

David …

Celia …

David These photos'll do.

Celia I have to cut them up.

David …

Celia Dad won't care.

David Maybe he doesn't even remember them.

Celia Maybe.

David …

Celia Do you want to see the photos of my mum?

David I think this is enough for now.

Celia Have you not found any old photos of your family at your house?

David I never saw any photos of my mother.

Celia Never?

David No. Not of my dad, either.

Celia …

David After they died, my grandma burned them all.

V

Those Ghosts

1993. October. Afternoon. The Medical School gym.

Josué   All of them. He burned all of them. Dad didn't like photos. Said there was no point remembering people after they were dead. You had to love them when they were still alive.

Sebastián   He wasn't wrong.

Josué   Love them when they're alive, and then forget them forever.

Sebastián   It's good to forget sometimes.

Josué   Well, I'd want my kids to remember me, even if it was just in photos.

Sebastián   Your kids will see you in person; they'll remember your face; they'll know how you laugh.

Josué   I hope so.

Sebastián   What about your wife?

Josué   …

Sebastián   Does she want kids?

Josué   Ooph, I hate doing abs.

Sebastián   Yeah, we'd best stop for a bit.

Josué   …

Sebastián   …

Josué   Elvira's the perfect age for getting pregnant.

Sebastián   You need to give her a hand with that …

Josué   I am doing.

Sebastián   Don't blush.

Josué   I'm crazy about Elvira.

Sebastián   …

Josué   We used to do it every day at first.

Sebastián   You've been married more than a year and half, right?

Josué   And I could stay that way my whole life … if it weren't for her.

Sebastián   Her?

Josué I think she's getting bored.

Sebastián …

Josué I must be imagining things.

Sebastián She's the … strictest lecturer we've got. I find her a bit intimidating.

Josué I promise you in bed she's quite relaxed.

Sebastián I can imagine.

Josué …

Sebastián You're so lucky, being with such a beautiful woman.

Josué …

Sebastián Is she from a medical family?

Josué No. She just wanted to be a doctor.

Sebastián She's done well.

Josué Already dean of the Medical School.

Sebastián She joined the Party very young.

Josué Only way to get ahead in this country: join the Party and start climbing.

Sebastián Keep your voice down; someone'll hear you.

Josué I don't care. I'd rather die than join the Party. If there were two parties instead of just one, I might think about it. But what use is a single party that decides everything for you?

Sebastián Shhhh.

Josué …

Sebastián Aren't you scared, saying those things?

Josué Scared of what?

Sebastián Well … I don't agree with it either. But you have to be careful here at school, right?

Josué Is the Party gonna feed your family when your doctor's salary isn't enough?

Sebastián Shhhh.

Josué …

Sebastián …

Josué So, why did you choose Medicine?

Sebastián There's something about it that attracts me.

Josué Yeah?

Sebastián   It tidies my mind. Helps me understand things.

Josué   …

Sebastián   Wipes the ghosts away.

Josué   What ghosts can a guy like you be afraid of?

Sebastián   I don't know. Things that come back to me.

Josué   Things you don't like.

Sebastián   …

Josué   …

Sebastián   …

Josué   Never heard you talk about your girlfriend.

Sebastián   Haven't got one.

Josué   …

Sebastián   No woman wants me.

Josué   Attractive guy like you?

Sebastián   They all drop me straight away.

Josué   Or you drop them.

Sebastián   Nope.

Josué   Until you find the one.

Sebastián   …

Josué   Yeah, I know it's not easy. What woman outside of the school would put up with this life? Hours and hours studying those massive books, all-night shifts … But she'll turn up; don't worry.

Sebastián   …

Josué   Aren't there any women in the school you like?

Sebastián   Shall we do another set of abs?

Josué   Why don't you spend this weekend with us?

Sebastián   You and Elvira?

Josué   Yeah, we're going to the beach, to Santa María, to her cousins' house.

Sebastián   No way; I'd be embarrassed.

Josué   Come on.

Sebastián   What about Elvira?

Josué She's a different woman outside this place.

Sebastián …

Josué Plus, I got hold of some weed.

Sebastián Weed?

Josué Have you never smoked?

VI

Old Stone

2015. December. The middle of the night. **Celia**'s *house.*

Celia Don't tell me you've never smoked weed.

Elvira Not for a lot of years. That's why I'm going slowly. I had a scare once …

Celia It is always best to smoke with company.

Elvira This is good weed you've bought, though.

Celia We've bought. You paid for it.

Elvira I was at the beach with my husband and a friend and we were smoking. I didn't want to but they insisted. I didn't feel anything at first. We got into an inflatable raft and went out to sea. It was night time. I remember them laughing at all the stupid things I was starting to say … I decided to start jumping up and down on the raft – can you imagine? – in the middle of the water … We nearly drowned. I don't even know how we got back to the sand … Oh, it all happened that night.

Celia You look happy.

Elvira I needed to relax.

Celia …

Elvira …

Celia So, you like the room.

Elvira Yes.

Celia The roof's peeling a bit but it won't fall in. These houses are some of the oldest in the city.

Elvira And the most solid.

Celia It'd be good to fix it up a bit, but everything's so expensive … And the builders are a disaster. I'll have to start scraping the walls myself someday so I can paint them.

Elvira You live on your own.

Celia Dad comes over sometimes but not very often.

Elvira Oh, you each have your own house.

Celia No, this is his house. He lives with a friend a few blocks away.

Elvira A friend?

Celia It's better. This way we don't spend too much time together.

Elvira ...

Celia I'm fond of my dad but he drives me mad sometimes.

Elvira Can I stay here a few days?

Celia Sure, as many as you need.

Elvira It'll be less than a week.

Celia When you called I never asked who gave you my number.

Elvira ...

Celia Well, it doesn't matter. My dream is to turn this place into a hostel, but until I've got enough money to invest in it, I'm going to rent it out bit by bit.

Elvira How much did you say it was?

Celia I'll give you mate's rates. What do you say to twenty dollars a night? To cover the water, the gas, the electricity.

Elvira I'll give you two hundred for a whole week.

Celia There's no need.

Elvira Here.

Celia Oh, thanks a lot ... I'll start saving for the hostel today.

Elvira ...

Celia Don't laugh; it's true. Straight into the moneybox.

Elvira ...

Celia So, you live Up North ...

Elvira In the States, yes. I felt like coming back.

Celia Has it been a long time?

Elvira Over twenty years.

Celia I'm twenty.

Elvira I left here before you were born.

Celia ...

Elvira I suddenly feel very old.

Celia You look fine to me. It must be all the great creams they have over there. The sun ruins our skin here.

Elvira I caught a lot of sun on this island before I left, I assure you.

Celia It must be great living there.

Elvira It's not all rosy.

Celia   That's what this government's spent years making us believe. But my friend Glenda says she got help as soon as she got there: she got vouchers for her food and even medical insurance for a whole year.

Elvira   She'll be breaking her back now.

Celia   How did you leave?

Elvira   On a raft.

Celia   Is that a joke?

Elvira   No. Half the island left on rafts. Rafts made of wood, with tyres so they'd float, with oars. Or the best ones had engines. If the police caught you with a raft in your house, you landed in jail.

Celia   …

Elvira   I paid a lot of money to get on that raft. We even had to bribe the coastguards when they caught us out at sea.

Celia   …

Elvira   They were crazy times. August 1994.

Celia   I've heard about it. They say people went out onto the streets to protest against the government, that there was a riot on the Malecón. That they smashed windows, shouted slogans. Dad told me he was scared. He hadn't graduated yet, he thought the whole system was about to come crashing down.

Elvira   The police responded with violence. And it was the people who lost out.

Celia   I've never seen anything like that. I've grown up in a country where you can't demonstrate. Where it's better to keep quiet.

Elvira   …

Celia   I don't like the system but I don't think I'd dare leave on a raft. It seems so dangerous. The sharks, the bad weather … No drinking water, praying you'll reach the other side, touch dry land … You need to be brave for an adventure like that. You must have wanted to leave for a long time.

Elvira   No. I'd never thought about leaving.

Celia   …

Elvira   But things suddenly got complicated.

Celia   Yeah, Dad says it was the worst time of his life, the crisis in the '90s. Constant blackouts, water shortages, hunger –

Elvira   I don't mean the hunger, or the blackouts. I'd lived with that my whole life.

Celia   …

Elvira   It was personal. Everything happened at once.

Celia   Why didn't you come back sooner?

Elvira   …

Celia   Couldn't you get permission to enter the country?

Elvira   …

Celia   Why now, after all this time?

Elvira   I don't know. I don't really know why.

Celia   Have you got someone here?

Elvira   Yes.

Celia   …

Elvira   I've come to see him.

VII

Such a Big Place

2015. December. The middle of the night. **David***'s mind/house.*

Josué   I've come to see you.

David   Is that you, Dad?

Josué   Shhh … Quietly or you'll wake Sebas.

David   He's sleeping like a log, can't you see? He won't wake up.

Josué   Just in case.

David   I'm so glad you're here.

Josué   …

David   I haven't seen you for ages.

Josué   You've not had time to remember me with so much going on.

David   Yes. It's been terrible with Grandma.

Josué   Do you miss her?

David   I don't think so.

Josué   Why not?

David   I feel liberated.

Josué   …

David   I closed her eyes on the bed.

Josué   I saw. I found it very moving. It felt like it was me doing it.

David   She used to call me by your name.

Josué   I know. I used to find it so funny.

David   I think she enjoyed getting mixed up.

Josué   She adored you.

David   She adored you.

Josué   …

David   Give her a kiss when you see her.

Josué   This is a big place. I might not see her for a while.

David   …

Josué So, you're going to Sebas's house for a few days?

David Later on.

Josué OK.

David What?

Josué Nothing.

David Is there something about him that bothers you?

Josué About Sebas?

David …

Josué I like him.

David But you'd rather we weren't together, right?

Josué Why?

David You'd rather I had a girlfriend.

Josué Are you bringing this up now for a reason?

David I just thought of it.

Josué He's good to you.

David He'd never betray me.

Josué He loves you.

David Yes, he loves me too much.

Josué You need someone to love you like that.

David Like the way you love me.

Josué But I'm inside you.

David Yes. And it's not the same.

Josué No. He's on the outside.

David And he helps me from the outside.

Josué …

David I think Celia's jealous of what we have.

Josué What about Celia?

David …

Josué Do you like her?

David What have you noticed?

Josué The way you look at her.

David ...

Josué The way you still get nervous when you see her.

David ...

Josué The way you pay her fees so she can stay on the photography course with you.

David ...

Josué The way you get embarrassed when she mentions you and her father.

David I don't get embarrassed.

Josué Are you sure?

David I don't get embarrassed, Dad!

Josué You asked me what I'd noticed and I'm telling you.

David You think I don't love Sebastián?

Josué I think you want a child.

David ...

Josué ...

David No, I don't. I'm too young.

Josué I was your age when your mother got pregnant.

David My mother.

Josué Yes.

David I'd never seen her before.

Josué You're right.

David Was that her?

Josué Yes. It was your mother who visited you tonight.

David But Sebas told me I was hallucinating!

Josué No, David. It was her.

David It can't be, Dad!

Josué ...

David It can't be!

Josué ...

David Dad!

Sebastián ...

David   Dad!

Sebastián   Hey …

David   …

Sebastián   Easy. You're all worked up.

David   …

Sebastián   Shall I get you something? … You were having nightmares.

David   No. I was talking to …

Sebastián   You know I have to wake you up when you start shouting at night.

David   I wasn't shouting.

Sebastián   …

David   …

Sebastián   Easy. Easy.

David   Yes. Hold me.

Sebastián   …

David   I can't sleep.

Sebastián   This is what I thought. That it wouldn't be good, the both of us staying here, surrounded by the memories of your grandma.

David   Can we go to your house?

Sebastián   At this time of night?

David   Yes.

Sebastián   …

David   …

Sebastián   All right. Let's go.

David   Sebas …

Sebastián   …

David   Who am I?

VIII

Boiling Water

2015. December. Night. **David***'s house.*

Elvira Do you know who I am?

David A friend of my grandma's?

Elvira In a way.

David I've never seen you before.

Elvira I've seen you.

David We buried her two hours ago.

Elvira I wanted to come before, but the plane was delayed.

David You came on a plane?

Elvira …

David I've never flown anywhere.

Elvira I prefer to avoid it. I hadn't been on a plane for over twenty years.

David That long?

Elvira But then I realized I had to come back.

David Because you're from here?

Elvira Yes.

David So, where have you just come from?

Elvira From the States.

David …

Elvira …

David Come in; come in.

Elvira Are you on your own?

David Sebastián went to walk one of the neighbours home.

Elvira …

David The house was full of people until just now. It was what Gran wanted. For us to come here after the burial and celebrate her.

Elvira And celebration for your gran means a good dinner, right?

David We made pork and potatoes.

Elvira   And rice pudding for afters.

David   How did you know?

Elvira   They were her favourite dishes.

David   You've eaten here before?

Elvira   Yes. Lots of Sunday lunches.

David   You came when I was a child.

Elvira   No. You weren't born yet.

David   …

Elvira   …

David   Do you want something to eat?

Elvira   No, no.

David   We cooked too much meat.

Elvira   I would be grateful for a glass of water.

David   We drink boiled water here. Because of the parasites. The city gets dirtier and dirtier.

Elvira   I get the impression there's more life here right now than when I left … More lights on in the streets. People opening small businesses.

David   It's all make-up. Varnish on the surface. The pipes under the ground are as disgusting as they ever were. I turned the kitchen tap on today and nearly threw up from the stench.

Elvira   You're right to boil the water.

David   We filter it, too. Sebastián says it's the best way to stop all the limescale from building up in your kidneys.

Elvira   …

David   He's a doctor.

Elvira   The water tastes very good. Thank you.

David   …

Elvira   It's like time's stood still in this house.

David   We've stopped the leaks, at least.

Elvira   You had leaks?

David   Until a month ago. We went up onto the roof terrace, cleaned all the tiles and put a new layer of cement on. But it's the same every year. I don't know how much longer these beams will last.

Elvira That's the problem with living close to the sea. The iron beams just keep rusting.

David Grandma saw the funny side, luckily. She was used to it raining inside the house.

Elvira So, what will you do now, David?

David Right now, you mean?

Elvira No, I mean tomorrow, the day after … What will you do now your grandma's not here?

David …

Elvira …

David Do you want me to tell you how to get to the grave so you can see her?

Elvira No, don't worry.

David …

Elvira I just wanted to see you and know that you're OK.

David You're leaving?

Elvira Yes, I should rest.

David How long are you staying?

Elvira It depends. Maybe until the end of the week. Why?

David …

Elvira Well, goodbye.

David …

Elvira …

David You're leaving again? Without telling me?

Elvira What?

David That you're my mother.

IX

Less Than a Week

2015. December. The middle of the night. **Celia***'s house.*

Celia   If Mum was here with us it'd all be different.

Sebastián   But she's not. And I keep this house that you live in going, so you have to do as I say.

Celia   Oh, Dad, you're barely ever here. I'm the one who looks after this house.

Sebastián   David was expecting you. I thought you'd be there.

Celia   We had a fight yesterday; I didn't feel like seeing him.

Sebastián   But his grandmother died.

Celia   I know.

Sebastián   His grandmother, Celia.

Celia   I don't like cemeteries.

Sebastián   You could've come to the house.

Celia   I don't like death.

Sebastián   There's no better excuse than a death for patching things up with someone.

Celia   …

Sebastián   You know his grandma was all he had left.

Celia   No. He's got you.

Sebastián   It's in very poor taste not to give your condolences to someone who's –

Celia   The only one with any duty to David is you. A duty you've invented for yourself. You know nothing about my relationship with him. You can't force me to love him.

Sebastián   Well, we're moving back in.

Celia   Into this house?

Sebastián   Yes.

Celia   And leaving his grandma's mansion empty?

Sebastián   It's not my business what he does with his house. We're going to live here now.

Celia   You can't do that, Dad. I've got the right to decide –

Sebastián Decide what?

Celia I've been living alone for years.

Sebastián David and I are quiet people. We barely make any noise.

Celia Drop the sarcasm, please.

Sebastián Why are you eating so late?

Celia You're joking about living here, right?

Sebastián Not at all.

Celia …

Sebastián I miss this house.

Celia Did David put you up to this?

Sebastián No. It was my idea.

Celia …

Sebastián …

Celia When are you planning on moving?

Sebastián Today.

Celia What?

Sebastián David's already in the bedroom.

Celia I moved into the big room months ago.

Sebastián That's why we'll sleep in the small room tonight, until you move again.

Celia But, Dad … You're sticking your nose into my life, into my plans.

Sebastián I'm going to sleep. It's been too long a day.

Celia I've just rented the big room out.

Sebastián What do you mean, 'rented it out'?

Celia To a woman, from Up North.

Sebastián How many times have I told you –?

Celia She's only staying a few days; less than a week.

Sebastián Have you lost your mind, Celia?

Celia Quiet or you'll wake her up.

Sebastián And to cap it all, a foreigner.

Celia She's not a foreigner.

Sebastián These things aren't allowed.

Celia Like you've never done anything that wasn't allowed, Dad.

Sebastián …

Celia Like we don't live on an island where everything we do and everything we get isn't allowed.

Sebastián How could you bring a stranger into my house?

Celia I needed the money.

Sebastián You could've asked me.

Celia And how much would you have given me? Five pesos?

Sebastián I'm not putting David through this kind of stress. First thing tomorrow, you tell that woman she's leaving.

Celia No, Dad.

Sebastián Either you do it, or I will.

Celia …

Sebastián …

Celia …

Sebastián So, where are you going to sleep?

Celia I was going to sleep in the small room, but now you've decided on a whim to come today.

Sebastián The living room's free. You can sleep on the sofa.

Celia Don't worry. I'll sleep on the roof terrace.

Sebastián You'll freeze.

Celia I'll blow up the raft. It's old but it still works.

X

Full Moon

1993. October. Night. Santa María beach. The weather.

Elvira Does that raft work?

Sebastián Yeah, it's new; I just bought it before I came.

Elvira But why bring a blow-up raft?

Josué I told him there was no need but he insisted.

Sebastián Just in case.

Elvira The sea's calm ... But going out on an inflatable raft at night?

Sebastián I brought it in case there weren't enough beds.

Elvira There's two rooms in the house.

Josué One of them's empty.

Sebastián I'll blow it up anyway.

Josué It's massive. You won't have any lungs left.

Elvira ...

Sebastián ...

Josué It's good beer.

Elvira Yeah, cold, at least.

Josué A weekend at the beach without beer is just wrong.

Elvira Lucky I managed to get these boxes from the store.

Josué One of them'll be left untouched, what with Sebas not drinking.

Sebastián I do drink.

Elvira Don't you like alcohol?

Josué You don't drink any alcohol, admit it.

Sebastián I do.

Josué I plan on getting you drunk tonight.

Elvira Leave him alone.

Sebastián Come on then, pass me one.

Elvira Don't let him force you. You do what you like.

Sebastián Everyone drinks beer.

Josué Here you go.

Elvira …

Sebastián …

Josué …

Sebastián Do you often come to Santa María?

Elvira We used to come more.

Josué I prefer the pool.

Elvira You're a weird one.

Sebastián Why don't you like the beach?

Josué I don't like getting sand stuck on me.

Elvira I don't like the sun but I put cream on.

Sebastián Well, I don't mind the sand or the sun. I love swimming.

Elvira You remember how you didn't know how to swim when we started going out?

Josué I did know; I just hadn't swum very much.

Sebastián Do you swim a lot?

Elvira Since I was a girl. You?

Sebastián Since I was a boy.

Josué Haven't you seen his shoulders? He did secondary school at the Sports Academy.

Elvira So, you've always liked it.

Sebastián My father liked it.

Elvira Why did you stop?

Josué Tell her the truth, Sebas: you got sick of swimming and not getting anywhere.

Elvira You're so annoying.

Sebastián When I was sixteen my asthma turned chronic.

Josué I thought your asthma was a recent thing.

Sebastián There's lots of things I haven't told you.

Josué I trust the beer will keep loosening your tongue.

Elvira …

Sebastián   …

Elvira   Let me blow the raft up a bit.

Sebastián   There's no need.

Josué   I'm not even gonna try, Sebas. I'm all out of strength and doing that hurts my mouth.

Elvira   Let me, go on. I'll help you … Has it only got one mouthpiece?

Sebastián   Just one.

Josué   Isn't there such thing as a foot pump?

Sebastián   Yeah, but the shop didn't have any.

Josué   You can never buy things whole in this country; only in pieces.

Elvira   Stop complaining about the country; it's not to blame for everything … Besides, it doesn't hurt to blow something up; it's exercise.

Josué   I'm sick of doing exercise.

Elvira   …

Josué   …

Sebastián   …

Elvira   Ooph, it really hurt my jaw.

Josué   Told you.

Sebastián   Press the valve so the air doesn't come out.

Elvira   …

Sebastián   Let me; I'll do the rest.

Josué   …

Elvira   …

Sebastián   …

Elvira   So, your asthma's under control now?

Sebastián   The school's very humid.

Josué   He always has his inhaler on him.

Elvira   But if you have a severe attack the inhaler doesn't control it.

Josué   You've got some suppositories too, right, Sebas?

Sebastián   Yes, but only for a crisis.

Josué   He puts them in himself. He gets embarrassed if the nurse does it.

Sebastián You're very drunk already.

Elvira It makes you unbearable.

Josué OK, I was trying to make a joke. I'll shut up.

Elvira How did you come to be friends with this buffoon, Sebastián?

Josué This is my best mate. You won't turn him against me.

Sebastián Yep, it can't be helped. Our whole school career together … I'm used to his clowning around.

Josué You too?

Sebastián Come on, don't start –

Elvira …

Sebastián Stop tickling me, stop it.

Josué This is so you learn to stop picking on me.

Sebastián …

Elvira I feel like a mother with two babies.

Josué Oh, a baby.

Elvira Come on, lie down here on my legs. Let's see if you can calm down for a bit.

Sebastián …

Josué Have I already told you, Sebas, I'm planning on having a child with the most beautiful woman in the world?

Sebastián Oh, are you?

Elvira We're not planning anything. It's in his dreams.

Josué The dreams of a poor drunk, destroyed by his exterminating-angel wife.

Elvira …

Josué Give me a kiss, come on.

Sebastián …

Elvira What about you, Sebastián? Do you want to have children?

Sebastián I need someone else to bring me up. How can I think about being a father?

Josué Well, I'm dying to be a dad.

Sebastián …

Elvira You've blown the raft up.

Sebastián Finished.

Josué What if the three of us get on it?

Elvira Will we fit?

Sebastián We will if we squeeze in.

Elvira Let's try.

Josué Not on the sand. Let's get in the water.

Elvira At this time of night?

Josué What does it matter? Look how bright the moon is.

Sebastián I can leave you two to it.

Josué No, no. We're all going.

Elvira What if it capsizes?

Sebastián We won't let it.

Josué Hang on. Let's have a photo, I brought the camera.

Elvira I'm in no state for a photo.

Josué You are, you are. Let's see: I'll get it out and put it here.

Sebastián You should go in the middle, Elvira.

Elvira It'll have a flash, right?

Josué Course it does. I'm pressing it.

Sebastián Run, you won't have time.

Josué Yes, I will.

Elvira Right, smile!

Sebastián …

Josué …

Elvira …

Josué Great.

Sebastián Print two of those so I can have one.

Josué OK.

Elvira So, into the water with the raft?

Josué Shall we have a smoke first?

Sebastián Again?

XI

Some Flowers

2015. December. Night. **David**'s *house.*

David You're leaving again? Without telling me?

Elvira What?

David That you're my mother.

Elvira …

David You are my mother, aren't you?

Elvira …

David I know I'm not hallucinating.

Elvira …

David You're here in front of me.

Elvira …

David I touch you and I know you're you.

Elvira …

David You were going to leave again without saying anything?

Elvira David, I …

David …

Elvira I don't want to upset you, Son.

David Don't call me 'Son' after all this time, please. My grandma's my mother.

Elvira Son –

David Don't say it again. It sounds like you're mocking me.

Elvira …

David I knew who you were from the moment I opened the door and saw you.

Elvira It's been hell being away all this time.

David I never saw your photo but I knew it was you.

Elvira Always wanting to come back and always terrified this moment would come.

David …

Elvira You'd have to have lived all those years to understand.

David   They can't have been worse than these.

Elvira   We were very young. I wasn't ready. I was so in love with your father –

David   Wash out your mouth before you talk about Dad!

Elvira   …

David   Dad's here, with me.

Elvira   How can I ask you to forgive me?

David   …

Elvira   You won't understand that it wasn't my fault … Son, I know perfectly well I have to take all the blame, and I don't care. There's no way to explain all the details to you, all the reasons. There's no way, and there's no point. Because nothing would make it clear to you; nothing would heal the pain of so much distance.

David   …

Elvira   So, I'm looking at you now with tears in my eyes, with all this guilt, from the deepest place inside me, begging you: listen to my voice, even if it sounds like a stranger's. My mother died giving birth to me and I never knew her. Think how lucky you are. It's all happened: love and horror. The world has turned. But your mother is right here, asking you for forgiveness.

David   …

Elvira   …

David   I don't have a mother. I've just buried my mother.

Elvira   …

David   …

Elvira   If we could calm down and talk normally –

David   But I'm not normal. Look at me. Do you think I'm normal?

Elvira   You're exhausted.

David   I'm not exhausted, I'm sick!

Elvira   I can find a way to cure you.

David   You think there's a cure for this?

Elvira   …

David   …

Elvira   I came here determined to explain to you, to tell you everything.

David   I know what happened! You died with Dad in an accident!

Elvira   No, I'm here.

David My grandma threw flowers and earth on your grave with her own hands.

Elvira Look at me, David. I'm flesh and bone.

David No, you're dead!

Elvira I'm holding you, Son!

David Why the fuck did you have to turn up now?

Elvira Come with me. I have money. I can pay for your passport, your ticket. I have contacts –

David What are you talking about?

Elvira You don't have to stay here. We can go to the States! You don't have anyone in this country any more.

David What about Sebastián?

Elvira Let's get off this island!

David Sebas! Sebas!

Elvira Listen to me!

David I want to wake up!

Elvira You are awake, David!

David No! Go away! I want to wake up!

Elvira Son!

David Go away! Get out of my head!

Elvira Listen to me, please!

David Dad, save me from this! Sebas! Dad!

Elvira Son, I can leave if you want but calm down!

David Save me, Dad! Get me out of here!

Elvira I'm leaving, David.

David Dad! Sebas!

Elvira …

David Dad!

XII

The Truth

1993. December. Night. **Elvira**'s *house.*

Elvira   Wait.

Josué   …

Elvira   I'm pregnant.

Josué   What?

Elvira   …

Josué   Really?

Elvira   Ten weeks.

Josué   I don't believe it.

Elvira   They confirmed it this afternoon.

Josué   Darling, that's the best news.

Elvira   …

Josué   We're really gonna have a baby?

Elvira   Don't squeeze me so tight.

Josué   Sit down, come on … You are pleased, aren't you?

Elvira   …

Josué   Was it the clinic at the school where you did the test?

Elvira   No, of course not. I didn't want rumours starting … I went to the maternity hospital. I've got a friend there.

Josué   Great, yeah, a friend.

Elvira   …

Josué   You're really pregnant?

Elvira   …

Josué   We have to plan everything properly … I'll finally have to get all the materials to build a room on the roof terrace … A brand-new room with its own bathroom. We can move upstairs with the baby and use this room as a living room … Or would you rather we moved to my mum's house? Did they say if it's a boy or a girl?

Elvira   …

Josué Wait 'til we tell Mum. She's dying to be a grandma.

Elvira …

Josué …

Elvira I'm not having a baby with a man I don't know.

Josué …

Elvira …

Josué You mean all that shit about the school?

Elvira …

Josué Darling, it's nonsense … If it'll put your mind at rest, I promise I –

Elvira I'm not just talking about your strange ideas, you not knowing how to keep quiet … All that does bother me, but I'm not just talking about that.

Josué Come on, let's go out for a bit. We can't talk about such important things stuck inside.

Elvira Like going outside will solve everything.

Josué We're talking about our child now and I'm not gonna shut up 'til I've convinced you what a blessing this is. We've talked about it a lot. This involves us both, we can't mix it up with stupid, day-to-day stuff.

Elvira …

Josué I'm at university because I promised my father. I love Medicine, but I love people more, and freedom … I've already made my mind up: as soon as I graduate, I'll make a living somewhere quiet, go inland, escape this model Revolutionary doctor they want to turn me into … Dignity means something different to me. I aspire to different things. I can't be so rigid, I can't force myself to believe blindly in something … that's impossible to believe in.

Elvira You don't think that way.

Josué Yes, I do. And I have to believe I can build something new for myself, something different to what I've always been taught. Leaving the country can't be the only way of having a life.

Elvira I don't know why you're throwing that in my face, I've never wanted to leave.

Josué Being a doctor at the highest level, dean of the Medical School, so in with the Party … Those things don't give you freedom.

Elvira …

Josué I understand that everything's against us. It always has been. And we've fought. No one in any university thinks it's a good idea for a lecturer to be hooked up

XII The Truth

with her student. And we didn't just hook up: we got married. You dared. You leapt. And we've built this little piece of the world for the two of us.

Elvira …

Josué When you're sick of it all, of being on duty all night, of the bureaucracy, the only refuge left to you will be your home. All you'll have, even if I'm not here, will be our child.

Elvira …

Josué …

Elvira My friend said I'm in the last week to interrupt the pregnancy.

Josué What's wrong with you?

Elvira I'd recover in a few hours.

Josué You're not doing that, it's crazy.

Elvira No one at the school would need to know.

Josué Did you not understand a word of what I just said?

Elvira Josué, I don't trust …

Josué …

Elvira I don't trust you.

Josué I've just told you everything! What the hell do you want me to do?!

Elvira I want you to look me in the eyes and admit you're sleeping with Sebastián!

Josué …

Elvira Just for once, take off your armour and tell me the truth.

Josué …

Elvira Let's see if I can believe you.

Josué …

Elvira Tell me and I won't get rid of the baby.

Josué …

Elvira …

Josué …

Elvira That's what I thought. That you wouldn't have the balls to do it.

Josué …

Elvira Not even for your own child.

Josué This can't be happening.

Elvira   …

Josué   Do you seriously think me and Sebastián …?

Elvira   Tell me the truth.

Josué   The truth is that baby you've got inside you, Elvira. There is no other truth.

Elvira   …

Josué   …

Elvira   I'm sick of it all, Josué. This dissident student who talks without thinking, saying anything, anywhere … Unaware of the damage he's doing to his wife, to me.

Josué   Elvira, don't –

Elvira   You have to get mixed up in everything. You have to have an opinion about everything, and you have to be allowed to do everything! You never listen to me, you don't care what I feel, what I understand … You think freedom means doing everything exactly when you want to! You say your dad was tough? No, Josué, he was soft! You're impossible! You kiss me now, you smile at me, you caress me, you tell me you dream of having a child … But for months you've been defying me, opposing me.

Josué   You've never believed in this deep down.

Elvira   I believed in you!

Josué   …

Elvira   And you've been cheating on me.

Josué   I haven't cheated on you.

Elvira   Because for you, freedom, your ideal of freedom, overrides everything. You can step on me, annihilate me, ridicule me. And you can sleep with Sebastián, with your best friend Sebastián, thinking that it won't hurt me, that I won't find out.

Josué   You're making a mistake.

Elvira   No. You know I'm not.

Josué   …

Elvira   …

Josué   …

Elvira   OK. You're not being honest with me, so this is what's going to happen.

Josué   …

Elvira   First, you'll get your things and you'll go back to your mother's house. Second, you'll go with me tomorrow, Friday, to the lawyer's to file for a divorce by mutual consent. Third, on Monday you'll present yourself at the secretariat and you'll ask to be released permanently from the school because of health problems.

No one will argue with you, no one will ask you any questions. As the dean, I'll sign everything off and I'll make sure you're free of anything that links you to me. And if you don't do any of those things –

Josué Are you threatening me?

Elvira I'm just informing you of the procedure.

Josué And what if I decide not to do any of that?

Elvira Then you'll be forcing me to tell everyone the real reason for our separation.

Josué …

Elvira …

Josué You wouldn't dare.

Elvira Try me and see.

Josué But you'd be lying!

Elvira There's only one liar in this story. And that's you.

XIII

A Bit of Calm

2015. December. The middle of the night. **Celia**'s *house.*

Sebastián Is that you?

Elvira I thought I heard you.

Sebastián What are you doing here?

Elvira I didn't think we'd bump into each other so soon, believe me.

Sebastián Have you been watching me?

Elvira …

Sebastián What did you say to Celia to get into my house?

Elvira Nothing, Sebastián. She doesn't know.

Sebastián How could you?

Elvira Listen to me, please. Everything's fine.

Sebastián No, nothing's fine.

Elvira I need us to talk calmly.

Sebastián I get up for a drink of water and I see you here –

Elvira Keep your voice down. It's best the children don't hear. We should sort this out between ourselves.

Sebastián They're not children.

Elvira …

Sebastián What did you do? Buy Celia off with a few dollars?

Elvira I just wanted to –

Sebastián So, it's true you spoke to David.

Elvira I had to.

Sebastián You turned up and spoke to him, out of the blue. Like it was the most normal thing in the world.

Elvira …

Sebastián I just can't believe it.

Elvira It's not comfortable for me either.

Sebastián Comfortable? You can't imagine what I feel, how much I want to …

Elvira …

Sebastián What are you doing coming back? You promised me –

Elvira I know.

Sebastián You weren't going to come back.

Elvira But I'm here.

Sebastián You can't, Elvira! You made a promise!

Elvira …

Sebastián God, you went to see David.

Elvira You didn't give me any choice.

Sebastián You went!

Elvira I saw you leaving and I took the chance and knocked at the door.

Sebastián And there was no better time than just after the death of his grandmother.

Elvira …

Sebastián It's been over twenty years. This can't be happening now. It's insane.

Elvira I think it's the sanest thing in the world.

Sebastián You cut yourself off.

Elvira What did you do with my letters?

Sebastián I spared David the pain. I burnt them.

Elvira And now you're the one reproaching me?

Sebastián It was your choice to leave the country!

Elvira I was going to come back!

Sebastián Has living Up North erased your memory? Have you forgotten how you cried, how you begged me?

Elvira I was ill, I needed to recover.

Sebastián And you were the only one who suffered? Only you felt pain? Don't be selfish. We all lost Josué.

Elvira …

Sebastián His mother lost him. You lost him. I lost him.

Elvira …

Sebastián I don't know how you didn't explode. Not even giving birth calmed you down.

XIV

Accidents

1994. August. Night. **David**'s *house.*

Elvira Nothing calms me down. They say motherhood transforms you? Well, I can't adapt to having a baby.

Sebastián …

Elvira I'm a bag of nerves.

Sebastián …

Elvira …

Sebastián That night on the beach –

Elvira I don't need an explanation.

Sebastián We'd been smoking. We'd been drinking.

Elvira …

Sebastián I know things started getting worse between you and Josué after that night.

Elvira Things had been bad between us for a long time.

Sebastián Yes, but if I hadn't turned up –

Elvira But you did.

Sebastián …

Elvira …

Sebastián Are you still not sleeping?

Elvira I sleep for half an hour, then I wake up screaming.

Sebastián Ever since then?

Elvira Yes.

Sebastián It's been more than six months.

Elvira It feels like yesterday to me.

Sebastián …

Elvira …

Sebastián David's beautiful.

Elvira Look at him pulling faces.

Sebastián   He's drooling.

Elvira   Thanks for the pram.

Sebastián   I thought it'd be a good present.

Elvira   Thanks for coming today.

Sebastián   …

Elvira   I haven't been able to stop thinking about –

Sebastián   That's not good for you and you know it.

Elvira   I had Josué in front of me, I mentioned the pregnancy, he was happy, we argued, I said so many things that I really didn't –

Sebastián   You'd got obsessed with that ridiculous idea.

Elvira   It was all too much for me … People gossiping, filling my head with smoke … I told him all of it.

Sebastián   And it wasn't true.

Elvira   It wasn't true?

Sebastián   No.

Elvira   I wasn't sure. I'm still not sure.

Sebastián   There was never anything between me and Josué. We were friends. Best friends. Nothing else.

Elvira   …

Sebastián   But that doubt wasn't your reason, not deep down. You were still angry with me and, by accusing him like that, you somehow got revenge on both of us.

Elvira   He didn't defend himself. He started crying, he couldn't speak. Then suddenly he shot out like a bullet …

Sebastián   …

Elvira   We've never talked about this, Sebastián.

Sebastián   Never. But we both know, with all that rage he had inside him –

Elvira   I'd rather believe it was an accident.

Sebastián   An accident.

Elvira   It's better for everyone.

Sebastián   …

Elvira   …

Sebastián   I've felt guilty too.

Elvira ...

Sebastián Because of the beach, because of what we did.

Elvira ...

Sebastián Because I didn't tell him.

Elvira We couldn't tell him.

Sebastián ...

Elvira ...

Sebastián Are you going to stay here with the baby?

Elvira Aurora asked me to move in here. I feel safer if I'm not alone.

Sebastián She is his grandmother, after all. She's got a big house. David can enjoy it his whole life.

Elvira ...

Sebastián They say at Med School you've requested to leave the Party.

Elvira ...

Sebastián You'll come back to teach, right? The routine will do you good.

Elvira ...

Sebastián It wasn't easy getting here. The bus was diverted. Some of the streets are closed. Have you seen how many people are going to the Malecón?

Elvira Yes, lots.

Sebastián Hundreds of people. It's really stirred up.

Elvira ...

Sebastián My neighbour's built a raft with lorry tyres. He's leaving at the weekend with his wife and daughter.

Elvira They say they've sent twenty boats from the States to pick up whoever wants to leave.

Sebastián The police'll get involved.

Elvira Yes, there'll be trouble.

Sebastián I'd better not stay too late.

Elvira ...

Sebastián ...

Elvira I can't stand being here another second, Sebastián. I can't walk through this house, I can't go into the kitchen without everything being a chaos in my mind. I can't rest. Every little thing reminds me of Josué. Everything brings him back to me. I'm suffocating on this island! I'm going mad. I can't even stand my own son! It disgusts me to touch him! I can't stand this smell on me, this stink of sour milk … I'm ashamed of myself, I feel so filthy … I'm rotting away.

Sebastián   What are you talking about?

Elvira   I'm leaving the country. Tomorrow, before dawn.

Sebastián   What?

Elvira   A raft with two engines. We'll make it across fine, it's not dangerous. I had to keep everything secret, I couldn't take any risks.

Sebastián   You're joking, aren't you?

Elvira   I've got the money and I'm doing it.

Sebastián   …

Elvira   I'll come back, though. I'll come back one day.

Sebastián   You're raving, Elvira. Calm down.

Elvira   No, I'm perfectly fine.

Sebastián   No one can just change their life like that!

Elvira   I have to do it now!

Sebastián   You'll never be allowed back!

Elvira   I'll come back when my head's clear and I can look my son in the eye.

Sebastián   You can't leave a baby on his own! You need to feed him, you need to –

Elvira   Aurora knows perfectly well what to do. And you're here too … I'll send you money as soon as I can.

Sebastián   Even dogs protect their puppies! How can you abandon him? He's just lost his father!

Elvira   No, Sebastián, no!

Sebastián   …

Elvira   No!

Sebastián   …

Elvira   David's your son.

XV

If You Weren't Here

2015. December. The middle of the night. **Celia**'s *house.*

Elvira I told you. And you were speechless.

Sebastián …

Elvira Josué couldn't have children. He didn't know that. But I did.

Sebastián …

Elvira So much time has passed since then. So many things have happened.

Sebastián Yes, I can see that. I can tell. You've got that arrogance that's brought on by money.

Elvira …

Sebastián Have you come here to throw it in my face that you live better than we do? That you've been able to build yourself a new world Up North? That you've eaten better, you dress better? That staying here was pointless? That you can put a few banknotes on the table and win over my children? Take David … and rub me out? Is that what you've come for?

Elvira I haven't come to fight.

Sebastián Now, because it's always been about what you want, about you feeling good about yourself, about healing your own sense of remorse … Now, because you're the centre of the world, you come with all your entitlement and turn everything upside-down.

Elvira I want us to talk like civilized people.

Sebastián Don't demand things of me that I can't give you! It wasn't civilized to abandon your child.

Elvira You think your relationship with him is civilized? The way you've won his affection, knowing who he was?

Sebastián Don't you dare talk about the way I love David. You have no idea about what's happened, about what we've been through here, together. You were a long way away, making a life for yourself Up North. No one forced you: you chose that path, you closed your ears so you wouldn't hear me. You cut yourself off, you left, you washed your hands! But things got very complicated here, Elvira. We had to carry on living here! Whatever news may have reached you is a pale reflection of the reality we've had here. How hard it's been to get the most basic things, to bring up a child, to feed him, to put shoes on his feet. The patience it took to watch him grow up and encourage him to study and become someone. The calm it took to struggle with everything that that child had in his head, to soothe him, to be beside him at every moment. Do you know what that is?! Do you have the slightest idea what I'm talking about?! Night after sleepless night! Praying that this teenager will stop wanting to kill himself ...! David only had me and Aurora. She didn't like me but we decided together, we made a pact: to fight tooth and nail to tame the beast that that child had inside of him. We turned him into a good man, a man with good feelings. And I think that alone is enough for me to demand some respect from you! I won't allow you to talk so lightly, to put labels on my sacrifice, my affection for David. It's not fair, after all these years, for you to come here and start judging. We did what we had to do to survive.

Elvira   ...

Sebastián   ...

Elvira   ...

Sebastián   ...

Elvira   OK. I'll be quiet.

Sebastián   ...

Elvira   But I'm still his mother. So, don't you judge the reasons why I've come back to find him again. To explain everything to him.

Sebastián   There are some things that can't be explained.

Elvira   ...

David   Like what?

Elvira   Son ...

Sebastián   ...

David   ...

Sebastián   What did you hear, David?

Elvira   ...

David   ...

Sebastián   I ...

Elvira   We could –

David   There's no need.

Sebastián   I swear –

David   It's all right, Sebas.

Elvira   ...

David   I've always carried Dad somewhere here within me.

Elvira   ...

Sebastián   ...

David   And I've always known that you're my father, too.

XVI

A Little Shell Surrounded by Sand

2015. December. The middle of the night. A wild, outdoor place for making love.

Celia …

David …

Celia …

David …

Celia …

David …

Celia I want you to be the father of my child. Of this little piece of you that's already inside me.

David …

Celia Yes. I know. And I don't care.

David …

Celia I always wanted it to be you. I couldn't meet anyone better than you.

David …

Celia And I want us to leave as soon as the child's born. Not to look back, never to return. To forget everything and start from nothing. To dream of an amazing future for our child, and we'll never tell him or her anything about this cursed island. We can do it now. It's in your hands. You've got that woman who'll give you everything. She'll do exactly what you ask, and what you're going to ask her is this: money for food until the baby's born, money for raising it, money for us to leave.

David But I don't want to leave here.

Celia …

David I'm not interested in travelling.

Celia …

David I liked making love to you like this, so urgently, in this corner under the moonlight.

Celia …

David I'll love holding my son. Playing with him. Laughing with him. We'll be inseparable. The best friends in the world. I'll love all of it.

Celia …

David But leave?

Celia …

David No. I've already made too many changes.

Celia …

David I don't want to go anywhere.

Outside the Game

**A File for the Reconstruction
of the Heberto Padilla Case**

Outside the Game and this English translation were originally commissioned by Cuban-Spanish artist and producer Dagoberto Rodríguez.

It premiered at Sala Versus Glòries as part of Grec Festival, Barcelona, on 28 May 2021, directed by Abel González Melo, with the following cast: Yadier Fernández, Ginnette Gala and Rey Montesinos.

For Raquel Carrió

Author's Note

Outside the Game: A File for the Reconstruction of the Heberto Padilla Case is a work of fiction. It is freely inspired by real people and real events which have been widely documented in multiple sources across several decades. As the text itself explains, the play in no way attempts to be a biography or a precise account of reality. Rather, it seeks to tell a new, poetic story that glimpses at how the events reimagined within it might or might not have happened. As one character remarks: 'Our way of understanding their lives and everything that happened around them. A way of understanding that, so we can understand ourselves.'

Parts of the File

I. Dawn in the Tropics
II. A Polish Story
III. Our Revolution Is Different
IV. The Good Advisor
V. The Attitude of the Nonconformist
VI. Provocations
VII. The Arrest
VIII. Villa Marista
IX. Absolute Scum
X. Pride of the Nation

Characters

Heberto Padilla, *writer*
Belkis, *his wife*
Their dedicated **Comrade**

The action takes place in Havana between 1967 and 1971. It also takes place in the present, in exile. And, perhaps, only in the mind of the protagonist.

I

Dawn in the Tropics

Belkis It all started like this …

1971. An apartment. Dim light. Violent knocking at the door. A quiet sound of concern.

Padilla Is it the end of the world or something?

Belkis You're still hung over from last night.

Padilla What did I do last night?

Knocking.

Don't they respect people's sleep?

Belkis No, they don't respect anything; they just turn up suddenly like this and –

Padilla It's seven o'clock; it's still dark; the sun hasn't come up yet.

Belkis And it's the weekend.

Knocking.

Padilla Why are they knocking at the door?

Belkis Who is it, I ask.

Padilla Who is it? They sound like animals.

Belkis I look through the spyhole.

Padilla It's the postman.

Belkis He says he has a very important telegram to give us.

Knocking.

Padilla The postman doesn't knock like that.

Belkis This time of the morning?

Padilla A telegram?

Belkis No one sends us telegrams.

Padilla Belkis, don't open it!

Knocking.

Belkis I know why they're here; I can sense it; I've been worried about it for months, imagining this very moment.

Padilla Is this a dream?

Belkis No, it's not a dream.

Padilla It's not normal: invading people's privacy like this, people's lives.

Belkis The knocking has just dragged me out of bed. It's dark, but the sun's about to rise.

Knocking.

Padilla Don't open it!

Belkis They'll knock the door down if I don't!

Knocking.

Padilla Will they not stop?

Belkis I know who it is! I have to open it, Heberto. I have to!

Much more knocking and then, suddenly, complete silence. Pause. It grows lighter.

Padilla Now, after all these years …

Belkis Here, far from the island …

Padilla On this side, in exile … Half a century away from all of that …

Belkis We can tell the story.

Padilla But can we tell it how it was?

Belkis It's like that morning's nailed to the middle of my forehead. In all this time I've never been able to forget.

Padilla The shouting. Her daughter coming out of her room terrified. The months before, the months after, the claustrophobia, the asthma …

Belkis But we're not the people we were back then.

Padilla No, we're not them. We couldn't be. We're actors.

Belkis We're only here now because they won't tell the story.

Padilla They wouldn't tell it, because they have –

Belkis We have –

Padilla We all have our own truth. Our private truth.

Belkis And when things have happened in the reality of history, it's hard, after time has passed, to tell those stories again, and for everything that was so real back then, to be just as real now, here, on a stage.

Padilla That moment we lived through.

Belkis A truly historic moment.

Padilla   The glorious days of the first years of the Cuban Revolution.

Belkis   Che Guevara had just died in the Bolivian forest.

Padilla   And we were just two young things who'd studied journalism and dreamed of being poets.

Belkis   He is Heberto Padilla.

Padilla   I'll be playing Padilla in this play. Because the real-life Padilla, the authentic one, died in exile in the US in the year 2000, from a heart attack, aged 68.

Belkis   By then we'd already been separated for some time. What happened to us was hard: the struggle to leave Cuba, starting from scratch in exile … We did split up in the end, yes … But during the time we're going to tell you about, we were together. Close together.

Padilla   She is Belkis.

Belkis   I'll be playing Belkis. Because the real-life Belkis, today, lives in the US. She's not a Communist activist any more; she's devoted herself to religion. And we haven't consulted her at all.

Padilla   In fact, she doesn't know we're making this play. Or maybe she does know.

Belkis   Or will know, if one of you here now goes and tells her.

Padilla   She, Belkis, is my widow.

Belkis   Heberto Padilla's widow. Loyally safeguarding his memory for nearly two decades. The memory of everything that happened.

Padilla   We've read some of the things she wrote about those events; she has a blog; but we haven't spoken to her directly.

Belkis   Because this isn't biography. This isn't strict historical faithfulness.

Padilla   Faithfulness can be a difficult word.

Belkis   This isn't faithfulness. It's scraps of information.

Padilla   Images, fragments … Even Heberto himself left his account of events in a book entitled *Bad Memory*.

Belkis   This isn't biography.

Padilla   This is a work of fiction. Pure fiction. Our way of understanding their lives and everything that happened around them. A way of understanding that, so we can understand ourselves.

Belkis   My grandma used to say, 'there's no God who can understand the Cubans'. We're too explosive a mixture.

Padilla   So explosive that that morning it felt like the knocking on the door would burst my eardrums.

Knocking.

Padilla Belkis and I have known each other for about … four years? We saw each other for the first time in '67?

Belkis That was when you first saw me; I already knew you … I'd read your work. Your name was already doing the rounds in literary circles, so –

Padilla Yes, I know what you're going to say … I'm ten years older than her.

Belkis That was never a problem for me.

Padilla Ten years is ten years.

Belkis It doesn't show so much now: I'm twentysomething and you're thirtysomething.

Padilla I have two daughters and one son from my previous marriage to Berta.

Belkis And I have a daughter from my marriage to Bernardo. María, the little girl who was frightened by the knocking at the door. She gets scared, poor thing: she's only seven and she doesn't understand.

Padilla We'd both had previous relationships.

Belkis And we'd finally decided to live together.

Padilla We were happy.

Belkis Yes. We were happy.

Knocking.

Padilla The knocking comes on March 20th, 1971 … And our only child together won't be born until the following year.

Belkis But lots of things will have happened before then.

Knocking.

Back then we didn't know what was happening to us.

Padilla We were living.

Belkis We'd go to the Coppelia ice-cream parlour to try one of their thirty flavours.

Padilla We'd write poetry.

Belkis But poetry can't describe a whole life.

Padilla It makes it too short.

Belkis Makes the real seem sublime.

Padilla And those were tumultuous years. Years that don't fit inside a poem.

Knocking.

Belkis You'd come home late the previous night. You'd been with that Chilean diplomat, Jorge Edwards, in the suite at the Riviera Hotel, and you didn't realize they were setting a trap for you.

Padilla I can still feel the hangover.

Knocking. The dim light and the quiet sounds of concern return.

Belkis You know why they're here, don't you.

Padilla We were just writers. We just wanted to live.

Belkis And through no desire of our own, we became the protagonists of the most violent episode in the history of Cuban culture and censorship.

Padilla Something that would mark a turning point in the way the world viewed the Cuban Revolution.

Belkis It would bear your name. It would be called 'The Padilla Case'.

Padilla But we couldn't have imagined that back then.

Belkis No, back then we loved Che Guevara.

Padilla We named our son Ernesto after him.

The sound has been growing unbearable. Much more knocking.

They're here.

Belkis I'm opening the door.

Padilla It's them, Belkis. State Security.

Belkis They're going to arrest us.

Police sirens are heard.

II

A Polish Story

1967. Office.

Comrade Do you remember that Polish story?

Padilla Which one?

Comrade That one where there's a writer who's an army private who can't criticize the poems written by a lieutenant, who has no choice but to applaud the short stories written by a captain, who, in turn, has to praise the novels written by a general, no matter how bad they are ... Do you remember? Who was the author?

Padilla Sławomir Mrożek.

Comrade And is he still alive?

Padilla Yes. Born in 1930.

Comrade So young.

Padilla The story's called 'The Process'.

Comrade It's delicious. 'About the en-masse militarisation of writers.' You said that once, at some meeting or other.

Padilla Do you always remember everything I say?

Comrade Mostly.

Padilla Even when you're not there to hear the conversation?

Comrade Even then. I have my methods. I'm not your dedicated comrade for nothing.

Padilla ...

Comrade I like that story. It's a shame about the Poles, isn't it. Not being able to be honest with their superiors ... Luckily we've wiped out capitalism in Cuba: all those critics trotting out sycophantic reviews, filled with bombast and dithyrambs ... Now Cuba has socialism, we can say things clearly, eye to eye.

Padilla And yet they've all fallen on me now like flies; attacking me because I supposedly dealt a 'hammer blow' to a comrade – that's what they're saying – with my opinions ... As if literary criticism had the power of a hammer.

Comrade They weren't just literary criticisms, Padilla.

Padilla ...

Comrade Why do you like looking for trouble?

Padilla   What surprises me most about this whole situation is that I had to find it out from the newspaper; it's out on the streets now and thousands of people have read it: how unhappy the editors were with my opinion about that little novel.

Comrade   *Urbino's Passion* by Lisandro Otero.

Padilla   And to cap it all, with that title: it sounds like one of Corín Tellado's romance novels.

Comrade   Don't be so dismissive: it's sold five thousand copies in a single week.

Padilla   Please: it's not even ninety pages long and it only costs forty-five cents … How could it not sell out?

Comrade   Suited to the Cuban pocket.

Padilla   If they wanted to publish reviews of contemporary Cuban narrative, wouldn't it have been better to choose José Lezama Lima's *Paradiso*?

Comrade   Or Guillermo Cabrera Infante's *Three Trapped Tigers*, like you suggest in your article?

Padilla   At least *Three Trapped Tigers* won the Seix Barral Prize. It was published in Spain just now to huge success.

Comrade   We'll never publish it here.

Padilla   Right: you all believe you have a duty to decide what the Cuban people should be reading.

Comrade   We know what the people need to read.

Padilla   And Cabrera Infante doesn't fit within this spectrum of magnanimous wisdom, of course.

Comrade   They like him in Spain? Let them eat him! I'm sure he'll do better with Franco than with us.

Padilla   I wouldn't say that with such sarcasm. Franco and our Commander get on very well, don't forget.

Comrade   Watch what you're saying.

Padilla   Both the sons of Galicians … They understand each other.

Comrade   Don't be too clever for your own good, Padilla.

Padilla   At least in Europe Cabrera Infante doesn't have to worry about them suddenly turning against him any minute.

Comrade   We gave him permission to leave Cuba.

Padilla   They won't humiliate him there, dragging him off a plane like they did here when he tried to go back to Brussels. He was cultural attaché: the government itself had given him the post.

Comrade   And the government itself decided he wasn't right for it. Many of us never believed, not even when they sent him there the first time, that he was the right sort ... So, if he's not in the post now, you have no right to use an opinion piece to call the Minister's decision into question.

Padilla   I didn't call anything into question! I just said it seemed to me they'd followed an irregular procedure with someone who'd represented this country overseas with such dignity. They treated him like a common criminal.

Comrade   You writers see ghosts everywhere.

Padilla   I see reality. Why did they make such a mess of things and no one own up to it? Why did no one tell him they were relieving him of the post? What reason is there for such a politically inept process? What were they accusing him of? A man who seemed to enjoy the ministry's full confidence. Because the accusations must have been serious for them not to give any explanation in public or in private.

Comrade   The people who had to know, knew.

Padilla   The first person to know should have been him. Now he's in a basement somewhere in London and he still doesn't know.

Comrade   What does it matter? He asked for permission to leave and we granted it.

Padilla   Right: that's the strangest thing. Cuban bureaucracy takes centuries to do anything, but when it involves getting rid of someone inconvenient, it's fast as lightning.

Comrade   We didn't like the road he was taking, Padilla. We don't like his novel.

Padilla   That's a matter of taste.

Comrade   He's a traitor and he's finally where he deserves to be, and Lisandro is here with us.

Padilla   Bravo! One constant in this country: expel the good and stick with the bad.

Comrade   You dislike *Urbino's Passion* because Lisandro wrote it.

Padilla   Maybe it was Lisandro who disliked Cabrera Infante. And now you all want to get into Lisandro's good books, you've paved the way for him.

Comrade   I can see it in your face. You don't think it's fair that Lisandro has a government job, or that the upper echelons like him so much.

Padilla   I have nothing against bureaucrats.

Comrade   You wrote that being a bureaucrat for the Cuban Revolution is a curse.

Padilla   I never wrote that. You have such a way of twisting words ... But I don't agree either with what the newspaper says ... Because it's you all who dictate things to the editors, right? Well, I'm saying it to your face: I don't agree that, as you say, being a bureaucrat is 'one of the greatest challenges a writer can find in the contemporary world'.

Comrade You know how much the Commander values the work of intellectuals.

Padilla Intellectuals like Lisandro, especially, who's capable of abusing his post as 'bureaucrat-and-novelist' to cancel two plays without even reading them.

Comrade You've worked for this government too, Padilla. You've had to take decisions too.

Padilla Luckily, I never had to ban anything.

Comrade Because we protected you from finding yourself in such a dilemma.

Padilla I'd never have agreed to it.

Comrade You were so busy overseas, old man, that you barely had chance to notice all we've done here for culture and education … In under ten years of Revolution, we've taught almost a million illiterate people to read and write, we've given grants to two hundred and fifty thousand students, we've published millions of books –

Padilla This is rhetoric: you're throwing things in my face that I'm just as proud of as you are.

Comrade From the way you behave it's obvious you weren't close to the process.

Padilla In eight and a half years of Revolution, I lived for just one year in Prague as a bureaucrat for the Ministry for Overseas Trade.

Comrade And could it be because you lost your bureaucratic post with all its perks that you feel a … certain envy now for Lisandro, who still has his?

Padilla I didn't lose that post.

Comrade Oh, didn't you?

Padilla I resigned.

Comrade It's so amusing how everyone designs the story to suit their own whims.

Padilla And I never had those perks you talk about. I froze in Moscow. And what little money I was paid all went on food.

Comrade And now, to cap it all, you're complaining.

Padilla You all want to make me out to be a man who only spent a few days living in his own country, but that's just a narrow and superficial view. None of my stays in the socialist countries were exactly a panacea.

Comrade The Commander himself came to me one day to tell me: 'Living and fighting in Cuba, day after day, is one privilege that Padilla has not enjoyed.'

Padilla But –

Comrade He's the Commander; how could I contradict him? Besides, he's right. He says it for your own good; because he's interested in you; because he's keeping an eye on your case.

Padilla My case?

Comrade Yes, your case.

Padilla What case?

Comrade The Padilla Case, he calls it.

Padilla There is no Padilla Case.

Comrade There is, even if you don't know it.

Padilla What the hell are you talking about?

Comrade He even looks upon your case with a certain … compassion.

Padilla What do you mean, 'compassion'?

Comrade Yes, the Commander is very compassionate. All of his speeches and heroic demeanour might transmit the image of an aggressive man, but his soul is filled with kindness. He says you've lived outside of Cuba for too long … He says it in a pitying tone, with a trace of pain, yes, as if blaming himself for your lack of political maturity.

Padilla That can't be. The Commander doesn't know me.

Comrade Doesn't know you? What country are you living in, Padilla? How could you think the Commander wouldn't know a person like you?

Padilla …

Comrade He knows your entire life story like the back of his hand.

Padilla I've done lots of things he can't have found out about.

Comrade No, no, no. You're wrong. He knows everything. What you've done. What you're going to do.

Padilla That's not possible. It's not possible!

Comrade Calm down! Don't get worked up: you'll have a heart attack, and we still have a long way to go.

Padilla *begins to calm down.*

Comrade That's it. Breathe. We don't want you having an asthma attack now: there might not be any medicine at the pharmacist's.

Padilla …

Comrade That writer … The Pole.

Padilla Sławomir Mrożek.

Comrade What a complicated name … Yes, him. Where was he born, exactly?

Padilla Southern Poland. Little village called Borzęcin.

Comrade You learned that well.

Padilla I love everything he writes.

Comrade It's incredible that from that village at the end of the world this Mrożek could already, at under forty years old, have gained such international recognition, such prestige … Just think: we've even heard of him on this Caribbean island and we joke around with his stories … Oh, life. Do you see, Padilla? He's only two years older than you, and he's already a fully-fledged star of world literature.

Padilla …

Comrade What do you think of that, Padilla? A star. Throughout the world. And only two years older than you.

III

Our Revolution Is Different

1967. The apartment.

Belkis   Are you writing again?

Padilla   Yes; it was what you said last night: it roused me.

Belkis   What did I say?

Padilla   You said you had an idea for a new collection of poems … It really cheered me up. You haven't written anything since *Letters to Anne Frank*.

Belkis   My head's been somewhere else for months; I've not been able to think of a single good line … It's just feelings, images coming to me. More a desire than anything else.

Padilla   You see: looks like you passed the inspiration onto me.

Belkis   So it's a competition?

Padilla   I'll never compete with you.

They embrace.

Belkis   I love you.

Padilla   And I you.

They kiss.

Belkis   I'm going to make chicken and rice.

Padilla   Chicken?

Belkis   I stood in a huge queue and managed to get the last ones … Did María fall asleep early?

Padilla   A little while ago, yes. I gave her what was left of the yoghurt.

Belkis   I'll try and get some more tomorrow.

She makes to leave.

Padilla   Wait. Tell me how it went.

Belkis   How what went?

Padilla   The meeting to decide what happened to Bernardo and the others.

Belkis   Oh.

Padilla   It was today you were meeting, wasn't it?

III Our Revolution Is Different 191

Belkis   Yes, today after lunch.

Padilla   So did you vote?

Belkis   …

Padilla   Belkis, did you vote?

Belkis   I had to vote against.

Padilla   Against them being expelled from the newspaper.

Belkis   No, Heberto. Against them staying.

Padilla   But –

Belkis   Yes, I know he's my ex-husband.

Padilla   We talked about this yesterday; you said you were going to defend them whatever happened.

Belkis   You weren't at the meeting; you can't imagine all the things they talked about there, the evidence they put on the table.

Padilla   No, I can't imagine what terrible things they can have made up to –

Belkis   It's not made up. I've known, you've known, for a long time: they're part of a microfraction.

Padilla   'Microfraction'; so now you're using that word too?

Belkis   It's what we call it in the Union of Young Communists. They're from the old guard.

Padilla   You know I don't always see eye to eye with the Popular Socialist Party, but they helped this Revolution to triumph too.

Belkis   I'm not saying they didn't, but that party doesn't exist any more, and with the new style of newspaper, their opinions –

Padilla   So is *Granma* going to stop publishing articles by people who think differently? There was room for everyone until now; everyone could be there; all that rich debate, and now suddenly –

Belkis   Sometimes things change overnight.

Padilla   Right, like this Revolution turned Communist overnight. I remind you that in 1959 the Commander himself gave a speech, which the whole world heard, saying we'd rather be dead than Communist, and then one fine day –

Belkis   Heberto, I don't want to argue.

Padilla   I'm not arguing, but I can't understand how you voted against Bernardo, who is a wonderful journalist and with whom you have a child, just because he belongs –

Belkis   The instructions came from higher up. It's a very tense situation.

Padilla A direct instruction from the Commander?

Belkis I saw him in the newsroom last week.

Padilla You saw him?

Belkis Yes, when I went to file the interview I did with Cortázar.

Padilla Is this a joke?

Belkis No, no, he was there. In the managing editor's office.

Padilla So it's true he goes to the newspaper.

Belkis …

Padilla …

Belkis I'd never seen him before; I'd just heard rumours that he came in when most people had gone home. They say he goes to the newsroom in the middle of the night, and to the printers too, and that he decides himself what goes on the front page of *Granma*, which photos get published, even what size font the headlines are written in and whether they should be in black or red …

Padilla …

Belkis I don't know what happened to me today … We were all sitting there, Bernardo just opposite me … The secretary took some papers out and started reading a series of … judgements about them and their work. About all of them, but especially about Bernardo. Saying his views didn't match the editorial line, that *Granma* should be highlighting other things …

Padilla And what did he do?

Belkis He kept quiet the whole time.

Padilla He didn't defend himself?

Belkis (*shakes her head*)   Not a murmur.

Padilla They ambushed him.

Belkis No, no; the Union of Young Communists doesn't work like that.

Padilla Oh, Belkis.

Belkis I swear I wanted to speak up, to say something to support them. I know what kind of person Bernardo is … He'd never go against all this, against the government; he loves the idea of the Revolution, socialism, that founding image … He loves it, but he has reservations, opinions; when anything has a whiff of Communism, he … He has to say things that sound like they're from a different time, that don't fit in with the mission we have now.

Padilla And what is the mission we have now?

Belkis To support this historic moment with our journalism.

Padilla Belkis, please, stop talking in clichés.

Belkis It's what we have to do.

Padilla No, the first duty of journalism is to be free.

Belkis We can write freely in *Granma*.

Padilla Freedom is freedom. With no interference.

Belkis …

Padilla Remember. It's what Cortázar told us that evening, before he said goodbye to us, praising your work: 'The work of journalists is sublime and cursed for the same reason: they must always tell the truth.'

Belkis The truth.

Padilla Was it unanimous?

Belkis No. Norberto Fuentes abstained.

Padilla Who?

Belkis A young reporter, a recent graduate.

Padilla So young, yet still with balls enough to stand his ground.

Belkis It makes me feel guilty when you say it like that … Do you think I feel good about all this?

Padilla I'm not blaming you; it's normal for –

She sobs. He hugs her.

Belkis All these weeks of tension and worry; it's been too much … Bernardo's eyes staring at me, accusing me, like I owed him something … But all my comrades were there, nodding every time the secretary said anything.

Padilla What will they do with them?

Belkis Redeploy them to construction, apparently.

Padilla Bernardo's never picked a brick up in his life.

Belkis They relocate them separately, to different districts.

Padilla But, construction?

Belkis Norberto was the worst thing.

Padilla …

Belkis He grabbed my arm as we were leaving. He said how could I have kept quiet, how could I have agreed …? Don't you remember that poem, he said, where first they come for the Communists and you keep quiet because you're not a Communist, and then the social democrats and you keep quiet because you're not a social democrat, and then the Jews and you keep quiet because you're not a Jew

... and in the end they come for you and no one speaks up because there's no one else left?

Padilla ...

Belkis He came out with it just like that. Looking at me like he wanted to pierce me right through. He told me it was useless, what I'd done, keeping quiet, voting in favour of the expulsion, because eventually they'd end up coming for me too.

Padilla ...

Belkis ...

Padilla Norberto Fuentes himself describes some of these events in his testimonial novel *Square under Siege*.

Belkis Although Belkis, the real Belkis, might recall them differently.

Padilla ...

Belkis ...

Padilla Don't listen to him.

Belkis I'm scared for María, Heberto. She's only three years old; I don't want –

Padilla Nothing's going to happen to María.

Belkis If something happened to me –

Padilla Nothing's going to happen to us.

Belkis They've had their eye on you for a while, too.

Padilla They can't open a file on me just because I think differently.

Belkis It's not just thinking, Heberto. You wrote it down. That polemic about Lisandro –

Padilla That's all forgotten now.

Belkis They don't forget anything. You're not even in the Party.

Padilla You're a Young Communist activist, that's enough.

Belkis I don't know what's enough here.

Padilla Having your own opinion isn't a crime.

Belkis Isn't it? Try telling that to Stalin.

Padilla Our Revolution is different. There's something that's ... beyond the Commander. He'll realize, he'll react. He loves journalism deep down; he loves literature. He knows he has to give us our space.

Belkis ...

Padilla ...

Belkis Those poems, by the way, the ones you're writing ... The book.
Padilla Yes.
Belkis Have you thought of a title yet?
Padilla *Outside the Game.*

IV

The Good Advisor

1968. The gardens of the Writers' Union.

Comrade   Padilla.

Padilla   Oh …! I didn't know you were here … What a coincidence.

Comrade   No, it's not a coincidence. Someone mentioned they'd seen you.

Padilla   And you decided to stop by and say hello to your friend.

Comrade   I came out of the office for a breath of air. Bureaucracy, it'll end up suffocating me … I needed to rest my eyes a little; I've been reading all afternoon.

Padilla   That is your job.

Comrade   Yes, it is my job.

Padilla   You love reading. You weren't voted president of the Writers' Union for nothing.

Comrade   Shame one can't always read what one chooses, isn't it?

Padilla   You're telling me: I nearly went blind correcting those translations we published in *News from Moscow*.

Comrade   Luckily you're back in the tropics now. Left your Soviet phase behind.

Padilla   One never knows.

Comrade   Yes, you've left it behind.

Padilla   …

Comrade   You didn't tell me you'd entered a book.

Padilla   A book?

Comrade   For the poetry prize.

Padilla   Oh, yes … That was about two months ago.

Comrade   And you'd forgotten about it.

Padilla   No … I just … I'm surprised at your mentioning it. What with it being under a pseudonym.

Comrade   I'd recognize your poems kilometres away.

Padilla   I think I read one at the recital last year.

IV The Good Advisor 197

Comrade Yes, the one about the man who hands in each of his body parts one by one to the Revolution, and whom the Revolution asks to keep on going even once he's completely dismembered.

Padilla So you do remember.

Comrade How could I not remember such a … surreal image?

Padilla I thought it was the jury who had to do all that reading, not you.

Comrade The jury does have to. And so do I.

Padilla No wonder you've got a headache. You can't do everything.

Comrade It's unavoidable when one takes on certain responsibilities.

Padilla …

Comrade I've come to advise you to withdraw from the competition.

Padilla What?

Comrade Yes, withdraw the book. It's not in your best interests. Those poems –

Padilla I write what I feel, what I understand of reality.

Comrade It's a very simple process. You go to the office, you sign the request, and that's it. Subject closed. No one will object.

Padilla Is this a joke?

Comrade No, it's advice.

Padilla And what makes you think I'd do something like that?

Comrade Your desire not to get into any more trouble.

Padilla I haven't got myself into anything. I just write.

Comrade All the same, you wrote another public defence of that turncoat Cabrera Infante a few months ago.

Padilla Cabrera Infante is still a brother above all else.

Comrade He declared himself a traitor to the Revolution, but even so you still supported him.

Padilla We each choose our loyalties.

Comrade You'll understand I couldn't defend you when they came from on high to tell me your position signified an attachment to the enemy. I couldn't argue with them.

Padilla And now, this advice you're giving me –

Comrade I've a soft spot for you. You've always seemed an intelligent man to me. Restless, yes, provocative, but clever.

Padilla   You're trying to please God and the devil.

Comrade   You're talking to me about double standards? You, who've spent all your time badmouthing the Writers' Union, publishing that article accusing us of cowardice, of opening our legs to the Revolution, when the only thing the Revolution has asked of us is that we position ourselves as intellectuals worthy of this historic moment?

Padilla   These are all clichés.

Comrade   You talk to me about double standards when you signed those papers filled with slurs against us, calling us a 'vault of pompous asses', and now you come with this parsimony and this butter-wouldn't-melt face to enter a book into a competition held by the very institution you spit on?

Padilla   Not that old tune again.

Comrade   If you were less of an opportunist, you'd withdraw that book.

Padilla   So these are the methods now? Sending a supposed friend to advise you? What's the name of that strategy? Stalinist warning?

Comrade   It's not about methods, it's about reason. You're not the young kid from Pinar del Río any more. You're quite the man of the world, after all the aeroplanes you've been on. Anyone else might be forgiven, but you?

Padilla   Forgiven for what?

Comrade   For talking about the Soviet Union like that in your poems, for example.

Padilla   Those poems are fiction inspired by my time there.

Comrade   You were lucky to travel overseas. Our Revolutionary government considered you worthy of the honour –

Padilla   I was already living in New York when the Revolution triumphed.

Comrade   But you came back. You chose to come back. And having come back, your duty is to adapt, to stay on track, to be one more link in the chain of the glorious endeavour. We all have to row in this boat in time, Padilla!

Padilla   And what do my poems have to do with that?

Comrade   The Revolution gave you the chance to go to the USSR. Your testimony before your contemporaries, before the people who will read it, ought to – how can I put it? – privilege the positive, the constructive ... I'm no great expert on the Soviet world, I'm not interested in it, I don't like the cold, I'm more a fan of the Antilles and the *Sóngoro Cosongo*, I'm more in my element here. But I have to recognize that the Soviets have been on our side ever since the Revolution triumphed: the money they send, the technology, the exchanges, entire magazines published in Spanish just so we can read them over here, and the canned Russian meat that's so delicious! ... So, even though I don't like Dostoyevsky or Chekhov or Tolstoy, I have to make the effort and at least read Mayakovski ... And Mayakovski, his poetry and his life, have taught me a lot, Padilla, about how an intellectual has to behave in a system like this one, in a social project like this one.

Padilla Mayakovski ended up shooting himself in the heart.

Comrade He was a great enthusiast for the Soviet process at first; he even praised Stalin ... Then suddenly he was filled with an indescribable disappointment ... What absurd behaviour, what a sudden change of heart, like a madman ... Poor chap. No one with a clear conscience commits suicide.

Padilla ...

Comrade Of course the Soviets made mistakes, and you're merciless about them in your book, by the way. You hide behind metaphors, yes, but if one looks closely, it's obvious ... Now, I ask you: are there not more achievements than mistakes? And the Bolsheviks, those impeccable revolutionaries, those men who are purer than our palms, how can you describe them with such historical imprecision, disrespecting them and showing such disregard for their sacrifice?

Padilla I'm not a History professor, I'm a poet.

Comrade A poet who wasn't here at the most difficult moments when we were confronting imperialism; we've talked about this before ... And in those poems – I think I can read between the lines – you try to justify that absence, that ... lack of personal militancy.

Padilla We're each revolutionary with the tools we're given.

Comrade Working with our intellect doesn't give us the right to underestimate others, Padilla.

Padilla I don't underestimate anyone!

Comrade Yes, you've always had a bourgeois soul. You don't like the worker, you scorn him.

Padilla What the hell are you talking about?

Comrade You're a spoilt brat. You find the proletariat clumsy and inept. You think they just nod, conform, obey blindly whatever they're told to do. In your poems you constantly hint at repressive atmospheres, persecution, ambushes, as if the Revolution were a Cerberus lashing out at anyone who dares to speak his mind ... This Revolution, which has always been characterized by its openness and generosity ... Right here in the Writers' Union – you know this – texts have been published whose ideology is quite different to what we consider politically acceptable, and we've done this with the express desire to give voice to multiple points of view.

Padilla And you should keep on doing.

Comrade But we can't, because this is Cuba: the land of devil-may-care and distraction, where you give people an inch and they take a mile. All of this editorial openness, all of that freedom, was useless: too many two-bit writers have started overstepping the mark and we can't let it get out of hand.

Padilla   An artist should be free to create.

Comrade   Who said otherwise? I'm an artist and I'm free to write ... I'm going to tell you this quietly because it's a secret, but I want you to know the trouble you could get into and that I have the moral duty to warn you about: Padilla, lots of those people – known to us, yes, who have even been or are our friends, who laugh and drink coffee with us at the recitals – are being paid by the foreign-backed counterrevolution that has been trying to sink us for almost a decade ... They're undercover agents for the CIA!

Padilla   Oh, please: how could they be agents for the CIA?

Comrade   They are. They're trying to undermine our principles!

Padilla   But they're just writers.

Comrade   Full of dangerous ideas. And we've only got ourselves to blame: we've been too lenient: a metaphor here, a simile there, this oxymoron here, fine, fine ... But it's got to stop, man; trying to sneak all those ideas in like we're idiots! Forget all this tolerance: the only thing we need is poetry that speaks to the masses, that glorifies our endeavours, that projects everyone together in the task of the infinite construction of the Revolution ... That's why Nicolás Guillén wrote that thing about 'To build this wall bring me every hand'! And look what foresight he had: he wrote that a year before the triumph, and in the new combat of the present his lines are more resonant than ever.

Padilla   Don't worry. Me, on the other hand, no one will say I was a poet with foresight.

Comrade   That's why I'm trying to guide you, Padilla, because you're in very muddy waters ... You won't get anywhere with those individualist poems.

Padilla   Have you ever been able to write anything that comes from anywhere other than yourself?

Comrade   It's all a question of perspective. Everyone finds their way. But this confessional tone, this personal, almost obscene intimacy that you want to impose on your readers, it won't take you down a good path. It's empty words. Your message doesn't work. Those poems can only reflect two things, Padilla.

Padilla   ...

Comrade   Overwhelming delusions of grandeur –

Padilla   I've never thought myself better than anyone.

Comrade   Or enormous resentment.

Padilla If you have so little faith in my poems, why not wait for the jury to read them and decide? There's nothing to fear, is there? If the poems are so bad, they'll no doubt give the prize to another book.

Comrade Don't give me an answer now.

Padilla I'm not withdrawing the book from the prize.

Comrade Think about your children. They're so little ... You've still got so many years left to enjoy with them.

V

The Attitude of the Nonconformist

1968. The apartment.

Belkis You've just won the prize.

Padilla What?

Belkis I tried calling the house from a public phone but it was engaged.

Padilla The Writers' Union prize?

Belkis For *Outside the Game*.

They embrace excitedly.

Padilla I don't believe you.

Belkis Congratulations, darling … I told you the prize was yours; I told you.

Padilla It can't be, Belkis.

Belkis Lezama Lima just confirmed it to me.

Padilla But Guillén has a terrible opinion of the book; he told me the other day … He's the director; I thought he'd put his foot down.

Belkis It was a masterstroke by the jury.

Padilla They went over the heads of the Union leadership?

Belkis Lezama's happy.

Padilla Where did you see him?

Belkis On the corner of 17th and H Street, before he got into his car. He was coming down the stairs, out of breath as usual. I was in the café; he came over to me.

Padilla Lezama himself?

Belkis 'Tell your husband we either gave the prize to his book or to no book at all.'

Padilla Is that what he said?

Belkis No small praise, coming from him.

Padilla I have to call him straight away to thank him. (*Goes to the telephone and picks up.*) There's no dial tone.

Belkis It's what I was saying: I think it's broken.

Padilla We'll have to tell the phone company.

Belkis (*takes out a piece of paper*) Lezama gave me this, to give to you.

V The Attitude of the Nonconformist

Padilla What is it?

She shows him.

His copy of the jury's statement?

Belkis (*reading*) '*Outside the Game* stands out for its formal quality and reveals the presence of a poet in full possession of his expressive resources' –

Padilla That's their reasoning.

Belkis 'With regard to the content, we find in this book an intense look at the fundamental problems of our era and a critical attitude to history' –

Padilla Right.

Belkis 'Heberto Padilla vehemently confronts the mechanisms that move contemporary society and his vision of man inside history is dramatic and, for that reason, agonizing, in the sense that Miguel de Unamuno gave to the word, that of struggle' –

Padilla Couldn't have put it better myself.

Belkis And there's still the best bit yet.

Padilla Let me see. (*Tries to grab the paper.*)

Belkis No, no ... I have to have the pleasure of reading this part too ... (*Reads.*) '*Outside the Game* stands beside the Revolution, is committed to the Revolution, and adopts an attitude that is essential to the poet and to the Revolutionary: that of the nonconformist, of he who aspires to more because his desires project him beyond the current reality.'

Padilla ...

Belkis What?

Padilla They're covering my back.

Belkis Lezama and Manuel Díaz Martínez wrote it.

Padilla My friend Manuel.

Belkis It's not a lie, what they say.

Padilla No, it isn't.

Belkis The attitude of the nonconformist.

Padilla 'Of he who aspires to more.'

Belkis It's not bad. They do have to justify their decision.

Padilla They're protecting me and protecting themselves.

Belkis That's normal.

Padilla Yes. The atmosphere's too heated.

Belkis Oh, and Lezama told me the theatre jury was still meeting when he left ... They'd been in the room for hours arguing and they couldn't agree. Apparently Antón Arrufat sent a 'problematic' play based on a Greek tragedy.

Padilla Yes, he told me he was writing it a while ago.

Belkis I hope he gets lucky.

Padilla He's a good guy, Arrufat.

Belkis I'm so happy.

Padilla So am I.

Belkis Why don't we go out to celebrate?

Padilla The strange thing is ... they haven't told me officially.

Belkis It's too soon for that. Don't invent ghosts.

Padilla They could have called me.

Belkis It was just a while ago ... They must be waiting for all the juries to decide before they make it public.

Padilla ...

Belkis The prize is yours. They can't revoke it.

Padilla Revoke it? ... They could. But it'd be a scandal: a prize already awarded, with Lezama chair of the jury –

Belkis No, they won't do that. Besides, the award ceremony's next week ... The book'll be out in three months and then everyone'll be able to read it.

Padilla I still don't believe it.

Belkis I had faith in *Outside the Game* since I read the first poems.

Padilla I have faith in you.

They kiss.

Belkis I got paid yesterday. Shall we go and eat at La Torre to celebrate?

Padilla Let's go to Monseigneur to hear Bola de Nieve.

Belkis You're not interested in Bola de Nieve: you're interested in Monsigneur's martinis; I know you.

Padilla Celebrating is celebrating, isn't it?

Belkis It's your day, so whatever you want.

Padilla Well, if I start telling you what I want ...

He hugs her and continues touching her sensually.

Belkis (*letting him*) I didn't mean that –

Padilla (*continues playing, kisses her neck*)   You said it yourself: it's my day to celebrate; you can't back out now.

Belkis   Heberto –

Padilla   I'll put the radio on really loud so you don't have any excuse.

The light dims. And from one corner of the apartment, or of the theatre, or of **Padilla**'s *mind:*

Comrade   There you see him. Having his way with his woman. Unbridled. I'd do the same. After a piece of news like that, who wouldn't? They're pleased as partridges … He's heard the warning voices but he's not paying them much attention. Still doing as he pleases. Drop by drop the glass spills over …. They're celebrating the Writers' Union poetry prize, the most prestigious in the whole country. He thinks he's got away with his mockery, that he's snuck his poems in without us realising the strategy he's following … He thinks, as he enjoys the flesh of his woman, that winning has made him untouchable. That those words from the jury, 'Padilla is committed to the Revolution', are a letter of safe passage … Imagine that, on this island. Untouchable? Yes, he believes it all, poor thing.

VI

Provocations

1968. Days later.

Padilla   They still haven't announced the official award ceremony.

Comrade   Ceremony? Why have an official ceremony? They're so dull.

Padilla   I haven't even had a call from the Union to tell me.

Comrade   Your telephone's broken; how do you expect people to call you?

Padilla   It's been broken for over a month. We've reported it several times and they still haven't fixed it.

Comrade   The technicians from the telephone company have a lot of work on; Havana just keeps on growing.

Padilla   It's quite a coincidence that it's broken just these weeks, isn't it?

Comrade   Why did you have to start writing such strange things, Padilla? When those lines were so pretty, the ones that made me admire you as a poet … That one that went: 'My hand sinks in the Revolution' –

Padilla   'And writes without bitterness.' That was years ago when I still thought –

Comrade   That all this was a bed of roses?

Padilla   …

Comrade   'For the love of your people, wake up!'

Padilla   'The time for human justice will begin!'

Comrade   Those really were good lines. Although there was a lot of padding in that book, too. You filled it with the leftovers from poems you'd written before the triumph of the Revolution, from that time when you didn't have chances to be published like the one you've been given now, Padilla. It was an uneven book.

Padilla   Yes, but it had good poems in it.

Comrade   *Outside the Game*, on the other hand …

Padilla   Did you read all of it?

Comrade   Did I read it? I didn't just read it; I re-read it, several times. I want to write an article for *Olive Green*.

Padilla   Why write an article about poetry in the magazine of the Armed Forces?

Comrade   Nothing one can write about your poetry is only about poetry, Padilla. Just like nothing you write is only about what you write, right?

Padilla I don't like tongue-twisters.

Comrade No. You like being clear. Like when you wrote that letter denouncing our horrific 'concentration camps for writers, artists and homosexuals'; that's what you called them, exaggerating.

Padilla That was a despicable episode in the Revolution and you can't say otherwise.

Comrade Were you there? Those places weren't as terrible as you've been led to believe. Besides, all societies punish those who stray and commit crimes. They made an exception with you, a writer always wanting to criticize, and look: they never took you to one of those camps ... Now I think about it, you've never been in prison, Padilla.

Padilla What's going to happen with my book?

Comrade The Union isn't at all happy about the prize ... They say you take every opportunity to throw poisonous barbs at the Revolution.

Padilla Who says that?

Comrade They say the poems are cheap, not just politically but also as literature ... They say the themes you discuss aren't worthy of a university-educated, well-travelled poet like yourself; that it's like you've lifted them from those CIA radio programmes.

Padilla Everything I write –

Comrade And it is true that, going through the book, you insist on this idea of censorship and persecution ... For example, you say: 'Let anything happen' –

Padilla 'Let them tear the page you love, let them smash down your door with stones.'

Comrade Anyone reading that would think you were being watched all the time in this country, Padilla. That you weren't being allowed to write and create freely ... And if the Revolution's offered you anything it's freedom to write. You've been given free rein. This violent system you talk about has only given you kindnesses: trips overseas, diplomatic postings, publications, prizes ... What lack of freedom are you talking about?

Padilla Let them give me the prize officially! Put the news in the press! Publish the book and stock it in all the bookshops in the country!

Comrade Oh ... We would have started with that, Padilla. This isn't about literature; it's about your vanity.

Padilla Vanity?

Comrade About you playing the victim and the troublemaker just to attract the attention of all those foreign intellectuals you rub shoulders with and take advantage of to artificially inflate your reputation.

Padilla I don't rub shoulders with anyone and I'm not trying to be a troublemaker.

Comrade We've just given you a prize and all you do is complain.

Padilla You didn't give me a prize; a jury did.

Comrade We gave it to you, Padilla.

Padilla A jury of great writers!

Comrade Do you think any prize gets awarded in this country, however great the writers on the jury may be, without our approval? Did an idea like that really go through your head?

Padilla …

Comrade We agreed to the prize. We were in favour of it. We have compassion for you.

Padilla I don't want your compassion.

Comrade I had to put up with the bureaucrats from the Union saying horrific things about you to my face: that you're a terrible example to young people because we let you circulate freely … Yes, 'freely', they said … That your poetry is full of hatred for the selfless State Security agency –

Padilla I don't hate anyone. I'm not interested in hatred.

Comrade I'm telling you all this so you know that no one is watching you or oppressing you, Padilla. While you're writing poems denigrating our soldiers and police, they're risking their lives for you, yes, for you. It's not fair of you to be so harsh towards them.

Padilla You're avoiding the subject, as usual.

Comrade No. I'm telling you things to your face so you understand them. We're happy you won the prize. We support it for that reason. Because the Commander, despite everything, believes in you.

Padilla The Commander?

Comrade Yes, like I've always told you. He's read you a lot. He admires you enormously and he still trusts you.

Padilla …

Comrade Those bureaucrats from the Union were reluctant to publish your book. But the Commander came to the office in person and defended you.

Padilla Me?

Comrade He said your book was fundamental to the Revolution. That it was his personal wish that it be published … It caused a frenzy in the Union, of course, but how could they contradict the Commander?

Padilla So the book is coming out.

Comrade It's coming out!

Padilla *is euphoric.*

Comrade We've come to an agreement with the Union.

Padilla What agreement?

Comrade The book will be published with all the poems, alongside a statement, written by them, explaining their disagreement with the jury's decision.

Padilla The same institution that awards the prize to the book including a note against it?

Comrade It's not just a note; it's a duly thought-out statement. These bureaucrats aren't idiots, Padilla, they do think too.

Padilla This is absurd.

Comrade It's not absurd. It's the Commander's reasoned decision so that the book can be published. He likes working with everyone and for everyone, that's why he's such a good leader.

Padilla And will Arrufat's play be published?

Comrade His too, of course. In the same way.

Padilla Well … We'll have books.

Comrade A considerable number of copies. It'll be our way of showing you how much we value you, Padilla.

Padilla Yes, yes, I know.

Comrade No, you don't know. You don't even imagine.

Padilla …

Comrade I hope this news will calm you down. I heard you'd been taking sleeping pills.

Padilla I'm fine now, thank you.

Comrade The last thing we want is for you to have a mental breakdown.

Padilla I won't get sick, don't worry.

Comrade Remember you shouldn't mix tranquilizers with alcohol. It's too great a shock to the stomach, and to the brain. That really is violence.

Padilla …

Comrade When the books come out from the printers, they'll send you a package to your home.

Padilla And there'll be a formal presentation at the Union.

Comrade Oh, you're such a bore with your obsession with formality ... You'll have the book in your hands, that's what matters.

Padilla There has to be a formal presentation ... I'll demand one.

Comrade Who will you demand it from? The men from the Union, with all the filth they say about you?

Padilla ...

Comrade Relax, Padilla. These are not times for demands. We're going to publish your little book, so show your gratitude to the Commander by keeping calm: enjoying your poetry here in your home, with your wife, drinking a coffee ... I know what I'm talking about. I've come here as a friend, to give you some more advice.

Padilla ...

Comrade (*pointing to the table*) What are those papers?

Padilla Notes.

Comrade Since when do you take notes?

Padilla It's some new poems.

Comrade New poems? And you didn't tell me? (*Approaches the table to pick them up.*)

Padilla (*gets in his way*) They're full of crossings-out.

They look at each other.

Comrade All right ... There's time.

Padilla They're just a rough draft.

Comrade I'll pop by tomorrow and you can read me something.

Padilla ...

Comrade You wouldn't have a title for those poems yet ...

Padilla Yes, I do.

Comrade And what is it?

Padilla *Provocations.*

Comrade How intriguing ... Quick. Direct. Like you.

Padilla ...

Comrade I'll come and see you again tomorrow. Rest up, Padilla. You've got bags under your eyes.

Padilla ...

Comrade And take care.

VII

The Arrest

1971. The apartment. Dim light. Violent knocking at the door. A quiet sound of concern. The **Voice** *will be the* **Comrade**, *speaking through a megaphone.*

Padilla   Don't they respect people's sleep?

Belkis   No, they don't respect anything; they just turn up suddenly like this and –

Padilla   It's seven o'clock; it's still dark; the sun hasn't come up yet.

Belkis   And it's the weekend.

Knocking.

Padilla   Why are they knocking at the door?

Belkis   Who is it, I ask.

Padilla   Who is it? They sound like animals.

Belkis   I look through the spyhole.

Padilla   It's the postman.

Belkis   He says he has a very important telegram to give us.

Knocking.

Padilla   The postman doesn't knock like that.

Belkis   This time of the morning?

Padilla   A telegram?

Belkis   No one sends us telegrams.

Padilla   Belkis, don't open it!

Knocking.

Belkis   I know why they're here; I can sense it; I've been worried about it for months, imagining this very moment.

Padilla   Is this a dream?

Belkis   No, it's not a dream.

Padilla   It's not normal: invading people's privacy like this, people's lives.

Belkis   The knocking has just dragged me out of bed. It's dark, but the sun's about to rise.

Knocking.

Padilla Don't open it!

Belkis They'll knock the door down if I don't!

Knocking.

Can't you slip the telegram under the door?

Voice Sorry. You have to sign.

Padilla Let them knock the door down!

Belkis They're there: on the other side.

Padilla Let them knock it down!

Voice State Security!

Belkis Was the shout we heard.

Padilla Violent. Crushing. And at the same time, the sound of the door falling to the floor.

Belkis A guard presses his secret-police I.D. into my face. He looks like a mastodon.

Padilla About fifteen men burst into the room, guns in hand.

Belkis I don't need to react. One of them grabs me by the shoulder and forces me to sit.

Padilla Another two come to the bedroom and order me to get dressed.

Voice You don't want them seeing you in your underwear in the street, Padilla.

Belkis You come out of the bedroom a few seconds later, still with your laces untied. But why are they pointing their guns at you as if you were a criminal?

Padilla You cry uncontrollably.

Belkis I'm scared; I can't stand it.

Padilla One of them, a short man, takes out a camera and starts taking photos, of the apartment, of the corners –

Belkis Of me. He takes photos of me.

Padilla They act like barbarians bent on destruction.

Belkis They throw the pots and pans on the floor in the kitchen, the clothes from the closet.

Padilla They open the drawers and empty all their contents onto the floor.

Belkis They take piles of books from the bookshelves and leaf through them one by one.

Padilla *and* **Belkis** Everything consumed in chaos!

Belkis   I can't hold in the nausea and they don't let me go to the bathroom so I throw up right there.

Padilla   It was like a gale blasting through the apartment in a few minutes.

Belkis   Suddenly the boss gives the order to stop. He looks at me and asks –

Voice   Where did you hide it?

Padilla   Hide what?

Voice   Don't play the innocent, Padilla. The novel, where did you put it? We'll rip open your arse if we have to!

Padilla   How could they know about the novel, Belkis?

Belkis   I don't know; I haven't told anyone –

Voice   Stop whispering! Where is it?

Padilla   There is no novel!

Voice   Do you think we're idiots, Padilla?

Belkis   He's about to launch himself at you when one of the guards tears a painting down from the wall.

Padilla   That exact painting.

Belkis   Whose frame, in the back, has a false lining where the manuscript is kept.

Voice   So there was no novel … I'll enjoy reading this, Padilla.

Belkis   A moment later they start tearing the other paintings from the walls. The knives pierce the wood and break all the frames. One by one the five type-written copies appear.

Padilla   In the back of the closet.

Belkis   In the first-aid box.

Padilla   In the oven.

Voice   You went to a lot of effort playing hide'n'seek, Padilla … You think you're as clever as the Road Runner but you're as stupid as Wile E. Coyote!

Belkis   I looked at you and you couldn't say a word. Two guards grab you and push you outside.

Padilla   They put me in the police car.

Belkis   I looked all around.

Padilla *and* **Belkis**   The apartment was a disaster!

Belkis   All of the mess we had in our heads was physical now, palpable.

Padilla A guard grabs you by the back of the neck and forces you out onto the terrace to watch the police car turn the corner with me in it. On the opposite side of the street, several neighbours look out to see what's happening.

Belkis But no one interferes.

Padilla No. You know no one interferes in cases like these. People watch it all from a distance.

Padilla *and* **Belkis** Happy it's not happening to them.

Padilla You're still crying.

Voice Now you're going to stop crying because you have to come with us too.

Belkis But I –

Voice You're going to come with us right now!

Padilla There's nothing to be done.

Belkis There's no point resisting, I thought.

Voice You're going to dry your tears right now!

Belkis They start boarding up all the windows.

Padilla They escort you down the stairs.

Belkis They put me in another police car.

Padilla The sun hasn't come up yet.

Belkis They turn on the siren and we drive off.

The deafening sound of police sirens.

VIII

Villa Marista

1971. Interrogation cells.

Comrade   Finally I can see you, Padilla.

Padilla   You, here?

Comrade   I swear I wanted to come sooner, but I had a few commitments I couldn't put off.

Padilla   They've had me locked in here since yesterday; no one will tell me anything. I don't even know how the children are; they haven't let me call them.

Comrade   Relax. They're with Berta. I popped by the house a little while ago.

Padilla   You saw them?

Comrade   Of course. I took them some sweets. Marshmallows. Russian. Delicious. They were delighted. I told them their daddy had sent them.

Padilla   Did you tell Berta?

Comrade   Tell her what? There's no need to worry her … She's your ex-wife. She doesn't need to know the details. I just told her you were fine.

Padilla   What about Belkis?

Comrade   We've got Belkis here, just next door.

Padilla   Here?

Change of cell.

Comrade   They tell me you haven't wanted to eat anything.

Belkis   I'm not hungry.

Comrade   You will be. You threw up everything you ate last night.

Belkis   What am I doing here?

Comrade   Are you sure you don't know?

Belkis   Where's Heberto?

Comrade   This situation isn't comfortable for me either, darling.

Belkis   I'm not your darling; I barely know you.

Comrade   Still, I'm extremely fond of you. And I know you very well. You and your poetry.

Belkis   I haven't done anything.

Comrade I know.

Belkis I'm very scared for my daughter.

Comrade Scared, Belkis? Why? She's with her father. They're going to spend the whole weekend together.

Belkis They were very violent when they grabbed me; it still hurts here.

Comrade They do go too far sometimes, yes. I apologize. They're thugs. They're not used to dealing with intellectuals ... But none of that will happen again. I'm here to take care of you.

Change of cell.

Padilla Is she all right?

Comrade Yes. She has quite an appetite. It's good for her to be eating.

Padilla But is she eating what – ?

Comrade What she's given. Why the concern, Padilla? We have very good chefs here ... They made her sautéed pork with black beans and rice. You can't even eat like that in El Potín these days.

Padilla ...

Comrade What do you think? That they'll poison her? That they'll poison you? Don't be silly, old man. That won't happen with me here. If anything did happen to you, how would we explain it to the Commander?

Padilla The Commander knows – ?

Comrade Of course. You're here because he wants to keep you protected.

Padilla Protected from what?

Comrade From all those diplomats trying to trick you, Padilla.

Padilla You were at the Riviera Hotel yesterday?

Comrade No, I wasn't. But news travels fast in this town.

Padilla You people ... You've been following me for months, haven't you.

Comrade Not that you exactly hide yourself.

Padilla What the hell do you want from me?

Comrade Why are you getting so worked up?

Padilla ...

Comrade They're not good people, Padilla. One has to keep a watchful eye. It's unbearable having to follow protocol and having to let them walk freely through our streets ... Journalists, foreign diplomats ... Lies. They're all infiltrated. They answer to the enemy. Don't look so surprised; they're on the Yank payroll ... I've been warning you. Have I or haven't I? I've been warning you for years ... They're bad, yes, but in the end they're foreigners, they end up leaving. They squeeze out all the juice, they mix you up in all their mess to make themselves more dollars, and then they go back to their homes and leave you well and truly screwed.

Padilla   ...

Comrade   We don't care about them, Padilla. But we do care about you. You're here. We care about you because you're one of us.

Change of cell.

The most important thing, Belkis, is the moral support you can give to your husband. That's the most fundamental thing for us.

Belkis   He got involved in ...

Comrade   In what? Don't be shy: we all know full well what he's done.

Belkis   I want to see him.

Comrade   ...

Belkis   How long will you keep us here?

Comrade   Oh, Belkis, if that were up to me –

Belkis   He's diabetic.

Comrade   They're checking him over.

Belkis   You can't afford for him to die here, of course.

Comrade   You talk about us with such disrespect.

Belkis   He needs his insulin.

Comrade   And we'll inject him. Every time he needs it. There's a nurse in charge of that.

Belkis   You've got the novel; you've got everything ... Why don't you leave us in peace?

Comrade   This situation is unpleasant for me, too, Belkis. Do you think I want to be stuck here, in this hovel, when I could be swimming at the beach?

Belkis   They turned the air conditioning up to maximum last night; there wasn't even a blanket to cover myself with; I was shivering all night ... Now, suddenly, this heat ... I think I'm going to be ill.

Comrade   There is a way for you to see him ... But you have to help me.

Belkis   ...

Comrade   You haven't wanted to eat today, either ... They don't treat poor Padilla as well as they do you: they haven't given him anything to eat since he arrived here the day before yesterday. This Revolution really is kind to women.

Belkis Why haven't they given him any food?

Comrade I don't know. I asked and they said: medicine, whatever he needs, but not food.

Belkis He has to eat!

Comrade That's what I think. But rules are rules, I can't break them just like that.

Belkis Please, I'm begging you.

Comrade Isn't life strange: you have the chance to eat and you don't want to. And he, who has to eat regularly because of his diabetes, can't.

Belkis Tell me what I have to do.

Comrade Trying to eat something would be a good start. Hydrating. You can take a shower. It's important you look good when you see him.

Belkis You're going to let me see him?

Comrade But I have to be sure you and I are playing on the same team, Belkis. I want to help him. We both want to help him, don't we?

Change of cell.

Poor thing. She had an attack of hysteria.

Padilla Where is she?

Comrade I didn't know your wife was so dramatic, Padilla.

Padilla What are you doing to her?

Comrade Us? She did it to herself … She fell to her knees, started crying, screaming, begging me to let her go.

Padilla I don't believe a word.

Comrade Imagine: she screamed so loud, the guards even came to the door. Have you ever thought of taking her to a psychiatrist?

Padilla Belkis isn't mad.

Comrade She rolled around the floor saying she was innocent. As if we were accusing her of something.

Padilla You want to finish me off!

Comrade Me? You're so ungrateful, Padilla … Saying that to me. (*Opens the briefcase, takes out a book, places it in front of him.*) First, this. What's it called?

Padilla …

Comrade What does it say here?

Padilla *Outside the Game.*

Comrade   That's right. *Outside the Game*. An authorized, published, award-winning book ... (*Takes out a manuscript.*) Then, this. (*Places it in front of him.*) Read what it says.

Padilla   *Provocations.*

Comrade   Pro-vo-ca-tions. Just like that, with all of its syllables. And on top of that, you treated yourself to reading these poems at a recital, and having some of your little friends applaud you ... (*Takes out another manuscript.*) And now, this. (*Places it in front of him.*)

Padilla   ...

Comrade   Read it.

Padilla   *Heroes Are Grazing in My Garden.*

Comrade   Pretty title, isn't it. The heroes of the Revolution grazing in your garden like cows.

Padilla   ...

Comrade   We've let all of that pass, Padilla.

Padilla   It's my work.

Comrade   Yes, of course, your work. Which we love. Your work, the pride of the nation. And that's why, look at the surprise I've got for you here ... (*Takes out a small tape recorder and connects it.*)

Padilla   ...

Comrade   Put them on, put the headphones on. You'll hear better that way.

Padilla *looks at the device with mistrust. The* **Comrade** *puts the headphones on him.*

Comrade   Oh, and I brought you a cigar ... Since I know you like them so much, I thought you'd enjoy listening to it more while smoking ... You prefer a shot of rum, I know, but alcohol isn't allowed in here.

Padilla   ...

Comrade   You're not going to smoke? Fine.

Presses a button on the tape recorder.

Padilla   ...

Comrade   ...

Padilla   ...

Padilla's *face begins to shift to terror.*

Comrade   What?

Padilla   ...

Comrade I thought you said something.

Padilla *removes the headphone desperately.*

Comrade You see how unfair you are? Telling me to my face that I'm trying to finish you off and forcing me to show you all of this that we've been collecting, classifying and storing for years, with no aim other than protecting you from these people who want to hurt you?

Padilla This ... I ...

Comrade I know; I know you didn't mean any of this, Padilla.

Padilla I never –

Comrade But you said it.

Padilla ...

Comrade But even so, the Commander is still certain you're one of us. He doesn't have the slightest doubt. He devoured *Heroes Are Grazing in My Garden* in one sitting, he laughed and laughed ... He loves you, Padilla, and he values you. He'd never have asked me to make you listen to these recordings. He only did it so he'd know that you know we have them.

Padilla *sobs.*

Comrade (*passes a hand over* **Padilla**'s *face*) Now, now ... It's not so bad.

Padilla ...

Comrade It's good to cry ... Cry. All that built-up tension.

Padilla ...

Comrade Oh, I was forgetting ... (*Goes back to the briefcase. Takes out a photo.*) Berta gave me this photo to give you.

Places it in front of him.

It was taken yesterday in Lenin Park. Lenin Park is looking very pretty; we're going to open it soon but the roller-coaster's already up and running ... The children enjoyed it; you can see in the photo ... Such a blessing to have children, Padilla. And to see them grow up ... They're so big. They asked me about you and I reassured them you'd be back soon. They miss you very much.

Padilla *bursts into tears.*

Comrade (*takes the photo from him*) The good thing is, you'll go back and they won't feel cheated, will they? ... Yes, you'll see them again soon, of course you will ... We're not going to do anything with this, with the recording ... Because it would be a shame for you to end up in here for fifteen years, accused of any old nonsense ... We'll forget everything. A clean slate ... You're a solid chap, Padilla. You've put your foot in it, you've put your foot right to the bottom ... But we're going to give you a chance. The Revolution always gives a second chance. The Commander loves you very much, old man, really ... He says you're a foolish dreamer, but he trusts you.

Padilla *rises.*

Comrade (*hugs him, trying to calm him down*) We'll fix it, you'll see ... Come on, calm down ... You're one of us. We'll fix it.

Padilla (*begins to release himself from the hug, slowly*) I ...

Comrade What's wrong?

Padilla *collapses to the ground.*

IX

Absolute Scum

1971. Days later. Hospital room. In a bed, **Padilla** *comes to.*

Padilla   Where have you brought me?

Comrade   To the military hospital.

Padilla   Why?

Comrade   You fainted.

Padilla   What have you done to me?

Comrade   Inserted drips. Taken blood.

Padilla   What about Belkis?

Comrade   You can't see her yet. You're still under our protection in theory.

Padilla   You mean I'm still a prisoner.

Comrade   You do like to play with words, Padilla.

Padilla   But has Belkis been released?

Comrade   So many questions, old man … You're not my interrogator.

Padilla   …

Comrade   Looks to me you're already feeling better.

Padilla   I think so, thank God.

Comrade   God and the Commander: he demanded we bring you straight away to the best room in the hospital.

Padilla   The Commander knows – ?

Comrade   And this affected him very much. He doesn't like you being ill. He wants you fit and strong.

Padilla   …

Comrade   I spoke to him earlier, on the phone. Reassured him you were still stable. He told me he'd come and see you this afternoon.

Padilla   Come here?

Comrade   Of course. You're staying here until you're fully recovered.

Padilla   The Commander's coming to see me?

Comrade   He wants to thank you for it in person.

Padilla   Thank me for what?

Comrade   For what you're going to write. What you're going to do.

Padilla   ...

Comrade   This is the moment we need you, Padilla. The Commander knows you'll take the step forwards.

Padilla   ...

Comrade   All of those foreign intellectuals have started protesting. They've published a letter in a Paris newspaper. Accusing us of not supplying information related to your arrest. 'Arrest', they call it. They say ... (*Takes out the newspaper and reads.*) 'The use of repressive methods against intellectuals who have exercised their right to criticize can only have wholly negative repercussions amongst the antiimperialist forces of the entire world, especially in these times when the Cuban Revolution represents a symbol.' Cheap rhetoric. And they go on ... 'We reaffirm our solidarity with the principles that inspired the fight in the Sierra Maestra and which the Revolutionary Cuban government has expressed so many times through the words and deeds of its Prime Minister, of its Commander Che Guevara, and of ...' Blah blah blah ... They've had a good time signing it! Mario Vargas Llosa, Julio Cortázar, Gabriel García Márquez, Italo Calvino, Marguerite Duras, Carlos Fuentes, Octavio Paz, there's almost thirty here ... Even Sartre and his wife, that de Beauvoir woman; we treated them so well when they came here, do you remember? And now they're complaining. Saying we're unfair. What an outrage. Absolute scum. They love the ideal of the Left, but they don't know what the truth is here inside ... And they think they're doing you a favour by causing all this fuss.

Padilla   ...

Comrade   But now this whole business is going to calm down, and all of them, one by one, will have egg on their faces, because you're going to write your statement with your truth.

Padilla   ...

Comrade   Yes, the truth. We only want your truth, Padilla.

Padilla   ...

Comrade   Because you do have a memory, don't you? You remember the recording I played you. And the photo I showed you.

Padilla   ...

Comrade   They've just brought me this briefcase. Look. You see what there is inside? ... Wads and wads of dollars. They say they found them in your apartment.

Padilla   In my apartment?

Comrade   Inside a mattress.

Padilla   But I never –

Comrade Those boys from State Security have no limits, Padilla ... When they want to find something, they pull it out from up their sleeves ... 'This amount of illegal dollars in his mattress, who knows who paid him them and what for?', that's what they said to me ... The conversations with the diplomats, your poems, your novel ... It's too many things, old man. The State Prosecutor won't like any of it. And not to mention the Commander; what a disappointment.

Padilla No one's paid me a single dollar!

Comrade I know that! Don't get worked up!

Padilla How can they say they found that in my mattress?

Comrade Maybe it was Belkis going behind your back.

Padilla She wouldn't take a cent!

Comrade It's a lot of money; look.

Padilla No, no! She loves this as much as I do.

Comrade When you say 'this', what exactly do you mean, Padilla?

Padilla This, all this.

Comrade All what? What?

Padilla The Commander! The Revolution!

Comrade Oh, it's good to hear you say that. That is a relief ... But, look: these boys say they found the money at your place ... And they brought it here, wad by wad, to prove it.

Padilla It can't be, it can't be!

Comrade Look: if you say so, I believe you. And I'll tell the State Security Service that the guilt they're pinning on you is unfounded. You're one of us. The Commander knows that, but it seems they need to be reminded.

Padilla ...

Comrade I'll tell them this: that we've made a pact. You write the statement and they forget the money.

Padilla ...

Comrade That's fair, isn't it? And that way we put an end to this once and for all, Padilla. And you'll see those children who are missing you so much. And we'll all get away and go on a holiday together. How do you fancy Guamá?

Padilla ...

Comrade Up you get: be quick about it; we only have a little while before the Commander gets here. (*Placing a pen and a paper in front of him.*) So we can welcome him with your speech already written to cheer him up.

Padilla Speech?

Comrade Yes, of course. We're going to ask you to recite it from memory later, as if it were off the cuff, in front of a select group of intellectuals and artists, many of your colleagues among them; we'll gather them together for a meeting … But, just in case, we'll preserve it in writing, with your signature.

Padilla …

Comrade It would be a shame for your words to get lost in the wind.

Padilla …

Comrade Come on!

Padilla …

Comrade Do I have to give you inspiration too? You could start, for example, by clarifying – and that way we'll avoid suspicion – that you requested the meeting yourself from the leadership of the Revolutionary government, to share with everyone present a fundamental part of your … experience.

Padilla …

Comrade Fine, I'll give you a hand. The main thing, in the long run, is that it's your handwriting … (*Places the pen between* **Padilla**'s *fingers and holds his hand with his, guiding the writing. He reads slowly, as he writes.*) As you all know, I have since March 20th been detained by our country's State Security Service …

Padilla (*removes the* **Comrade**'s *hand. Looks at him. Looks at the audience*) I was detained for being a counterrevolutionary.

The **Comrade** *watches as* **Padilla** *continues writing.*

X

Pride of the Nation

On the backdrop, a fragment of the video of the real **Heberto Padilla**'s *appearance before the Writers' and Artists' Union of Cuba, 27 April 1971, where he says:*

'*I even attacked, mercilessly, a comrade from the State Security agency who informed against the activities of Guillermo Cabrera Infante, saying that ... Talking about literary style ... As if literary style had anything to do with the truth, or as if the truth were not more important than literary spirit. These things that you are hearing me say now, you may think I should have thought them before. Yes, it's true. I should have thought them before. But such is life: men make mistakes. I've made these mistakes. Mistakes that are unforgivable. I know, for example, that my appearing here tonight is an act of generosity from the Revolution, that I did not deserve to stand before you like this; that I did not deserve to be free. I believe that sincerely. I believe it over and above this international fuss, which I appreciate on a personal level, because I think they are comrades who live other experiences, who have a completely different view of the Cuban situation. A situation that I have falsified in some way, or in every way, because I wanted to equate a particular Cuban situation with a particular international situation and particular stages of socialism which have been overcome in those socialist countries, to equate those historical situations with this historical situation that has nothing to do with them. And those comrades who have supported me, who have shown solidarity with me internationally, lack a deep knowledge of my life in recent years. Many of them do not know that I was involved in those activities, that I had adopted those attitudes, that I had taken such positions and acted in accordance with them. It's a natural instinct among writers in the capitalist world, which I hope that these comrades, when they realize the generosity of the Revolution, when they see me here able to speak freely with you ... Because if these were not my ideas, the first thing that should be demanded of me would be the bravery, in this moment, to say what my ideas really ought to be, even if tomorrow that meant going back to prison ...*'

Belkis *appears, lit by the images from the documentary.*

Belkis   The rest is the most well-known part of the case. The part everyone remembers, the part that was published in the articles, the books. The retraction. The shame. Herberto incriminating himself at the Writers' Union. Everything he had to write and memorize. Everything he was forced to say. Why did he do it ...? The 1970s were starting, the most perverse, crudest decade of the whole Revolution. And this was the trigger. The punishment. Throwing Heberto into the ring. Exposing us. Fabricating this circus ... There were lots of us there. We were part of the game, that pathetic performance, that witch-hunt. Heberto pointed the finger at us, laid the blame on us ... And we lowered our heads and we accepted it. A perfect, premeditated script: we all had to admit guilt ... One by one we stood up, confessed our failings before the powers that be, before those filthy people ... They weren't our minds, they weren't our tongues: it was just terror making us talk ... The cameras recording, the photographers ... Such shame. Heberto was the worst, degrading himself, sarcastic, manic, exaggerating everything in such a feverish way, making an unconceivable, absurd defence of the Revolutionary process. Heberto, intoning such a disgusting *mea culpa* ... That was when the destruction began, the downfall. From that day on he was never himself again. (*A suffocation.*) Now, half a century later, it might be hard for you all to understand. You might think us servile, cowardly. But when you're there, in that moment, when they show you the instruments, like they did to Galileo, yes, like they did to us, then everything changes ... If only it had been different ... Is it worth regretting it now? He's not here. He's dead. But there are still others ... So many others ... There. Here. Such loneliness ... Oh, History. That infamous exercise repeating itself. And repeating itself. And repeating itself.

Slow blackout.

Tell Me the Whole Thing Again

An Age-Old Spell

This English translation of *Tell Me the Whole Thing Again* was originally commissioned by Arca Images.

The play premiered at the Miami-Dade County Auditorium, 6 August 2021, produced by Arca Images, directed by Larry Villanueva and Abel González Melo, with the following cast: Laura Alemán and Adrián Más.

For José Luis García Barrientos

Structure of the Spell

I. Maybe I Shouldn't
II. A Half-Hour in the Cafeteria
III. Welcome Home
IV. Don't Let Go of My Hand
V. The Greatest Role of Your Life
VI. Such a Light Blue
VII. A Typical Small-Town Bar
VIII. A Carnival in the Penthouse
IX. May I Sit with You?
X. That Time We Were in Mourning for Someone
XI. Bewitch Me
XII. My Urge to Escape
XIII. Tell Me How It All Was

Characters

He *and* **She**, *two age-old figures from the spell,*
two people from today,
telling each other the whole thing again

I

Maybe I Shouldn't

She   Was there anything else important to tell you?

He   I don't know. We hadn't spoken for several days. Several weeks?

She   Actually, only a few hours.

He   A few minutes.

She   We hadn't spoken for a few minutes but for him it was like an eternity.

He   It was an eternity.

She   You'll tell him to come? That we want him to come to our home?

He   …

She   Did you go deaf or something?

He   …

She   What I'm saying is: let's accept the invitation to invite him. After all that's happened, he wants a truce. It's been tense between us for weeks, not even looking at each other … The business at the bar, everything coming out in the press all mixed up, the pictures from the premiere next to pictures from the fight and the award and then the TV stations hounding us for weeks and weeks … He wants to make a deal. He likes you deep down.

He   He likes you.

She   You're insane.

He   He wants to come because he likes you.

She   No. He's coming because he feels better here. With you. With us.

He   It's not us he's coming for.

She   Well, he's coming because he has to, because that's how life goes, because he's grateful to you somehow.

He   He is?

She   For not reporting him. For not opening your mouth in front of the cameras and saying terrible things about him, for not telling them what goes on in there.

He   …

She   He's thanking you in his own way, inviting us to invite him to come. To break bread. To celebrate our success with us here, in our home. So we can raise a glass to you.

He   But right here, now … Having to put up with them all? Smiling? Pretending not to notice them getting drunk? Did it have to be that way? Did it have to happen that way? Putting up with him in my own house that night?

She   We could change the story but this is the story we've got.

He   Maybe I shouldn't.

She   Why shouldn't we?

He   …

She   Maybe it'll work. Maybe we'll find some solution to all this torment. Stop you suffering so much.

He   There's no solution to this.

She   Are you sure?

He   …

She   He needs you. He needs you on his side.

He   …

She   You're everywhere now. People adore you. It doesn't suit him for you to be angry.

He   …

She   He trusts you again. Let's take advantage.

He   He trusts me?

She   …

He   Yes. Maybe.

She   …

He   But I don't know how to pretend.

II

A Half-Hour in the Cafeteria

She   May I sit with you?

He   It was the first day of rehearsals after Easter and I didn't pay much attention to her. Actually, I didn't even hear you. You had to ask again.

She   May I?

He   Yeah, sure.

She   Did you not hear me the first time or were you just pretending not to hear me?

He   We're in the theatre cafeteria and I'm having a coffee with a dash of Baileys. I always order my coffee that way. Coffee with Baileys to take away all the bitterness.

She   Coffee is bitter, that's the best thing about it.

He   But I've never liked bitterness.

She   Don't give me that. Tell them, see if they believe you.

He   You're not having anything?

She   I asked for a decaf but the machine's broken.

He   Order something else.

She   He says that and goes back to his newspaper.

He   The best thing to do before rehearsals is read the newspaper. Lose yourself in the endless stupidities the journalists tell you. Forget the script. Forget the character you have to play. I don't say any of that to her.

She   Do you always read the newspaper instead of going through the script? I mean, before rehearsals.

He   It's just, my character spends all his time onstage reading the newspaper. So actually, I'm already rehearsing.

She   And I burst out laughing.

He   No, you didn't so much as smile. You thought I was arrogant.

She   And you insisted on ordering me a coffee.

He   Are you the new intern?

She   Don't worry, I'm fine with my bottle of water. You don't have to get me a coffee. Caffeine keeps me awake.

He Nothing wrong with staying awake. Don't want the intern getting caught sleeping on the rehearsal room floor on her first day.

She I've been in the company for a month and a half.

He Oh, you have?

She We'd seen each other days before. Several times. So I didn't believe him. He'd noticed me. He knew who I was. I didn't believe him that day in the cafeteria. We'd bumped into each other in the dressing room when I was taking that basket of apples out for the forest scene; I'd been asked to go get the basket and when I was about to open the door he stepped out in front of it without seeing me and all of the apples fell to the floor. Our eyes met. You don't remember?

He I remember that's the version you always tell. But it can't really have been that way. I'd have been onstage at that moment. I never went to the dressing room. I never saw the apples. I'd never seen her before. What day are you talking about?

She Oh, I'm sorry!

He No, no, my bad ... I'll help you pick them up.

She There's no need, I'll do it.

He No, no, I'll help you, it'll be quicker ... This is crazy, we've been rehearsing for two weeks with the same apples, they're almost rotten now, they ought'a buy apples that don't smell.

She That don't rot?

He Plastic apples. They sell them in stores.

She But how could they be plastic apples when you have to eat them onstage?

He That's true.

She And there, crouching down picking up the apples, smiling, I saw it all. Your lips for the first time. Your eyes.

He I'm sorry about this mess but, well, there we go: apples back in their basket.

She I knew it all there and then.

He We're so close. The smell of the apples. The smell of your mouth.

She Well, see you later ...

He Are you the new intern?

She Did you ask me that in the dressing room or in the cafeteria, or are you asking me now, here, so softly, like you'd never asked before, as if you were dying to relive that moment, that moment our eyes first met, the first day we saw each other? Are you asking me now? Here, in the theatre?

He So, what are you doing for your internship?

She I run out along the corridor and leave you behind. You go to put on your make-up. You're going to become someone else for the forest scene.

He I'm still the same person. Even when I become someone else, when I change, I'll still be me.

She It's nearly time for rehearsal.

He I never have time to finish my coffee.

She Because you never get here early enough.

He I've been sitting here in the cafeteria reading the newspaper for half an hour.

She No. You only just got here.

III

Welcome Home

He I'll tell you who everyone is.

She Stop texting me, it's distracting.

He Put your cellphone under the table, no one will notice.

She I want to know what's happening. I want to listen to the meeting.

He No, you don't. I can see it in your face.

She You've been here for years, with you they'll let it pass. But I'm new, if I keep texting you …

He No one cares about these meetings, trust me.

She …

He People bring work here they want to get ahead with … See that guy in the corner? He's learning his lines; see how his lips are moving … We're here because we have to be here, let's just be discreet.

She You've got it good here.

He You mean '*we've* got it good'. Don't complain, you're part of the pack now, too. You've only been here a month, but you're quite the potential beast already … There'll be time to work your ass off soon enough onstage.

She Gee, you're poetic.

He Gee, you're sarcastic.

She You get angry too easily.

He You haven't seen me angry yet.

She …

He Even the guy reading the report doesn't care what he's saying, look: he doesn't even know how to read, his voice is sending me to sleep, I'm starting to snore.

She Ha ha.

He His whole life he's wanted them to give him a part but he's only ever been an assistant.

She His only lines are on the report he's reading, right?

He Ha. The only lines he'll ever read in his life.

She Those glasses look terrible on him.

He What would I do without my cellphone at times like these?

She The vice of texting.

He The one on the right of the guy who's reading, the fat guy.

She He's not so fat.

He He's the treasurer.

She You have a treasurer here?

He Yeah, an administrator.

She Him?

He Not that he really administers anything. He's a puppet. Just does what he's told. He's not the one holding the purse-strings.

She So who is?

He Officially or really?

She Officially. And really.

He Look two chairs to your left. See her? That's the director's wife.

She His wife?

He Yeah, she's got her iPad in front of her like she's taking notes but really she's on Facebook.

She Isn't she that super-famous actor?

He Too famous, yeah.

She What's her name?

He I don't know.

She Yes, you do.

He I forgot it. I forget the names of people who are too well-known.

She I'll make sure we never get to know each other, then.

He Trust me, I'll remember you.

She So it's the wife who hands out the money?

He The perfect woman.

She She's looking at you.

He …

She She just winked at you.

He …

She And you're smiling at her.

He She likes me.

She Oh, she does?

He And I let her.

She So I see.

He You're jealous?

She No. Why?

He I don't know.

She …

He The director hasn't taken his eyes off you, either.

She …

He He keeps looking at you and smiling.

She Stop it.

He You're the new jewel in the crown.

She …

He Or should I say 'the latest untamed shrew'?

She …

He He likes you. He'll soon start sticking his claws in.

She Stop it.

He The director's a dumbass anyway.

She Are you gonna go on?

He …

She And who's that on his left?

He That's the lead actress.

She Is there something in her hair?

He It's a wig.

She For a character?

He No. She's going bald.

She Oh.

He But don't mention it to her. You'll earn her hatred for life and you need her as a friend.

She She glared at me when we passed in the cafeteria.

He Welcome home.

She And there's no romantic lead?

He Me.

She Oh. Right, sure.

He I get farther from the romantic-lead age-range every year, it's true, but … no one else has joined the company. I sit in on all the auditions and I don't like any of the men.

She You must have had some good guys come.

He No. At least not here.

She I had to prepare a lot to pass the audition.

He Who saw you?

She The red-head.

He Oh, she's very funny, very noble. Always smiling. She's the one who brought the cupcakes. Did you try them? … She has nodules in her throat, you can hardly hear her when she speaks.

She And she acts?

He Yeah. Well, she says she does.

She Oh. Nodules. Poor thing.

He No, not 'poor thing'. She should retire. It's torture working with her. She's past forty and still playing ingénues.

She I'm grateful to her.

He She has a reputation for hiring the worst actresses.

She …

He It's a habit.

She Is there anyone here you do like?

He What do you want me to say?

She …

He They do it to protect themselves. So they don't have young rivals.

She …

He Although they do screw up sometimes.

She …

He They probably screwed up with you.

She Don't try sweet-talking me now.

He I'm telling you what I feel. An actress with no voice. It's not my fault, the nodules destroyed her throat. It should be you playing her parts.

She The good thing is, I'm in now.

He Until they kill you.

She How nice.

He I'm being serious.

She I love your sense of seriousness.

He Whatever happens, I'll be here to protect you.

IV

Don't Let Go of My Hand

She Was I the first one to scream?

He Or was it her?

She The gruesome scream of the artistic director's wife.

He She screamed with a truth I'd never heard from her onstage.

She It's incredible, when she's screaming, in so much pain, that you stop to think about those things.

He She's been making your life impossible for years. Don't start defending her now.

She But why is she screaming?

He We're in our house on the outskirts of town.

She We've been together almost five years.

He Five years since the apples, since the coffee?

She Last night, just last night it was five years.

He And we're celebrating at home.

She We invite the whole company over.

He They love coming here. They love the glamour of our house outside of town.

She They live in the city. They get bored there. They get polluted there. We have our home in the countryside, our healthy lifestyle. They love coming here.

He It's chic, to come to this house now and then.

She It's chic, thinks the lead actress, and she brings a cheap bottle of wine.

He It's chic, think the members of the ensemble, the dinner is exquisite and they even have maids.

She It's chic, especially with the rumor spreading –

He The idea spreading that I'm about to make peace with the director.

She Especially with you rising like bubbles in recent years, darling, you're a greater and greater actor.

He And I owe it all to you.

She And that's what they like most. Your success. That's why the director wanted to come. Thank you for inviting them, for acquiescing … I'm so pleased we can negotiate with him in our own way.

He Yes, you're so pleased the director's come to the house.

She To our house, at last.

He …

She But why is she screaming?

He Deafening screams.

She We're lying in bed.

He The dinner was fabulous.

She All so drunk they had to sleep here.

He We have plenty of rooms. They shared them out however they wanted.

She It's the dead of night.

He We made love last night like never before.

She We rolled around the bed and you did things to me you'd never done before?

He Last night you turned me on like never before.

She We did it all.

He Celebrating the wonderful dinner.

She And our fifth anniversary.

He But in the dead of night, almost at dawn, something wakes us up. It's her, and she won't stop screaming.

She 'It can't be! Come here, all of you! Come quick!'

He So I go down the stairs, barely dressed.

She I throw on whatever I can and follow you.

He We go into the room. It's still dark.

She Everyone's drunk. We've woken up hung over, we feel terrible.

He But you didn't drink all night.

She I didn't?

He No. You were sober.

She What's happened?

He You ask the wife.

She Her eyes are red.

He Your eyes are red.

She 'It can't be! My husband! How could …?'

IV Don't Let Go of My Hand

He She stops mid-sentence.

She Suddenly she looks at us, her face filled with hatred … Do you remember her face when she looked at us?

He You felt so powerless, you couldn't hold it in, and you screamed, like a character from a classical play, you held your head in your hands and you screamed:

She Oh, horror without measure! Wherefore are we witness to such great terror? Fateful day, etched forever in my eyes! That such a happy night should end so bitterly! The director dead in the guest room of my house? I could never have imagined such dishonour! In our own house!

He Are those your words?

She Hold me tight, please.

He I hold you and you burst into tears.

She …

He They all look at us.

She Waiting for us to give an order, to take the initiative.

He Are they hoping we'll call the police?

She But is he really dead?

He 'He's not breathing', says one of the actresses, who's approached the bed somewhat fearfully.

She Who slept in this room with him?

He He was coughing all night.

She All night. A hellish cough.

He The wife began to rise from the bed, her eyes red, she began to stand and, looking at us all, marking her words, said:

She 'He wanted to sleep alone. I went to the living room, beside the fireplace. It's your fault for having such a big house and insisting we stay. We should never have listened to you. This is a conspiracy! You've all hated my husband for years! And he's given everything for this company! My husband turned all of you into actors! He took you all to the top! Why should he have to die now, suffocated in this backwater? He didn't have the good fortune to die in a city, instead of this shack in the middle of nowhere, in this rickety old bed, in the middle of this freezing-cold night! But our time in this company doesn't end here! I won't let you get away with this! You've murdered him! With stories, with lies! You gave him that rotten punch to drink! You gave him those chorizo croquettes to eat! It's like an Agatha Christie novel, you've poisoned him! And then you suffocated him! I don't trust any of you! I hate you all! I'm getting out of here! You're going to pay for what you did! You'll regret this bloody slaughter!'

He   She said.

She   And then she shot out like a bullet through the forest.

He   What's that buzzing sound, like insects?

She   You're imagining things, calm down.

He   'You'll regret this bloody slaughter!'

She   What bloody slaughter is she talking about? There's not been any bloodshed here.

He   Should this have been a bloody death perhaps?

She   He died of natural causes. You look at them all, surrounding the body. You squeeze my hand and you say to them:

He   We all agree he died of natural causes, right?

She   Yes, they say. They agree. We all agree.

He   Call an ambulance, please, and call the police, too … A wife can't run out like that when her husband dies. She's the suspicious one, don't you think? Insulting us like that, saying all those terrible things about us? The police need to know about that. It doesn't make sense, it's not human, her treating us like that. I can understand her pain but she doesn't have the right to throw … such disdain in our faces. It's absurd, her running away like that, insulting us all, then running away when it's still the middle of the night! It's absurd, unless she … has something to do with this, has something to hide in all this! We have to tell the police that she ran away, because … who gains from his dying apart from her …? Just think for a second … You all know her. Enjoying all those privileges for all these years … It's made her tough, covered her with an armour of insensitivity! What if the director didn't die of natural causes? What if she had something to do with it …? We all need to stick together. We have to be, like always, loving comrades. Now, more than ever … Not just colleagues at work, but a family … I feel so desolate, sharing something like this with you. As host I can only beg your forgiveness.

She   You fall onto the couch and burst into floods of tears.

He   They all gather around me and hug me.

She   The lead actress even kisses you on the forehead.

He   They come to console me.

She   Showing their affection, their support.

He   Slowly they leave, some go to the bathroom, others go out to smoke.

She   All except that one actor from the ensemble.

He   He doesn't leave?

She   He approaches, leans over, and whispers in your ear:

IV Don't Let Go of My Hand

He 'You can't deny this death is good news for you.'

She He looks at me. His eyes bore into me. And he goes on.

He 'How curious that this has all happened in your house.'

She Is he threatening us?

He How dare he? He's just some bit-player! I can't stand being threatened.

She Is he really doing this?

He Tell him not to threaten me! Tell him!

She What are you insinuating?

He Yes, you ask him, but he doesn't reply, he laughs and walks away. He's a nobody from the ensemble; exactly what aspersion is he trying to cast?

She You've always defended him, you said he was your friend.

He He's not my friend! I have no friends in this company! How many times do I have to tell you?

She Don't take your anger out on me! And keep your voice down. No one should know what's happening to us. I'm here. We're in this together.

He I'm sorry.

She My hand starts to burn.

He Don't let go, it's burning!

She I squeeze tighter and tighter.

He My hand burns and drips.

She Liquid drips from our intertwined hands.

He And when I look down …

She When I finally look down …

He There's a puddle of blood on the floor.

She Or there's nothing. Because bloody murder is a thing of the past.

V

The Greatest Role of Your Life

He   That time you read my palm … You went quiet, you didn't tell me everything.

She   I told you what I saw.

He   But the silence … The look in your eyes … As time's gone by I've remembered that moment and I can't stop thinking about it … You were so insistent.

She   I just wanted to touch you.

He   We were in the cafeteria. We'd known each other for about a month.

She   We'd only just met.

He   What?

She   It was the day we met.

He   She often changes the dates. Tries to confuse me. I don't know if she does it on purpose or if she just gets mixed up … She changes the places, the days … You don't remember?

She   You weren't having coffee that morning because the machine had broken.

He   And the actor from the ensemble appeared.

She   Smiling like a dumb kid and smelling of tobacco.

He   But he's my friend.

She   He says terrible things about you behind your back but he's your friend.

He   …

She   Just when I have your open hand in mine, just as I'm looking at the lines on your left hand …

He   Just when you're saying:

She   I'm not sure if it's an M or an A I can see.

He   Let's see.

She   Just then, the actor from the ensemble appears.

He   'What's going on … You get off on having your hands tickled now?'

She   He cackles, I look at him, and you say:

He   Pull up a chair, I'm having my fortune told.

She   And we enter another dimension.

V The Greatest Role of Your Life 251

He We were still sitting in the cafeteria but everything started to fade.

She The atmosphere changed.

He We listened to you, like in a medieval legend.

She I see so many things … I see all that is to come, all that is to heal you. I tell you everything. I tell you, as I look at the lines on your hand, that you will continue to rise. That there's still so much more to achieve. I tell you the time will come when you will be filled with glory and people will cry as they watch you playing the greatest roles, on the greatest stages, when they see you directing the company with such majesty, stripped of useless artifice and building the universe anew with every word.

He 'And no critic will ever insult you again?'

She Asks the actor from the ensemble, because he's jealous.

He 'You, directing the company?'

She He's furious.

He Because you haven't said anything to him.

She Because it's only your palm I'm reading. It's you I'm interested in. Your future. Because through your hands, I work my way into your bones, into your blood.

He You're seeping into my blood.

She Because by doing this, by telling you the whole thing, I can save you.

He The actor from the ensemble can't keep quiet; he insists, 'And there's no good news for me? I'm not getting a pay rise? Come on, read my hands, they're clean, look … I don't use them for anything you couldn't imagine, trust me.'

She He's so vulgar. I detest people this vulgar.

He Why don't we cut him out?

She We could cut him out, yes. Now, to relive the moment, sure, we can cut him out. But he was there that day, he heard everything.

He Everything you told me.

She It annoyed him.

He It annoyed him when you came out with them giving me the lead in that play. Those comedies beloved by old ladies fresh from the hair salon. He didn't even like the part, but he couldn't stand the idea of me playing it.

She And what about you? Could you have stood anyone else playing it?

He …

She …

He I'm cutting the actor from the ensemble.

She Cutting him completely?

He No. Not yet.

She He's not annoying you too much yet?

He You made that up about me getting the part.

She I didn't make anything up. I was just reading your future.

He How could you know?

She It was in your hands. Everything's inside you, in the end.

He Everything's always inside us?

She Our reality and its reflection.

He How could you tell?

She And everything I didn't tell you.

He You didn't tell me but it happened.

She And when the bell started to ring, that long bell, that beat of monotony, that drip that hangs there and never quite drops …

He When the warning bell rings for the start of the show …

She Here, backstage, the bell rings.

He Now the bell rings and I have to go onstage, to act the part.

She To act in a play, as if it were the greatest role of your life.

He Even though I know it isn't. Even though it's not enough for me.

She Because the greatest role of your life is you.

VI

Such a Light Blue

He Easter vacation. The city empties. The heat suddenly returns. All of my friends have gone. To the beach. In cars, in trains, in planes. Off to enjoy some rest with their children, to recharge their batteries for when we come back, because when we come back we're starting the new play, the dazzling premiere of the spring. They're happy, they post pictures on Facebook, they comment, they dream. And I stay here. I don't leave. I don't enjoy the rest. I'm single. I have no children. I don't recharge my batteries. I'm stretched out on the couch and the hours pass by. I ruminate on the paradoxes of life: the wonderful play I hold in my hands, and the shitty part I've been given to play in it. The one I've been playing since I joined the company fifteen years ago. One of those. One that talks and appears in a corner, one that's in several scenes with the protagonist but doesn't really add anything, just the necessary blah-blah-blah for the latest dandy to express all the richness of his inner world. Ring any bells? The one you see wedged in the corner of the poster or the press photos, in those photos mothers keep framed in their living rooms, the one who's always in the second row, the whole team and me behind them, my character in the background, slightly hidden behind the lead actress's shoulder. One of those who's first to come out during the curtain call, the one who gets least ovation, the one who has to put up with the humiliation of receiving reluctant applause, and seeing that applause increase more and more with every other cast member that comes out onstage. A nobody the audience only claps out of courtesy. Who no one interviews, no one asks for an autograph … The script is on the living-room table and I've highlighted all my lines in blue marker, it's silly but it helps me, it helps me to see that I do have some lines, some colour, even if it is such a light blue. But I don't go back to the words, I resist going back. I turn on the TV and it bores me. I go to buy bread and it bores me. I go for a bike ride and it bores me. I go onto Facebook and compare everyone's enthusiasm: the artistic director's kids playing in the sand and him behind them with an enormous bream he's just fished out of the water, and his wife watching me … The lead actress covering her skin with sunscreen lest a single ultraviolet ray compromise her splendid whiteness … The return home from vacation draws ever closer: each comment, each smile reveals everyone's delight at starting rehearsals again. I, on the other hand, feel sad. Holy Week is far too short to do justice to the scale of holiness its name evokes. Stretched out on the couch it seems infinite but short, yes, too short, shorter than the lines I have to say in the play. 'You do have quite a lot of lines', the director says when he gives me the script, when we bump into each other in the men's room. With his sarcastic smile, his usual acid wit, that sonofabitch smirk that I hate. And yes, I look at the script, I flick through the pages. I do have some lines, I do have a part that many would die for, I do get a stable salary from the company, I can cover a very wide age-range within a cast, I do grotesque characterization and psychological intensity equally well, I do melodrama with ease and I've even sung in vaudeville. I'm not an actor who's side-lined, my fellow cast members respect me, admire me, love me, I'm almost the protagonist of this performance, I have just as many lines as the lead actress, I speak enough at the press conferences, a major newspaper just called me to ask me questions about the upcoming premiere, I'm appearing on the front of more and more magazines, the media talk about me more and more, I get stopped more and more in the street and teenage film students take photos with me. The director says that one sentence to me, 'You do have quite a lot of lines', and I believe it and I know it's true. And I can switch on the TV and cheer myself up with some reality show, and smile at the baker who sells me my favourite whole-grain cookies, and cycle to the park and lie on the grass and watch the clouds float by and feel happy at the life I have, at the job I have, at the opportunity I have always to be someone else and somewhere else, beyond the heavens, or further still, with my solitude and with myself and with the others who aren't here, who don't exist, who don't even exist in the beyond. I know all this, but now, when I ride the subway, now, when I walk along the sidewalk, now, as I cross the square to walk into the theatre, all I can think is that being grateful is not enough, being grateful doesn't matter to me, being grateful doesn't fulfil me. I reach the cafeteria with scarcely time to spare, just as the bell is about to ring for the start of rehearsals, I order a coffee and when it's served to me, as I drink it, I barely manage to think that in my life, in myself, in the depths of myself, this is not enough. This is no use to me. I need more.

She ...

He And then I turn around and see you.

She I can calm your anxiety.

VII

A Typical Small-Town Bar

He Yes, hello …

She I can't hear you, log out and log back in again.

He OK.

She I'll call you.

He …

She Are you there? Can you hear me now?

He I can hear you now. It's patchy but I can hear you … Turn your camera on, I can't see you.

She Now?

He Now I see you.

She What happened?

He It was terrible, the director's lost his mind … I don't know, I don't understand it … You noticed he was acting strange in the rehearsal last week, right? He's been that way for a while, he treats me … He plays the scenes like he's ignoring me, not looking at me.

She He's a pirate, he never looks me in the eye.

He Well, with you it's because he has the hots for you, because he can't stand you being with me.

She Don't be ridiculous.

He You don't remember that dumb excuse he made not to come to our wedding?

She I'm being serious, he doesn't even look at me when we act together. Not even when we had to kiss each other in that piece of post-dramatic bullshit we did … He doesn't look, he's a creep … There's nothing worse than having the artistic director acting with you in the cast. Why does he insist on performing?

He But really, this time it was terrible. You know he's changed the order of the curtain call because he said I'm getting too much applause?

She Of course you're getting too much applause! What's wrong with him? You're the best thing in the show.

He Right, but, imagine, he's not getting a single 'bravo', it's made him hysterical.

She That's so stupid.

He The curtain came down and when we were changing in the dressing room, he came up to me and told me to quit upstaging him.

She Upstaging him?

He Yeah, except he uses some foreign phrase, right … You know he likes throwing in exotic words, like he's some kind of international jet-setter.

She So how are you upstaging him?

He He says I put ad-libs in to win over the audience, says I improvise too much … He says I laugh too much in the scene where he's talking on the phone.

She But you have to laugh in that scene. It's in the stage directions.

He Oh, but now he's gotten it into his head that I'm sabotaging him … And in the middle of the scene, he yells at me to shut up! He says into the phone, 'I can't hear you very well, because this clown in front of me has been laughing since I came in.'

She He said that? In the middle of the show?

He He said that. It was … jaw-dropping.

She But did you laugh more today than other days?

He Look … I don't know. I do laugh at him, it's true I don't waste a second to … You know. I don't like getting bored onstage. But I always stay within the scene, within my character …

She You pissed him off.

He He pisses me off every day! On and off the stage!

She I'm not disagreeing with you, I know –

He I'm a professional and he's a schmuck.

She OK, don't get frustrated … Don't let it get to you.

He And in the dressing room, one of the other actors was there and he said nothing. He could have said something, I was right, but people … It's just the director says any dumb thing and they're all scared to death he'll fire them. And he can't. He ought'a fire all the assholes who grow in this company like weeds, but he can't.

She So, what did you do?

He I didn't reply. Didn't open my mouth.

She Did you apologize?

He Why?

She Because it's politic, because it's good business … Because he's dying.

He He's not dying. I'm the one on the verge of a heart attack.

She No. You're stronger than that.

VII A Typical Small-Town Bar

He There's more. We all went for dinner together … I didn't feel like it but the lead actress practically forced me, she begged me with that melancholy face like some saint from a painting, took my arm and made me walk with her to the restaurant … The typical small-town bar, because this isn't a city, it's a small town, but very pretty, very lively … Anyway, we start eating and drinking and the night starts getting tense, we're drinking beer and laughing, we're all kind of making digs at each other disguised as jokes … I'm not so much, I wanted to get back to the hotel to sleep, I'm exhausted, but I made one comment, said one dumb thing, I don't know what, and the director stands up from the other end of the table and comes over to where I am. I stood up, one of the bit-part actresses held out her hand to hold me back and make me sit back down, but the director started insulting me, laughing, no one else was laughing but he was, he was drunk, do you know how often he does the show half drunk? He'd already been drinking but now he was even drunker … He started insulting me, and then he slapped me in the face, so I pushed him against the wall and then … Oh, I'm not enjoying telling you this.

She You hit him?

He Yes. But everyone saw how it happened. They pulled us apart right away. Everyone knows it was his fault.

She What about his wife?

He She was frightened. She stood up and didn't know what to do … There were journalists there, they took photos, the same journalists who'd been in the theatre, so tomorrow the news about the premiere will come out with the news about the fight.

She How very folkloric, right?

He His wife apologized. She asked me to excuse him, said he's not been well these past few weeks.

She Five years I've been in this company and I still can't get used to you going on tour alone, I don't like you touring with shows that I'm not in, I don't like you being alone.

He …

She …

He There is some good news. I just found out. The festival ended today and they've given me the acting award.

She Really?

He Yep, the big prize. They just called me. And it's quite a lot of money, which I'm most happy about.

She Oh, congratulations, honey, I'm so pleased for you.

He Yeah, there's that, at least … They've only told me unofficially but they'll confirm it tomorrow and then the word will be out.

She You're the best.

He …

She So the director knows?

He Maybe he could sense it and that's why he went crazy.

She Yeah …

He …

She Are you sharing a room?

He No, they put us in single rooms, thank goodness.

She So much the better.

He Yes. So much the better.

She …

He This can't go on.

She I know it can't.

He I've had enough of being humiliated.

She …

He I'm going to bed. We'll talk tomorrow.

She I love you.

He And I love you.

She Kiss kiss.

VIII

A Carnival in the Penthouse

He I walk down the avenue at night.

She The carnival lights have gone out. It's still cold.

He I don't like mixing with these kinds of people but one time I had to do it, come to this alleyway, knock on this door.

She It's a year now since the old director died and nine months since they appointed you.

He Do you think the people in the company like me?

She That's not a question you should ask yourself. Look how well we're doing. Living in this penthouse, in this paradise, in the heart of the city at last, in the heart of the world. How did we ever think it was healthier to live in the countryside?

He It's chic to live in the heart of the city.

She I adore the heart of the world. I hate our past in the countryside.

He But do they like me?

She You're making your mark on the company. You have the support of the critics. You're starting to create a magnificent repertoire. And you're acting, too. You're the star. What more could anyone want from you?

He But I'm still so jumpy all the time.

She There's no need to be. Come here, give me a hug.

He I forget everything when you hold me.

She But you don't forget the actor from the ensemble still saying things to you like:

He 'This didn't happen under the old director.'

She And you gave him an excellent part this season.

He It's just, people don't learn. They don't know how to be discreet. People don't want to look away and keep quiet. They insist on crossing the line.

She So now, walking alone in your overcoat. Lost in the immense darkness.

He I turn into the alley.

She Into that corner of your past life, of your plunges into the lower depths. You always were attracted by the margins.

He I never liked the margins. This world disgusts me.

She   You move through the margins with total ease. You handle the knives. Manipulate the whores.

He   I did all that?

She   Even though no one ever found out. Why do you think you're an actor?

He   I don't know if I'll ever learn to act.

She   He's a North African kid, no older than twenty.

He   I talk to him under a street light.

She   It's a brief meeting, furtive. An instant that no one can find out about. You slip the envelope into his pocket and say to him:

He   You know what you have to do, right?

She   You make sure he knows to tell you when he's done.

He   And that he's memorized the actor from the ensemble's face.

She   …

He   A toast to life and the joy of being together!

She   This penthouse is a dream for throwing parties.

He   And did you notice the cold has gone?

She   It knows we're happy so it's calling a truce. You should have a huge party to celebrate the premiere!

He   I did really bring the house down.

She   And now, here we are again, our home filled with all our resplendent company.

He   Like that night when … he died.

She   Let's not talk about dead people now, OK?

He   …

She   …

He   They all look happy. Bread and circuses.

She   I told you they'd calm down as soon as we opened. You see there was no need for you to worry?

He   You were fantastic that night. It was so believable when you came down the stairs behind me stunned at the death of the king … It made my hair stand on end, I swear.

She   You're making me blush.

He   It's the God's-honest truth! I'm with you onstage and it scares me, when you start convincing me –

She You're really good when you're doubting, when it looks like you're not going to listen to me … And the banquet? You go wild in the banquet scene!

He I just can't hold it in.

She You've got a message.

He Let's see …?

She Was it him?

He Yes. It's done.

She …

He …

She Your cellphone rings. It's the actor from the ensemble. You talk to him.

He You really don't know who could have sent you those photos, buddy? The kid looks, what, North African …? Hey, take it easy, don't take it out on me … I didn't picture you getting your kicks with North African boys, you're a married man … Oh, now I'm the sonofabitch? You're the one who hooked up with a … If you like it that much … Stop yelling, calm down … What do you mean I wanna take you down?

She What?

He He hung up.

She …

He …

She 'Why didn't that actor from the ensemble come to the party? He's so nice.'

He Says the lead actress, coming over. She doesn't mention what a success the opening night was. She doesn't congratulate us. She comes over with her squinty eyes and halitosis and the first thing she comes out with is that, in our own home, at our party, on the terrace of our penthouse. And she goes on.

She 'Because you did invite him, right? He deserves it … He was really good in the show tonight. Why didn't he come to the party? Why? Why?'

He Because he just didn't, you old bitch! He didn't come because, if he did come, all of the happiness I'm feeling right now would disappear in an instant and I would have no other choice but to grab you by the throat and throw you over the balcony! He didn't come because he's a bare-faced, social-climbing good-for-nothing who's been wheedling his way into the company like a cancer! He's not coming because he's a terrible actor who will never be anything more than just one of the ensemble, and who is worse than all of the rest of you put together, worse even than the worst performance that you've ever given, you, who, rather than being called the lead actress, ought to be called the rear actress! He's not coming because he is envious riff-raff of the lowest kind, because he thinks the world is his for the taking, because he thought he could keep threatening me for the rest of my life, that he could blackmail me, that he could say whatever he wanted about me and my wife, that he could discredit us, and insinuate that we killed the old director! And today, on our big opening night, just so you know, he was not as good as you say he was! He was terrible! My wife and I were brilliant, even though that's hard for you, even though you hate us! We were better than you've ever been! But he was not! He made me suffer, from the first scene to the last! Every single moment was painful to me! He was deficient! You were all deficient! Worse than deficient! You're a fourth-rate company! We hire a big-name director from overseas to direct you and I die of shame that he has to work with such terrible actors! If I had the power, I'd throw you all out onto the street! You're like leprosy!

She …

He …

She Everyone gathers around us. They look at us, with their glasses in their hands. They're all speechless.

He …

She Don't mind him … He gets anxious sometimes and starts playing these unpleasant little games, talking nonsense.

He A trap … Wipe him out forever …

She Don't mind him, he's had too much to drink.

He But … I didn't say that last thing, right? Please tell me I didn't say that.

She We were on the terrace, in the middle of the party, it was all like a dream and then suddenly … A spirit possessed you.

He I don't know what came over me, I don't know, I don't remember anything … Just that actor from the ensemble's face in front of me, I could see him through the eyes of that old woman and everything that came out of my mouth …

She Everything that spewed out of you …

He All those things I said were meant for him.

She …

He Tell me no one else heard.

She They were all there.

He But we have the power. We still have that, right? The power to switch it all around and go back to that night when we were all celebrating our success.

She I'm not a queen. I don't have that power.

He But this is our space. This is our reality. We can change it here.

She Will we change it?

He Give me your hand.

She   Don't let it go.

He   ...

She   The lead actress starts to come over.

He   She asks us. She asks me where the actor from the ensemble is.

She   And you smile.

He   I know why I'm smiling.

She   You know, but she, there, in front of you, she can't know. She can only see you smiling.

He   Darling, my darling lead actress, the greatest there'll ever be ... That actor from the ensemble, as you rightly say, so talented, he sent his apologies, he's not coming, he had to stay home to take care of his baby, he has a newborn baby, that's how it goes, the responsibilities of being a parent ... That's why my wife and I will never have children.

She   That speech came out really well.

He   I hug you, I kiss you.

She   They all go on enjoying the party. You sigh. You start calming down.

He   ...

She   ...

He   You don't want to have kids, right?

IX

May I Sit with You?

She I have the stain of love right here. Look at my hands. Do they look clean to you? And yet, they hide the impossible. These lines don't trace the course of my life. These lines are markings, just simple markings for the game. If I sink through them, I'll see it all, I'll understand it all. And the future, how can I see that? How can I interpret it with certainty? Even with everything planned, everything rehearsed down to the last detail, even with this line so precisely drawn, so minutely designed, this line that's so faint but at the same time so deep, that starts at the tips of my fingers and stretches all the way to the soles of my feet ... Even with my life planned out so carefully, how do I respond to the unexpected? When my eyes cloud over and my reason no longer serves me and all I see in my hands are lines that can't be crossed, when instead of stories on my arms there's skin, when in my head the murky landscapes blend with the orderly words, when the actor and character get confused, when I stare at you and can't get inside you, how will I get out of the maze? ... None of my classmates could believe I'd gotten into this company. That afternoon, when they told me, I didn't move, they told me over the phone and I couldn't even say thank you. So young and in that company? Was it really what I wanted? After so many years in school, after preparing so much for those exams, for those impossible auditions, was this the moment? Was this happiness? Was this what I'd been training for? For a stable job and a salary? And then I asked my friends, 'What about our idea of flying?' They looked at me like I was crazy, looked at me like they wanted to kill me, 'Are you stupid? When you want to fly, take a plane and go to a desert island.' But what about the island of my heart? Or the desert of my life? Why, if everything was so great, did I feel so alone? ... None of those sad ideas cross my mind. I say nothing to my friends. From the moment they tell me the news, I don't stop feeling euphoric for an instant. I have to enjoy this terror, this terror of everything that's coming, the raging sea that's approaching. I have to go into my new life silent, almost imperceptible, I'll go to the cafeteria and sit quietly in a corner with a coffee. And when I see him reading the newspaper, when I see him come in, worked up and sweating, so enigmatic, anxious inside, opening the door, about to start the rehearsal, the bell about to ring, when I see him and he says to me:

He May I sit with you?

She I'll know it's him. I'll recognize him right away. I'll notice every feature of his face and imagine the cafeteria dissolving, the walls falling, the theatre falling. I'll forget all the stories, all the images, all the characters that have been and will be, and when he comes in ... I can only be myself, look at him, and think of one thing. I could only think of one thing when he came in, when he came in and said to me:

He May I sit with you?

She   The two of us walking a tightrope. Eyeing each other, face to face, walking from opposite ends, from the margins to the centre, one foot in front of the other, not taking our eyes off each other, knowing we have to lift our foot each time and that each time we run the risk, sensing the abyss but not looking at it, knowing there's a risk of forgetting our lines, forgetting our moves as we stare at each other, the breath of the immediate, the whisper of what's coming and wanting to cast us into the emptiness, and the tightrope holding us up, the rope being born from every new step, the tightrope, alone in mid-air with all our desire and suffocation and desperation to keep on going forward, all of that bursting out in the gesture of our outstretched hands, our hands reaching each other's, my hands covered in stains ... Is it really him? Is the cliff-edge of loving him worth it? I feel the stain, the spot. You don't see it but it's here, hidden by this make-up, by this heat, by these words. It might be any artificial red liquid, I've cut myself on the edge of the crown. It could be, it is, it would be, it surely would have been, once, a drop of blood, a drop of my very own flesh.

X

That Time We Were in Mourning for Someone

He   What was that show where I played your father?

She   You're not old enough to play my father.

He   I was in that show. We both fell in love with the same guy, didn't we?

She   You fell in love with a guy?

He   And you wanted to make apple pie.

She   No. The apples are from this play. I drop the basket in the dressing room and you help me pick them up.

He   No, no. I mean some other apples. That play where we were in mourning for someone.

She   We were mourning your son?

He   I slapped him in the face and he stopped talking to me. Then he killed himself.

She   No. The guy you were sleeping with killed himself.

He   The guy you were sleeping with?

She   What about my brother?

He   My son?

She   He got stabbed twice.

He   …

She   …

He   That's horrible. I never did like blood.

She   I couldn't stand you sleeping with another woman, you know.

He   What about another man?

She   I'm very orthodox. I went to a convent school. I don't care if it's a girl or a guy.

He   You don't care?

She   Either way I'd kill you.

He   I won't give you that pleasure.

She   Try it and you'll see.

He   …

X That Time We Were in Mourning for Someone

She …

He Have we already told the story of what you did when we met?

She Do we really know each other?

He We were at the beach. I'd gone for my Easter vacation. I was playing in the sand with the old director's kids … We always were like family. He was taking a photo with a bream he'd just caught.

She While you were laughing with his wife.

He I love you.

She 'You love that I'm the artistic director's wife.'

He Don't be stupid.

She 'You're such a strange guy … Maybe it's your voice that makes you mysterious?'

He Do you wanna find out?

She 'No, because I'd have to get close to your mouth.'

He The kids play on the sand and she, his wife, comes close to my mouth.

She …

He …

She Was it her or me who came close to your mouth?

He The old director's wife never could stand you.

She It's because of me?

He Maybe it's because of me.

She Had you promised her something?

He …

She What had you promised her?

He …

She Tell me, before I go crazy, what the hell did you promise her?

He Hey, take it easy!

She Why have you hidden this from me all this time?

He Calm down!

She Why couldn't you tell me then, when I asked you, that you two almost ran away together?

He That was all in her head. She meant nothing to me. I never liked her. I didn't like kissing her, I didn't like being in bed with her. I swear none of it was real!

She Were you still seeing her when we were together? Were you still seeing her after we got married?

He Why are you bringing this up now? What does it matter?

She Don't tell me it doesn't matter! I've been here all these years! I've waited for you here every night, awake but pretending to be asleep, waiting while you had your meetings with the director and her … And I understood, it was your work, it's the basis of everything we've built, the foundations of our crystal island. I never said anything, out of respect, because it's our life, even if you came home way after midnight, even though you got in so late … But from the very first day I noticed it, from that very first meeting in the green room, it was my first day with the company and she, the director's wife, she had her iPad out and she was pretending to make notes, you told me so yourself, she was pretending to make notes but she was on Facebook and suddenly she looked up at you … You were messaging me and suddenly she looked at you … And for a few seconds you stopped messaging me. You looked at her. Yes, you looked at her! I've never been able to forget the way you looked at her that day … That was where it all started. How did I not realize then? The way you were so rude to them, the way you detested them, was that all a lie so I wouldn't suspect, so I wouldn't know you were secretly still in love with her? … 'The perfect woman', those were your words. Etched on my hard drive. I told you! I told you! Why did you have to cheat on me? Why? If there's one thing I can't stand in life, it's betrayal!

He …

She …

He You said all that to me so loudly, so desperately … And I turned to stone.

She I wasn't at the beach the day she kissed you. But believe me, it's as if I were. I have it nailed here. On the centre of my forehead.

He So was that the day we met?

She …

He …

She The director's wife is coming over here.

He She's been gathering evidence against us for a year.

She Evidence that incriminates us, so she says.

He Evidence that makes us her husband's murderers.

She Us, can you imagine?

He Two actors like us.

She She's filled with rage.

He We've usurped her empire. Would you think a theatre company in a country like this could be led like the feuds of ancient Scotland?

She She hates that we took over the company, that we can do whatever we want with it. That we won.

He But the thing she hates most is you.

She Which is why I take it personally.

He We should let her come here. Let ourselves make a pact with her.

She You want us to talk about how much I like the pacts you make with her?

He I don't say another word. But I watch.

She I feel.

He I foresee.

She I make a date myself with the wife of the old director, in a tea house. I won't let anyone ruin our happiness … No one is throwing me out of the penthouse, no one is stopping me from buying expensive dresses. She stirs her tea with her little spoon, I smile at her, I can tell she's anxious to know what I have to say, to know what agreement we might come to, because yes, she's smart and she'd rather negotiate than throw this business to the animals from the press and the police … No one's gonna get in the way of my life with you. She turns, barely for a second, and I take the chance to pour these drops into her tea.

He You're sick with jealousy. You're not going to kill her. I'm going to arrive just in time, when she turns back, and throw her cup to the floor.

She So we can talk here the whole time about your loneliness, your abandonment issues, your anxiety, we can talk about you for the whole play, crown you, make you a hero, a star, and I have to stay here in silence, supporting you, agreeing with you, taking care of you?

He Quiet. Don't go down that road.

She 'Quiet, quiet!' You think I'm scared of you?

He You're taking things to where they shouldn't go.

She Let go of me. I'm going to kill her!

He She's married. She has another life.

She What do I care about that?

He She's pregnant.

She Get out of my way!

He With my child!

She You told me like that, out of the blue?

He I told you so you'd calm down.

She You're telling me she's going to give birth to your child?

He I told you so you'd calm down but it made things worse. Don't do it! You promised me we wouldn't get to this point.

She I grab her by the ears.

He The director's wife tries to defend herself but you're blind, mad with rage, you bang and bang her head against the deserted counter of the tea house.

She Until she stops breathing.

He Now the police will come looking for us. Committing a crime ain't what it used to be. It always leaves a trace, a trail.

She There's no trail. There's no trace. This is a play, and there was nothing I could do except kill her.

He Nothing? Even though there's nothing left between you and me?

She There's everything left.

He …

She Choose the version of the death you prefer.

He So shall we call this chapter closed?

She Some chapters are never closed.

He I lied to you. It wasn't my child.

She I know.

He You know …? So why the hell did you do that?

She Don't shout at me!

He Why? Why?

She I know you can't have children.

XI

Bewitch Me

He   I spent the whole night dreaming in English.

She   You woke me up at this hour to tell me that?

He   In English ... Do you realize how strange that is?

She   What? Dreaming in a language?

He   I spent the night dreaming that I was reading our play, but in English. That I was standing in the middle of the square reading it out in English.

She   That makes sense. It was written in English, we translated it.

He   But still, some phrases ... The inner life of my character, the words echoing through the inner courtyards of his castle, the wind blowing through the corridors of our home ... All that heroic magnificence opposing the pain, the intimate intensity, that feeling of ... poverty.

She   But he's a rich guy. He wants for nothing.

He   Don't I want for everything?

She   Let me sleep.

He   His ideas, his words in English, they're confusing, they fire off in too many different directions ... When he says to his wife, 'You bewitch me' ...

She   We'll talk about this tomorrow.

He   When he says, 'You bewitch me' ...

She   Yes, he's saying he loves her. She's charming.

He   Charming, yes, but 'charming' is not the word he uses. That could be ambiguous. Open to interpretation. What he actually does ... is call her a witch. 'You bewitch me.'

She   ...

He   He's saying she's put a spell on him.

She   She's put a spell on him?

He   Yeah.

She   ...

He   He's talking about magic.

She Please, I've read that play a thousand times … The witches are a whole other thing, they appear at a different moment … When your character says that to the wife … he's talking about love, about fascination, he's talking about how much he loves having her beside him, how he's dying of passion, like the way I'm dying for you, look, watch me kissing you, see? Like that, desire … That's what he's saying. 'You bewitch me', sure, but, that phrase is imbued with his sexual urges, his fear of the very idea of ever losing her … It's like you looking me in the eye so hard that I could never get away from you again.

He No. I listen to you now and it's clearer and clearer to me. He's not talking to her about love. He's talking about witchcraft.

She What witchcraft?

He Hers. Hers, making him have feelings he could never have imagined.

She No one can make someone else have feelings … that are not already there.

He You did, to me.

She …

He The English is ambiguous.

She Why set love and magic against each other? Why do you see them as opposites? They're not so far away from each other. They're practically the same thing.

He Still, there's a certain nuance.

She Just because in English the word is 'bewitch'?

He If she, his wife, didn't exist … If they hadn't met one day, if they hadn't gotten married … If we hadn't smiled as we drank that coffee, hadn't stumbled together over the apples … If that moment, when, for the first time, they realized they were destined for each other … If that chance meeting had not taken place … Would he not have been bewitched? Afflicted with passion? Would we not have achieved a single one of our dreams? Would she … not have cast a spell on him?

She Maybe he'd have died of sadness.

He He does get killed in the end anyway.

She Yeah, you get stabbed with a sword.

He But when that happens …

She We'd already had it all.

He We'd reached the top?

She Who knows?

He Right. Who knows?

She You'd already dared to do everything.

He At least I'd found love.

She Yes.

He …

She We both had.

XII

My Urge to Escape

She   Let's see, give me your hand.

He   I don't cut my nails properly, I don't like showing my hands.

She   I, look … I bite my nails and I don't care if people see my hands. In school I always used to have to wear false nails for acting. Except when I played a boxer, then I wore gloves.

He   You played a boxer?

She   I don't want to intimidate you, but I did learn to box.

He   OK.

She   And I took fencing classes for that period drama.

He   So how are you with a sword?

She   With a sword … Yeah, a sword has something about it … How can I put it ? … You grab it by the hilt, raise it up, touch the tip, discover that swishing sound the blade makes when you twirl it in the air … It was tantalizing. I used to get strangely excited, it was like I could conquer everything. It took me to the edge.

He   Of what?

She   Of myself. Of my urge to leap, to escape … to another time, with those outfits, that valour.

He   With that excitement we've lost now?

She   To escape to that planet where the characters talk about a palace and about love … It took me to the edge of all those things but most of all … to the edge of my urge for other people to disappear.

He   …

She   Although it's different when it's for TV. You can't actually kill anyone. It's not like in theatre.

He   You don't actually kill anyone in theatre either.

She   You don't?

He   …

She   On the stage you look the other actor in the eye and …

He   The way you're looking at me now?

She   We're not onstage now. Now we're here, you and me.

XII My Urge to Escape

He And when she placed her palm on mine it felt frozen.

She It was hot, like everything was boiling up inside me.

He As cold as the hand of a dead man.

She So hot I thought my skin would burst.

He I'm going to read your future.

She There's no need. It's already upon us.

He What are you going to make up?

She I like the director. The way he looks at me, talks to me.

He He always disgusted you.

She No, that's what you imagine. You haven't stopped interpreting this play according to your own tastes, and for that reason I come across as the most lovable, loving woman. You want the truth? Here it is. I've been seeing him for years. I've been sleeping with the director for years.

He That's not you!

She I've had pleasure with him I never had with you.

He …

She He's not going to die meekly in our country house. I'm not going to encourage you in any more of your obsessions. Look at me, pregnant with his child. Your dumb excuses are over, your anxiety, your envy. Now, if you want to kill him, you have a real reason.

He …

She You're not going to do it, are you. I figured. You don't have the balls!

He …

She Here's what's going to happen. In spring we're going to get married. What did you think, that I'd put up with your stupidity my whole life? How long did you think I'd tolerate your self-centredness, your egotism, your delusions of grandeur, your paranoia? Until it drove me mad? Until I found myself walking in endless circles around the house rubbing my hands like someone crazy? You can agree to the divorce or you can force me to use all this as evidence against you. We've filmed everything today. Everything that's happened on this stage has been recorded and I'm going to edit it to suit me and make you look like the guilty one.

He …

She I could give you a thousand reasons for my decision. I don't feel loved. My baby needs to grow up with its father and not with a stranger. I'll be much better off as the director's wife. In every way. I could give you a thousand reasons but the main one, perhaps the most authentic one, is that I can't stand you.

He   …

She   And if you dare add one single scene after this one, if you try to make this puzzle fit together differently, if by any chance you dare to confuse them with another lie about me, I swear … I swear, in front of all you people … I swear I will go to the police and tell them that all these marks from all the nights of pleasure I've spent with the director are your fault, because you locked me in the attic and beat me.

He   …

She   You've been warned.

XIII

Tell Me How It All Was

He   They're asleep already?

She   They're drunk. It's time.

He   Should I go down the stairs?

She   Silence inhabits the whole palace. Hear it?

He   …

She   …

He   Are you going to give me the dagger?

She   There's no dagger. This is our house.

He   It's not Scotland?

She   It's right now. All you have is your hands. All you have is yourself.

He   And the words.

She   Yes, and the words.

He   And when the audience sees me? What if I can't do it when they're all there in front of me?

She   We've rehearsed it lots of times. It's going to be perfect. We've been planning it for so long.

He   False face must hide what the false heart doth know.

She   …

He   But you'll go straight away, right?

She   And you'll already have done it.

He   What's that noise? That furore that deafens me?

She   The beating of the leaves. The howling wind.

He   Is this the end? … Will my destruction come?

She   You're the director of this company. You're the actor in this scene. You have to do it.

He   And what about what I'd feel here, inside? In that moment, when he's … When I see him in his bed and he's … Where will I put my feelings at that moment? When his eyes really flash before mine and I have to do it, how will I behave to keep myself sane? Where will I find the strength?

She   Don't look at me with those eyes, not those eyes again … Not as if you were starting to doubt now. You can't doubt now!

He   There are a few seconds left.

She   You have to go down there!

He   Wait.

She   What?

He   I'm begging you. One more time, just one more time, it's the only thing I need before I finally go out there, finally out there on the edge, before I hear the applause, there, once all of this anguish is over … One more time, please, and then I'll go down, I promise you.

She   What?

He   Tell me how it all was.

She   …

He   Tell me the whole thing again.

Abyss

A Tightrope

Abyss and this English translation were originally commissioned by Arca Images.

The play premiered at the Miami-Dade County Auditorium on 17 March 2022, produced by Arca Images, directed by Carlos Celdrán, with the following cast: George Akram, Luz Nicolás, Alina Robert and Larry Villanueva.

For my brother Josep Maria Miró,
maestro of abysses

Sections of the Tightrope

I. Indigenous Charm
II. A Scent from the Past
III. The Rigour of Our Craft
IV. The Risks of Intimacy
V. A Dazzling Legacy
VI. Pure Gold
VII. The Edge of the Desert
VIII. The Big Premiere of the Season

Characters

Isabel, *chair of the board of a large theatre*
Adolfo, *artistic director*
Lorena, *his daughter, company stage manager*
César, *her husband, actor*

The action takes place in the present day, in four locations in the theatre: the artistic director's office, the cafeteria, a corridor and the stage. Four spaces which, perhaps, are only one.

I

Indigenous Charm

Friday. Office. **Adolfo** *has a cellphone in his hands. Beside him,* **César**.

Adolfo   Did you read what happened at the gallery?

César   What?

Adolfo   It's scandalous. They just censored a Gauguin painting.

César   Gauguin, the French guy?

Adolfo   Yeah, this spectacular painting, look. (*Shows him on the phone.*)

César   I don't recall ever seeing it.

Adolfo   What? It's very well-known. From his indigenist phase. When he went to live in Tahiti.

César   Tahiti?

Adolfo   An island in the Pacific.

César   Gauguin lived in Tahiti?

Adolfo   They say it all started with a comment on the gallery's Instagram.

César   I hate Instagram.

Adolfo   One anonymous message and everything turns on its head.

César   What happened?

Adolfo   They took the painting down this morning and replaced it with a sign. It says … (*Reads.*) 'This work by Paul Gauguin has been withdrawn following confirmation that its content is inappropriate for public exhibition, in accordance with the moral principles of our institution.'

César *lets out a laugh.*

Adolfo   What are you laughing at?

César   'Moral principles.'

Adolfo   You think it's funny?

César   How did they not notice its 'inappropriate content' before?

Adolfo   The problem isn't the content. It's the fact they took it down. The anonymous comment went viral and they started getting dozens of complaints, from associations, people who felt insulted.

César   Insulted by what?

Adolfo   What's really insulting is the censorship.

César   This isn't fake news?

Adolfo   No.

César   Let me see the painting again.

Adolfo *shows him.*

César   I just see happy Indian girls … A nude man on a horse … And a lot of colours. Why are people scandalized?

Adolfo   According to the anonymous post, Gauguin painted those girls by day, and then by night, he …

César   Huh?

Adolfo   Yeah, the anonymous message accuses him of …

César   No way. (*Looks at the painting again.*)

Adolfo   They're just girls.

Cesár   Lying on the grass.

Adolfo   Laughing. Relaxed.

They look at the painting.

César   So, it's been proven that he …?

Adolfo   Well, it's on record that he lived there. He went to Tahiti to escape the vicious circle of Parisian art, in search of the exotic.

César   In search of the exotic?

Adolfo   I read somewhere he felt free to create there.

César   But the girls … He did something to them?

Adolfo   How would I know?

César   Didn't you say you read about his life?

Adolfo   Yes, but I didn't live with him there!

César   It's not the kind of thing you read about and forget.

Adolfo   I don't know. I'm interested in his paintings, César, the kind of artist he is.

César   You're interested in an artist like him?

Adolfo   Not just me. Millions of people like Gauguin the world over; his work gets exhibited in museums; he appears in Art History books –

César   That doesn't mean he can't have –

Adolfo   Of course, it means nothing more than that: he was a great painter.

César   You'd like to have one of his paintings in your house?

Adolfo   Don't be ridiculous, a Gauguin painting costs millions.

César   But if you could afford it, you'd have one?

Adolfo   What are you talking about?

César   You'd like to have one.

Adolfo   Who wouldn't?

César   In your living room, for example.

Adolfo   It's a classic!

César   This painting?

Adolfo   It's one of my favourites.

César   Even though you're not sure if the painter did things to those girls? I can't stop thinking about it since you told me.

Adolfo   Why are you thinking about that?

César   Painting girls over and over …

Adolfo   They're just a motif. His work is much more than that. Besides, maybe they're not girls exactly, if you look closely –

César   I see girls.

Adolfo   It's just a painting!

César   Sure, but a real person painted it.

Adolfo   Who died a long time ago.

César   Let's see … (*Looks for something on his cellphone.*)

Adolfo   He died in the early twentieth century.

César (*still looking*)   Of what?

Adolfo   I don't know. Old age?

César (*finds it*)   No. Syphilis.

Adolfo   You're sure?

César   The Internet says so.

Adolfo   A lot of people died of syphilis in those days.

César   Especially if you went around sticking it in everywhere.

Adolfo   You're an expert in his sex life now?

César   Doesn't take a genius to see he was promiscuous.

Adolfo   You worked all that out based on this painting?

César   No. (*Referring to the cellphone.*) It says here he got several adolescent indigenous girls pregnant ... and then abandoned them ... Bet you didn't know that.

Adolfo   ...

César   So?

Adolfo   What?

César   So what do you think?

Adolfo   Obviously, if he did that, it was wrong.

César   They're right to take his painting down.

Adolfo   Actually, if you look at it, the painting's more famous now than ever.

César   How come?

Adolfo   It's in all the newspapers, on all the websites.

César   ...

Adolfo   Imagine the thousands of people the world over looking at those girls right now?

César   ...

Adolfo   You hadn't seen it before and now you're an expert.

César   I did my research.

Adolfo   About something you knew nothing about fifteen minutes ago.

César   Of course I knew who Gauguin was!

Adolfo   Yeah, sure you knew.

César   What, you think I'm some kind of –

Adolfo   I'm just saying it's obviously backfired on the gallery.

César   It's the journalists, they always –

Adolfo   Journalists just report the news, that's their business. But they're not the ones who throw the shit. If the folks at the gallery hadn't made such a fuss in the first place, if they hadn't listened to that bunch of dumbasses screaming for an artist of his stature to be excommunicated, you and I wouldn't even be talking about this.

César   You still call someone like that an artist?

Adolfo   What?

César   When you know what he did.

Adolfo   You read four things on the Internet and –

César   You read what happened at the gallery on the Internet.

Adolfo   Yes, it was news, something that happened right here just a few hours ago. But all that business with Gauguin, if it happened, happened over a century ago and thousands of miles away. It's not the same, César.

César   People have a right to protest.

Adolfo   So let them.

César   They don't want their kids to be exposed to a piece of work … that they have doubts about, however important the artist is.

Adolfo   And doubting's for the wise, of course!

César   It's right they should ban the painting when he's suspected of something like that, Adolfo!

Adolfo   Sure, let's ban ourselves all the way back to the Stone Age!

César   Don't treat me like I'm an idiot!

Adolfo   Your words, not mine.

César   You can't stop me thinking he's abhorrent!

Adolfo   And you can't stop me thinking he's a genius!

Lorena *enters.*

Lorena   Dad.

Adolfo   Right, we have to start rehearsal.

César   We're coming.

Lorena   It's not that … Something's happened …

Adolfo   …

Lorena   You're not gonna like it.

II

A Scent from the Past

One week earlier. In the office, **Isabel** *and* **Adolfo**.

Adolfo 'I'm your grandma', she said, 'and now you're gonna go to bed and I'm gonna snuggle you up and sing lullabies until you go to sleep. Don't be a bad boy.' And then she started patting me on the back.

They laugh.

She's unbelievable.

Isabel How old is she now?

Adolfo Three.

Isabel Kids today, the things they come out with.

Adolfo She's like that every day. She plays at turning into a superhero ... And of course, she loves pretending to be members of the family ... Oh, and if you curse, she tells you right off, 'Grandpa, we don't say that word!'

They laugh.

Isabel Artist's DNA. That's what happens when you're born into the home of people with so much talent for theatre.

Adolfo It makes me so happy when she comes to wake me up every morning.

Isabel Lorena's back living with you, right?

Adolfo Yeah, after the separation. She wanted to rent an apartment on the Avenue or close to here. Not to be a burden, you know her. But I said no way.

Isabel It's good for you to have company. Since Estela died –

Adolfo Yes, it is.

Isabel Doesn't help to be alone.

Adolfo I feel very spoiled.

Isabel And so you should.

Adolfo …

Isabel You can count on me, Adolfo.

Adolfo I know.

Isabel A man like you doesn't deserve to stop having a love life just because of an accident.

Adolfo Thank you, Isabel.

Isabel I've been alone a long time. I know what I'm talking about. (*Moves a little closer.*) Maybe if –

Adolfo No, please.

Isabel I just think you and I –

Adolfo Please. Not again.

Isabel …

Adolfo …

Isabel I've always cared about you very much.

Adolfo And I've always been grateful.

Isabel …

Adolfo …

Isabel Well. The reason I came –

Adolfo The gala on Saturday.

Isabel The gala, yes.

Adolfo I've been meaning to ask … Ever since I read the email, I've been wondering if … Couldn't we do something more discreet?

Isabel What do you mean?

Adolfo The homage. Something more intimate.

Isabel Like with fewer people?

Adolfo Right, fewer people.

Isabel But it's an award in your honour. We're celebrating your whole career, an entire life dedicated to –

Adolfo That's what I'm saying. A homage without the excess.

Isabel Excess?

Adolfo You know I don't like being the centre of attention.

Isabel The official invites already went out. More than eighty people have confirmed, including the Secretary of Culture. He wants to give you the prize personally.

Adolfo I should have realized.

Isabel This award isn't just for you.

Adolfo It isn't?

Isabel It has your name on it but it's an award for our theatre, for our institution.

Adolfo   Such responsibility.

Isabel   Yes, they're acknowledging all of us. As chair of the board, I'm thrilled.

Adolfo   So am I.

Isabel   Can we talk about the dinner?

Adolfo   …

Isabel   I want to make sure it's all to your liking.

Adolfo   Whatever you decide is fine.

Isabel   No, I'm not having standard fayre or delegating it to your PA, this isn't just any dinner … I want every detail to be perfect. For example, since I know you like bacon –

Adolfo   Who said I like bacon?

Isabel   Huh?

Adolfo   …

Isabel   People.

Adolfo   People talk … about my tastes?

Isabel   Well, everyone knows –

Adolfo   Everyone?

Isabel   I did some research … I wanted to organize it without you finding out but in the end I decided it was better to come here and tell you all about it. Since I also know you don't like surprises.

Adolfo   But the bacon thing?

Isabel   It was just a comment, Adolfo. Don't be upset.

Adolfo   …

Isabel   If you don't like bacon, we can –

Adolfo   I do like bacon.

Isabel   So which is it?

Adolfo   I just didn't know it was public knowledge.

Isabel   It's not public knowledge.

Adolfo   It's not as though I like it especially.

Isabel   Fine!

Adolfo   How did we wind up talking about bacon?

Isabel   …

Adolfo I have to focus on the premiere. You really ought to ask Jenny these questions, she's much more practical than I am.

Isabel I don't want to ask Jenny, I want to ask you. Personally. I've had the courtesy to come here in person –

Adolfo We open in a week.

Isabel And it'll be another hit, I have not the slightest doubt. We've all put a lot into this production. *The Crucible*, directed by you, it'll be an event. Glory, Adolfo. A great title for a great occasion.

Adolfo …

Isabel Is there anything I can help you with? What about the technical department?

Adolfo All in order.

Isabel And the cast?

Adolfo All set.

Isabel No problems?

Adolfo None.

Isabel And that issue?

Adolfo Solved.

Isabel I'm glad to hear it. We're a family. We should keep it that way.

Adolfo …

Isabel …

Adolfo Is the mayor coming?

Isabel Wouldn't miss it.

Adolfo He's given us a lot of support lately.

Isabel I had dinner with him last night.

Adolfo He's getting better?

Isabel Still stable.

Adolfo I'd like him to come and give him a hug.

Isabel Politics and heart problems don't really go well together.

Adolfo No, they don't.

They smile.

Isabel He seemed on edge. There's some kind of trouble at the gallery.

Adolfo Trouble?

Isabel Yes, with the opening on Thursday.

Adolfo I read they're bringing an exhibition of impressionists … No, post-impressionists, who've never been seen in the city before.

Isabel I don't know what it is exactly. He didn't tell me.

Adolfo Probably nothing important.

Isabel …

Adolfo Are we done?

Isabel …

Adolfo Can I go?

Isabel Yeah, sure.

Adolfo It's just, I have a date with the dentist. A molar … giving me grief.

Isabel I was about to leave too.

Adolfo Need a ride someplace?

Isabel No, thanks. I'll call a cab.

Isabel's *cellphone pings; she has received a message. She looks at it.* **Adolfo** *makes to leave.*

Isabel Wait.

Adolfo (*stopping*)   What?

Isabel I don't know who sent this … I don't know the number.

Adolfo Ignore it.

Isabel It's a photo of you.

Adolfo Of me?

Isabel Yeah. An old photo … (*Shows it to him.*) That is you, right?

Adolfo …

Isabel And who's that guy next to you?

III

The Rigour of Our Craft

Friday. **César** *and* **Adolfo** *in the office.*

César Don't treat me like I'm an idiot!

Adolfo Your words, not mine.

César You can't stop me thinking he's abhorrent!

Adolfo And you can't stop me thinking he's a genius!

Lorena *enters.*

Lorena Dad.

Adolfo Right, we have to start rehearsal.

César We're coming.

Lorena It's not that … Something's happened …

Adolfo …

Lorena You're not gonna like it. I'd rather tell you … in private.

Adolfo Now you've got me worried.

César What is it, Lorena?

Lorena César –

César Please, what's the mystery?

Adolfo You'd better –

César Fine, I'll wait for you in the green room.

He exits.

Adolfo What's going on?

Lorena They're upset.

Adolfo Who's upset?

Lorena The cast … Not all of them, but several of them … They say until things are cleared up –

Adolfo This same thing again?

Lorena They're refusing to rehearse.

Adolfo Like they have a choice.

Lorena They don't think the committee acted properly.

Adolfo   The committee did what it had to do.

Lorena   I know, but –

Adolfo   Isabel listened to them.

Lorena   They insist the complaint wasn't properly heard. Ana, Marietta … They're not happy.

Adolfo   There's no reason for –

Lorena   It's mainly them, but there are others, who were unsure, and they've joined them … I told them to get ready to start rehearsing again and …

Adolfo   They ignored you?

Lorena   They stayed sitting down. Ana had her legs crossed on top of the table and she gestured at me like this, with her hand, totally inappropriate.

Adolfo   She's so vulgar.

Lorena   That's not the point right now.

Adolfo   I don't know how she got into this company, how her contract gets renewed year after year.

Lorena   Don't start with that.

Adolfo   She's such a mediocre actress.

Lorena   Dad!

Adolfo   Her diction is terrible, she trails off at the end of every sentence, you have to correct every detail, she overacts all of her lines … I've had to put up with it throughout this whole process. For weeks she's had a face like she's just smelled a fart.

Lorena   Those kinds of comments –

Adolfo   Yes, I know, they don't help.

Lorena   It was the first piece of advice the lawyer gave you: be polite, stay composed.

Adolfo   It's just the two of us in here.

Lorena   Walls have ears.

Adolfo   Can't I have a cast that's normal? My God, that's all I ask.

Lorena   You have the cast you chose.

Adolfo   Not those two, they were foisted onto me.

Lorena   This is exactly what I mean when I ask you not to talk that way.

Adolfo   Just because they're women, right?

Lorena We work together. We have to try to fix this.

Adolfo It already was fixed.

Lorena Maybe for you, Dad, but it feels very different out there.

Adolfo …

Lorena *pours a glass of water and gives it to him. He drinks slowly.*

Adolfo I'll go talk to them.

Lorena I don't know if –

Adolfo We have to calm things down, we open tomorrow.

Lorena They're threatening –

Adolfo They've lost their minds –

Lorena – not to do the premiere.

Adolfo How can they be so unprofessional?

Lorena I agree with you.

Adolfo How dare they?

Lorena They don't care.

Adolfo Those two little brats are not going to cancel my premiere.

Lorena Dad!

Adolfo They're just bitter.

Lorena Yes, but –

Adolfo They've never played a decent role in their lives! They get the chance to work with me and … this is what they do? Conspiring behind my back?

Lorena People feel what they feel.

Adolfo Half the city is coming tomorrow, the whole theatre's sold out, and they're trying to stop the premiere?

Lorena You're still talking in that tone and you don't realize –

Adolfo What tone?!

Lorena That tone, Dad!

Adolfo …

Lorena What's happening out there is serious. There's no point insulting anyone.

Adolfo So now I'm to blame.

Lorena I'm not talking about blame. But you're the one they accused a month ago over what happened at the rehearsal.

Adolfo …

Lorena They did it, Dad. However much it upsets us. Even though we know it's ridiculous. They raised a complaint of verbal and physical assault. In that Facebook post they insinuated –

Adolfo You were there that day, Lorena … I just spoke a little louder so they'd understand they were still getting it wrong, I went over to Marietta, I took her by the arm –

Lorena You don't need to explain yourself to me.

Adolfo A rehearsal room is not a monastery! We can't tiptoe around whispering and not touching each other!

Lorena Of course not.

Adolfo Theatre is made with blood, with pain, with rage!

Lorena And with the people you work with. In a collective. People who are all different and who don't have to put up with certain things.

Adolfo What things?

Lorena You say you took her by the arm, she says you pushed her and hurt her.

Adolfo I didn't hurt her, you saw it yourself.

Lorena I don't know, Dad, you're from different generations.

Adolfo Respect for the theatre, for a playwright, for a premiere … comes above generations and these … susceptibilities.

Lorena They're demanding respect too. In their way.

Adolfo It's the rigour of our craft. I didn't assault her, I've been this way my whole life.

Lorena But times change.

Adolfo I'm getting the impression … Are you taking their side?

Lorena Don't talk nonsense. I'm just trying to be neutral.

Adolfo …

Lorena …

Adolfo Why have they waited until now to bring this up?

Lorena They've been dropping hints on the WhatsApp group for days … It was inevitable.

Adolfo Why, when the committee reported back and found it had all been a … misunderstanding …? Why didn't they complain then?

Lorena Well, why do you think they waited until the last minute?

Adolfo I should have had them replaced.

Lorena You know that wasn't an option. It would have been worse. They'd have felt … even more assaulted.

Adolfo …

Lorena …

Adolfo I'll go talk to them, before this whole thing turns into chaos. Convince them.

He approaches the door. She stands in his way.

Lorena They don't want you to convince them. They don't want to talk to you until –

Adolfo I'm their director.

Lorena They want another meeting, with witnesses, and for you to admit –

Adolfo What are they talking about? We open tomorrow.

Lorena They want a meeting with all of the board, not just a handpicked committee. A meeting with a union representative present and someone from the City Hall gender equality department.

Adolfo What?

Lorena They don't trust that decisions made internally … will be fair. Impartial.

Adolfo And they want the guy from City Hall to guarantee what?

Lorena The woman from City Hall.

Adolfo Right, that figures.

Lorena They're probably with Isabel right now.

Adolfo Just like that, they go to her office? With no appointment or anything?

Lorena They'll try to make her see them.

Adolfo She'll stop them in their tracks.

Lorena Let's hope so.

Adolfo …

Lorena …

Adolfo Marcos, Aníbal … Have they said anything?

Lorena They've kept quiet.

Adolfo Typical.

Lorena They haven't supported them.

Adolfo They haven't challenged them either.

Lorena You think they're …?

Adolfo No. I don't want to get paranoid.

Lorena …

Adolfo Having to deal with this, Lore … We have a dress rehearsal in a few minutes, that's the only thing we should be worrying about.

Lorena We have to sort this out first, Dad.

César *enters.*

Lorena What?

César Isabel. (*To* **Adolfo**.) She says she wants to see you right away.

IV

The Risks of Intimacy

One month earlier. Cafeteria. Seated, having a snack, **Lorena** *and* **Isabel**.

Lorena   Good sandwich, right?

Isabel   Too much mustard for my taste.

Lorena   I like mustard.

Isabel   I like home-made mustard. But this mass-produced stuff … tastes of plastic.

Lorena   Home-made mustard is a thing?

Isabel   I make it at home for oily fish.

Lorena   You eat oily fish with mustard?

Isabel   Always have.

Lorena   Really?

Isabel   My grandma used to make it.

Lorena   I never would have thought of that.

Isabel   Well, it tastes great.

Lorena   You'll have to have us over some day, now it's just me and Julia again.

Isabel   Just you two?

Lorena   …

Isabel   Lore …

Lorena   We're separating.

Isabel   Oh, no … But César's such a good guy.

Lorena   …

Isabel   You're the perfect couple …

Lorena   …

Isabel   …

Lorena   I can't stand how cheery he's being, seeing him smiling every morning.

Isabel   He's trying to make the days easier for you.

Lorena   He's acting … as if nothing had happened. Rehearsals, routine … He takes Julia to the park, plays paddle tennis with her …

Isabel It's normal for you to feel like this after such a loss … But it's not good for you to be alone.

Lorena …

Isabel Don't take it out on César.

Lorena I've felt so fraught lately, I just think maybe I need some time to myself.

Isabel …

Lorena Thanks for always being there, Isabel.

Isabel …

Lorena I've been too close to death … Something so sudden, so unexpected …

Isabel Yes, it's horrible.

Lorena Now I need to fight to get better. I want to focus on the things that are really important in my life. My daughter. My work.

Isabel You're getting divorced?

Lorena Not for now, we're going to give it some time. I'll move out with Julia, it'll be good for the three of us.

Isabel That's for the best.

Lorena Why?

Isabel I don't know … There's no need to rush, maybe you'll work it out.

Lorena What difference does it make if I get divorced or not?

Isabel None, Lore. Calm down. You just caught me by surprise, is all … Everything's so stirred up …

Lorena …

Isabel You know what I'm talking about.

They stare at each other.

You know.

Lorena …

Isabel …

Lorena I should have known this was why you wanted to see me.

Isabel I –

Lorena Let's cut to the chase. We haven't sat down to talk in months. Why else would you suddenly ask to meet me?

Isabel …

Lorena She's been to see you.

Isabel I wish you had. Not your father, I wouldn't have expected it from him, to come, he's too proud ... But you, I trust you, you're the company stage manager, you should have come and told me.

Lorena I thought it was just a squabble. That it wouldn't leave the rehearsal room.

Isabel But it did.

Lorena ...

Isabel I always like to be the first person to hear about any trouble, so I can deal with it.

Lorena I'm sorry.

Isabel I know that after Estela died –

Lorena Mom dying has nothing to do with this.

Isabel Adolfo, just like you, has had a difficult time, and that's normal. Something so traumatic takes ... months to get over. Years. He's been restive. I talked to the doctor, he insisted he rest for another couple of weeks, maybe another month. There was no hurry for him to come back ... Don't you think he started working again too soon?

Lorena The date was already set for the premiere.

Isabel It would have been easy to change.

Lorena He wouldn't get better staying at home.

Isabel People would have understood ... A normal period of mourning, it's the least ... But instead he comes back so soon, starts the project again in such a rush –

Lorena He's always been that way, you know that, he's very strict with his theatre commitments.

Isabel It almost seems arrogant of him to assume ... that he can do everything, when in reality –

Lorena Dad is perfectly well enough to be directing!

Isabel You're sure about that?

Lorena He was when he came back two weeks ago and he is now.

Isabel That's not the impression I got when I went to visit him.

Lorena ...

Isabel Yes, when I went to his house, a few days after the funeral.

Lorena So, what impression did you get?

Isabel He was kind of withdrawn. He was absent, Lorena.

Lorena Of course. At home. After losing his wife, depressed, shut away, not even picking up the phone ... He wasn't seeing anyone, but you're his best friend so he saw you. And the one thing you picked up on was that he was 'absent'? What the hell did you expect?

Isabel   …

Lorena   I should go. (*Makes to get up.*)

Isabel   Wait a second, please.

Lorena *breathes. She sits back down.*

Isabel   I'm sorry, I'm … on edge. Marietta came to the office and … I don't want this getting out of hand.

Lorena   That day, before you visited, I went to his place and we talked a lot. I convinced him to start taking the pills. It's thanks to them that he stabilized.

Isabel   …

Lorena   He would never go into a rehearsal in a state that would prevent him from …

Isabel   …

Lorena   Did Marietta insinuate something?

Isabel   No, no … It's me, I want to be up to speed so I can head off any –

Lorena   What exactly did she say to you?

Isabel   She said 'deranged'.

Lorena   Deranged?

Isabel   That was the word she used. 'Adolfo's deranged and I'm not putting up with it.' She said she didn't like the way he looked at her or the way he spoke to her … Said she felt isolated and sometimes wouldn't dare ask a question for fear of getting an unpleasant answer … But that this time he'd gone too far: he'd grabbed her angrily by the arm, she even showed me the marks, the indents from his fingernails … She says he pushed her –

Lorena   She's making Dad look like a –

Isabel   – and threw her to the floor.

Lorena   No, Marietta tripped and fell, we all saw it. Do you really believe – ?

Isabel   I'm telling you exactly what she said. A few minutes later, Ana came in and added to the story, she gave more details, and some from other days, too.

Lorena   …

Isabel   Apparently, they felt uncomfortable when one of the male actors –

Lorena   Who?

Isabel   Aníbal. There's a scene where Marietta and Aníbal –

Lorena   It lasts two seconds.

Isabel Well, she felt uncomfortable.

Lorena Aníbal made her feel uncomfortable?

Isabel No, Adolfo did. He directed Aníbal to touch her.

Lorena Well, actors in theatre touch each other.

Isabel According to them, in this case, he insisted it be unnecessarily forceful. They say Aníbal tried to do it more gently, but Adolfo insisted on it being aggressive.

Lorena Dad didn't insist on anything, he's just staging the scene as it is, the way Miller wrote it.

Isabel Scenes can be interpreted in a lot of ways.

Lorena Yes, but this is his way. The way he imagines it, the way he sees it. It's his taste, it's his point of view. He's the artistic director for a reason.

Isabel No one's saying otherwise, but you have to understand they have a right to an opinion.

Lorena What they're saying is not objective!

Isabel And when the subject is your father, neither are you.

Lorena …

Isabel …

Lorena I thought it was clear that I'm professional enough to separate family from work.

Isabel I'm not questioning your professionalism, Lorena. But at least admit that in a situation like this you can't help but take a position.

Lorena I'm not taking a position.

Isabel Unconsciously, you are.

Lorena …

Isabel If this got reported, if it went to a jury –

Lorena Why are you talking about a jury?

Isabel – you wouldn't be allowed to defend him because you work with him and you're his daughter.

Lorena It was you who agreed to me having this job.

Isabel I've never had any hesitation supporting your career, standing beside you, helping you grow this far. I know how good your father is. I know how good you are. Your dedication, your discipline. You're his right hand, especially at a moment like this. Which is why I need your help.

Lorena …

Isabel You say he's in a fit state to direct, and I trust you. This is the most hotly awaited premiere of the season, Lorena, and I only want to read headlines about art, you understand? You remember what happened at the Opera House last winter, don't you? We can't allow a scandal like that here.

Lorena There's not going to be any scandal.

Isabel Most of the company is loyal to Adolfo, but those two young girls ... They have ideas that they believe are irrefutable ... The way they promote themselves on social media, the comments they post ... But lately I've seen public opinion support all kinds of things, I don't know ... Maybe I was wrong to renew their contracts ... But the fact is they're in the cast now and we have to make a deal.

Lorena ...

Isabel I'll put a small committee together to look into it. There's no need to tell the whole board, it would only arouse suspicion ... The committee will give Ana and Marietta an official response and that will satisfy them.

Lorena ...

Isabel I also thought ... I could hire an intimacy director.

Lorena An intimacy director?

Isabel It's working very well in other places.

Lorena Is this a joke?

Isabel No, I read about it. I have friends – directors, journalists – they applaud it.

Lorena It's quackery.

Isabel It's someone who ... makes sure things don't go too far when actors have to touch each other.

Lorena You were laughing at this just months ago, you said it was moralist nonsense.

Isabel We didn't have a problem like this just months ago.

Lorena It's absurd to have someone come and –

Isabel It's not absurd if it keeps peace within the company.

Lorena So this holy intimacy director comes armed with a magic wand?

Isabel My duty is to protect the reputation of this theatre. That's the only thing that concerns me. Adolfo will accept this intimacy director. I'm doing it to protect him. The committee will analyse what happened and, above all, apologize to those two girls.

Lorena It was just a misunderstanding in the middle of a rehearsal.

Isabel Whatever it was, Lorena. Whatever it was. I want this issue buried. And I want to know I can count on you.

V

A Dazzling Legacy

Friday. A corridor. **Isabel** *faints.*

César Isabel …

Helps her.

Sit here, come on.

Isabel I'm all right.

César That's it, sit here.

Helps her to sit on a bench.

What's wrong?

Isabel I just felt kinda woozy.

César I'll get you a coffee.

Isabel I think so. I could do with one.

César *approaches the coffee machine, inserts a pod and presses a button.*

Isabel …

César …

Isabel You were with Adolfo?

César Yeah, in the office. We were heading to the rehearsal when –

Isabel Did you know about all this?

The coffee is ready.

César You want sugar?

Isabel No, thanks.

He passes her the cup.

Did you know anything?

César You mean …?

Isabel Yes.

César Well, only what all of us who were there at the rehearsal that afternoon know … What the committee said.

Isabel But you knew those girls were still upset, offended?

César They never stopped being.

Isabel That day … Did you think he shouted at them? That he lost it with Marietta, that he pushed her on purpose?

César He has a strong character, you know him … He's been my teacher ever since I started acting school, I'm used to him sometimes –

Isabel So he did do it.

César Adolfo's a great director.

Isabel And that scene where Ana gets dragged along the floor …

César Yes, after she's accused.

Isabel Is that scene completely necessary?

César It's in the text.

Isabel But is it necessary?

César You haven't been to any of the rehearsals this week?

Isabel I was supposed to go today.

César Supposed? We are having the dress rehearsal today, right?

Isabel …

César What's going on?

Isabel They ambushed me outside my office again.

César Who?

Isabel Ana and Marietta … Then Sonia came and some of the others. They said a whole bunch of things …

César …

Isabel Marietta says she's been affected psychologically. Says she can't sleep, says this whole situation has left her traumatized. She says Adolfo terrifies her.

César Terrifies her?

Isabel …

César …

Isabel When I agreed to be chair of the board … When they painted such a great picture, so I'd accept, of course … I said to myself, 'It'll only be a few years, you'll focus on taking the theatre forward, upholding its reputation, getting even more international exposure, turning it into a beacon of good taste … And then you'll hand the baton to someone else who, thanks to the seeds you'll have sown, will continue with your work on solid foundations.' Ever since then I have lived and breathed this place, lain awake thinking about it, felt happy about it, about everything it's achieved and how much what we do here means to people … Just a few years, I said … And how long has it been now since that day I accepted? You'd have been a kid … Was

I dutybound to say yes, for family, for tradition? To continue the empire my uncle and my mother had built up, getting themselves into debt, fighting with all the people who didn't believe in them, overcoming all the adversity, almost turning it into a temple? I said yes without realizing I'd be mortgaging my whole life.

César   No one can say you haven't more than fulfilled your mission.

Isabel   This building's my home. Everything I love is here, everything I fear, everything that makes me happy … I used to run through these corridors as a girl. We said goodbye to Mom forever on this stage … I thought I knew everything that went on between these walls.

César   …

Isabel   And now I'm tormented by the idea that something terrible could have happened here without me being able to see it.

César   …

Isabel   Someone sent a photo to my phone the other day.

César   A photo?

Isabel   It was kind of blurry, but you can make out Adolfo laughing with some young guy. An old photo, years old, in black and white. Adolfo has a hand on the kid's shoulder and he's laughing. They're both laughing. In profile. I couldn't tell who the guy was at first.

César   What was so strange about it?

Isabel   It seemed … odd that someone should send it to me, and from a number I didn't recognize.

César   You showed it to Adolfo?

Isabel   Yes.

César   You asked him about it?

Isabel   It was his reaction that alarmed me most.

César   …

Isabel   He was surprised, and then … he seemed confused. Like he was hiding something from me.

César   What would he want to hide?

Isabel   …

César   Couldn't it be a joke?

Isabel   That's what I forced myself to think … until this morning.

César   …

Isabel   I had a letter from Henry Méndez.

César Henry Méndez?

Isabel He worked with Adolfo on that *Hamlet* you'll have heard about.

César …

Isabel He played Horatio very young, barely seventeen years old, I remember it well … He was a student at our school. I never liked him, he was too conceited. But Adolfo defended him, there was something about Henry that drew him to him, and he insisted on giving him the part … These days we'd think twice about casting a student, a minor, in a professional production. The closeness, the contact, you can imagine … But at that time it didn't occur to us it could be a problem.

César …

Isabel He spent … two or three seasons with the company. And then he disappeared.

César How come?

Isabel Life. He wasn't a good actor.

César What does he say in the letter?

Isabel He found out about the award Adolfo's getting tomorrow and, according to him, he can't stay silent any longer.

César Silent about what?

Isabel He's giving a TV interview tomorrow and … accusing Adolfo of assaulting him.

César Adolfo?

Isabel He says he wants to talk about how Adolfo forcibly seduced him when he was a teenager. Forced him to have sex with him.

César No way.

Isabel Right here, in the theatre.

César …

Isabel …

César But … if it happened so long ago … why go digging it up now?

Isabel He's asked me to meet him before the interview. Out of respect for me, he says.

César And you said yes?

Isabel My head's so jumbled up right now.

César But where's this guy been all these years?

Isabel I lost track of him ... I searched his name online yesterday and ... there's not much there. He made a short film, taught a mime workshop ...

César Maybe he's done nothing major since he left here ... How long ago was it?

Isabel I don't know ... Thirty years.

César So ... in the photo ...

Isabel Adolfo's at least ten years older than him.

César ...

Isabel ...

César Who took the picture?

Isabel God knows.

César ...

Isabel Why is everything coming all at once?

César You think Marietta and Ana – ?

Isabel They refuse to perform at the premiere tomorrow unless he publicly acknowledges –

César They can't do this to us. What about the others?

Isabel The company's very divided.

César They signed a contract. Actors don't have the legal authority to –

Isabel Trust me, people's legal authority is the least important thing right now.

César ...

Isabel ...

César This can't be a coincidence ... The homage, this obsession of theirs, the letter ...

Isabel ...

César I owe you a lot, Isabel. Whatever decision you have to make ... I'll support you.

Isabel ...

César ...

Isabel You ... You've been very close to Adolfo for years ... You were his student. You're his son-in-law.

César ...

Isabel Did he ever ...? With you, did you maybe ever notice that he ...?

César …

Isabel Not even – ?

César Never. Absolutely nothing.

Isabel …

César …

Isabel I'm sorry.

César Don't worry.

Isabel …

César …

Isabel Could you ask Adolfo to come in here?

VI

Pure Gold

Two and a half months earlier. The stage of the theatre. **Adolfo** *speaks to the cast and creative team of the new production.*

Adolfo   The device constructed by Arthur Miller is fascinating: by taking us to another era, to a seemingly distant conflict, recreating the Salem witch trials, he speaks about his own time, exposing the horrors of McCarthyism, an out-of-control, ideologically motivated purge. We cannot, therefore, begin rehearsing this play without bearing this in mind: although we may find the plot and the characters extremely seductive, we have also to intuit that the playwright is asking us to delve into something beyond these words, landscapes and behaviours. There is an invisible thread that connects centuries and spaces, presenting us with this small Massachusetts hamlet in 1692 as if it were our country, our city, our time. Even when the parallels are not immediately obvious, the aura of intolerance and blindness continues to besiege us. I would even go so far as to say more today than at any time in the past few decades.

Silence.

Over the past week we've exchanged all sorts of ideas about the text, its dramatic structure, the behaviour of the characters and the unfathomable ethical map that emerges from the storyline. I'd like to return to some of your observations on Monday. For example, Elizabeth Proctor's lie to the court, a white lie intended to hide her husband's moral failings, becomes the key to John's downfall. As if the playwright were punishing the fear, the shame, or the strange impulse that led an irreproachable woman to lie, albeit for the first and only time in her life.

Silence.

The title of the play, *The Crucible*, is in of itself a powerful metaphor: the receptacle in which certain materials are melted down at very high temperatures. Did you know that the industrial process used for refining gold is called 'the Miller process'? But not for Arthur Miller; rather, for someone who was born almost a century earlier, in England: Francis Bowyer Miller. His famous method for refining and hardening gold using chlorine gas was patented in London in 1867 and in a very short time spread throughout Australia, New Zealand, Europe and the United States. This curious connection between the two Millers has always fascinated me: the idea of purification. The playwright chooses a highly poetic title, combining semantic force and exquisite phonetics: *The Crucible*. As if the delicacy of its pronunciation were trying to mitigate the violence of the chemical processes that will be used to cleanse the most precious of metals.

Silence. His cellphone rings. He rejects the call.

But the crucible also refers to a place, a situation where human beings and their ideas are put severely to the test. A test from which something new and exciting will result. Just like what happens onstage, in this difficult romance we establish with the audience. In reality, Arthur Miller gives his play a title that is addressed to us, the actors: our bodies will be the impure metal, and the stage, the crucible in which the purification will occur, before a courtroom occupied by the audience. Embodying Miller's characters means nothing less than discovering ourselves and facing our own deepest demons. Discovering, if this were possible, the roots of our very truth.

His cellphone rings again. He rejects the call again.

You will understand now why I find some of the translations of the title into other languages alarming. Calling the play, as it's known in Spanish, *Las brujas de Salem*, *The Witches of Salem*, when its original title is *The Crucible*, strikes me as a frankly unacceptable act of vulgarity. Because the title is incorrect and imprecise not only linguistically, but also conceptually, turning the parabolic magma of a noun that blends the abstract and the concrete into the extreme crudeness of literal nomenclature.

His cellphone rings.

Sorry. I don't know what's going on. I'll just be a second. (*Steps away briefly. Speaks into the phone.*) Yes, what is it?

Silence.

Yes, of course, she's my wife.

Silence.

What?

VII

The Edge of the Desert

Friday. Office.

Adolfo Having to deal with this, Lore … We have a dress rehearsal in a few minutes, that's the only thing we should be worrying about.

Lorena We have to sort this out first, Dad.

César *enters.*

Lorena What?

César Isabel. (*To* **Adolfo**.) She says she wants to see you right away.

Adolfo …

Lorena Watch what you say, please.

Adolfo She's in her office?

Lorena Listen to her carefully.

César I left her on the second floor, sitting by the coffee machine. She said she'd wait for you there.

Adolfo Why there?

César You should use the stairs by the dressing rooms.

Adolfo By the dressing rooms?

César Don't go through the green room.

Adolfo *looks at* **Lorena**. *He exits.*

Lorena What's going on in the green room?

César When I went back in there … Ana called me over, she asked me whose side I was on.

Lorena What does she think this is, a boxing ring?

César I'm just telling you.

Lorena Now you're defending her.

César I'm not defending her.

Lorena First you're bitching about her, calling her 'vulgar'; now you're sleeping with her.

César Why do I have to put up with – ?

Lorena   You are together, right?

César   Lorena –

Lorena   You're a terrible liar.

César   …

Lorena   You sure got over our break-up quickly … What happened to that emptiness you were feeling? Barely three weeks pass and you're already rubbing up against her.

César   You're the one who decided to leave!

Lorena   Apparently, the best thing I ever did!

César   Why do you have to treat me like a piece of shit? Why do you have to be so angry with me? There's been no peace between us for months, Lorena. We had … so many dreams … We have a daughter to bring up together … What happened? Why could you suddenly not stand me any more?

Lorena   None of this was sudden.

César   I've been putting up with this horrible situation for so long … Even folks here at the theatre have noticed. You're so withdrawn, more and more closed in on yourself, more serious. Ever since your mom died –

Lorena   Don't bring Mom into this.

César   Ever since she died … you've been a different person. Everyone, all the magazines focusing on Adolfo, following him, hounding him, but what about you?

Lorena   …

César   What's going on, Lore? (*Approaches her.*)

Lorena   Are you with Ana?

César   Quit stonewalling. That's not what's bothering you.

Lorena   How do you know?

César   I don't have feelings for Ana. Yes, something happened one night, we'd been at the bar, I thought you wouldn't find out … It was stupid … You're not home and I can't get used to … to being without you, without Julia.

Lorena   Don't bring my daughter into this.

César   She's my daughter too. And these past weeks I've settled for seeing her for a little while once every two days. You said you wanted space and I gave it to you. But it's not the fix you want it to be. It's pointless being apart like this, it's not working for either of us. It's driving me crazy. And you're still sad, you're still suffering.

Lorena   …

César   There's no one I care more about than you. There's no one I love more than you and Julia.

Lorena ...

César Forgive me, please. Come home. We'll talk it out, whatever it is.

She sobs slightly. He approaches slowly.

César Honey ...

Lorena I feel like ... everything's falling apart ...

César (*takes one of her hands*) Easy, easy ...

Lorena ...

César We're in this boat together, Lore.

He hugs her tightly. She slowly moves away.

Lorena We open tomorrow and I'm freaking out about these things!

César These are the things that matter.

Lorena An opening night we might not even have.

César Of course we'll have an opening night. This will all get fixed. Adolfo and the girls ... They'll work it out.

Lorena I'm not so sure.

César They will.

Lorena Dad has not been well these past few weeks. I shouldn't have let him start work again so soon, not before he'd gotten better.

César We talked about this at the time, when Isabel had her doubts. You thought he was ready.

Lorena Maybe I just didn't want him shut away at home any more.

César He's put so much into this. He's made a beautiful show, it's visceral. I've never known his imagination soar this way ... He's directed us so well, we can all feel it.

Lorena So how come some of them are so upset?

César It's just those two. They started this and now they're trying to infect everyone else.

Lorena Do you think he mistreated them?

César I don't think so, but ...

Lorena But you're a man.

César There are plenty of women in this theatre who love your father. Even in this company, Norma was saying to me just today how happy she's been.

Lorena They're good friends. And besides, she's playing the lead.

César Laura really respects him too. She's thrilled about the award, she thinks he more than deserves it.

Lorena Dad doesn't hate women, does he?

César What the hell are you talking about?

Lorena He is a good man, right? He's not one of those sleazebags who take advantage of their position, the ones in the news the world over who've been accused of –

César No, Lore.

Lorena I'm so close to him I can't tell. I feel like something's about to break.

César …

Lorena I woke up in the night screaming again, in the middle of that stupid nightmare.

César …

Lorena Mom and Dad arguing on top of a mountain of sand. She's talking really loudly, he seems kind of stunned … Mom takes a rotten apple out from her pocket and he, he's dumbfounded, he tries to run away but it's hard because his feet sink deeper and deeper into the sand, until he grows wings that carry him away. Mom follows him, she's on metal wheels, I don't know, or are they bristles? She tries to catch him, but she can't … The desert ends, over in the distance, at a precipice. Mom runs, I shout, I scream for her to stop, but all she can see and hear is Dad, flying up high, too high … She runs and runs faster, Dad disappears into the clouds. And then Mom, who's been looking up at the sky all this time, she reaches the edge of the desert, the end of the world, she trips on a little stone, a tiny pebble, and she falls, with a deafening roar, into the abyss.

César …

Lorena …

César …

Lorena Today I had to put up with Marcos telling me I was going to end up like Mom.

César …

Lorena Hanging myself from a rope.

César What the hell's wrong with him?

Lorena No, César –

César He's been goading me for days to break his face open.

Lorena Please, let's not make things any worse.

César   They don't want us here, Lore. They never have. They've always thought of us as freeloaders.

Lorena   …

César   So close to your dad, taking advantage of him, the legendary Adolfo Sierra. Movie icon. The most famous theatre director in the country.

Lorena   …

César   They can't stand that he respects me so much. That he cast me as John Proctor.

Lorena   …

César   They think they have the right to judge us all the time, for anything.

Lorena   …

César   And he's been fair. We argue a lot, yes, but he's fair … He makes me think, confuses me sometimes … I admire his knowledge, his wisdom, his generosity … He's been a role model for me for years, he's the actor I'd like to become one day … And despite all that, deep down, I think I don't know him. But isn't that where his charm lies? In the mystery? Isn't that what fascination is? Never quite understanding someone?

Lorena   …

César   I don't know where that philosophy sprang from.

Lorena   Do you think it was his fault Mom killed herself?

César   What?

Lorena   Suddenly –

César   He's your father. Don't do that to him.

Lorena   …

César   Don't do that to yourself.

Silence.

Lorena   I'm not sure all this will make any more sense tomorrow.

César   …

Lorena   Me and you. Us.

César   …

Lorena   This isn't because of you. I have to work this out for myself. And it isn't about Ana. Or that deafening noise threatening to destroy us.

César   …

Lorena I admit it, César: I can't put us back together. So much time spent with you, with Dad, within the dark walls of this stage … It hasn't exactly made me more enthusiastic. Or more insightful. I know onstage I might seem like the calmest, most exceptional woman there is, there, hidden behind the curtains, giving all the cues so meticulously and brilliantly. But after the curtain call, when I have to go home, that's when I fall apart inside.

César …

Lorena I don't want this agony anymore. I don't deserve it. Maybe I never did.

César *goes to speak.*

Lorena Not now. All I want is to stop this whole thing from sinking.

Silence. **Lorena** *makes to leave. Suddenly,* **César** *speaks.*

César Did you ever hear of Henry Méndez?

Lorena (*stops*) From *Hamlet*? … He hated Dad.

César He did?

Lorena He never forgave Dad for being such a success … Some folks say Henry fell hopelessly in love with him.

César …

Lorena Why are you asking me about Henry?

VIII

The Big Premiere of the Season

The corridor.

Adolfo Why are you hiding here like a stowaway?

Isabel There's a revolt in the green room … You'll have heard that from Lorena. Three times they knocked on my office door and I had to see them. They've gone crazy … I needed some peace. Somewhere quiet to think for a few minutes.

Adolfo You have to let me talk to them.

Isabel This wouldn't be happening if you'd listened to me and we'd kept the intimacy director in the rehearsals.

Adolfo What?

Isabel Yes, I offered you a simple solution, you just had to yield a little, but –

Adolfo It was ridiculous.

Isabel Why do you have to be so difficult?

Adolfo You should have seen him. I couldn't concentrate. The face he made when César and Laura were touching, in the scene where they embrace … They were fine, but there he was, behind me, muttering.

Isabel Maybe Laura wasn't so fine.

Adolfo What?

Isabel You don't think maybe she just keeps quiet, rather than refusing to do what you ask?

Adolfo I have always given my actors freedom, they're the ones who come up with –

Isabel No, they don't always feel free.

Adolfo Where are you getting this from?

Isabel Marietta had to go to her doctor, she's been put on treatment for her nerves.

Adolfo What does that have to do with me?

Isabel Laura told her she's uncomfortable but she's scared to tell you.

Adolfo Scared?

Isabel They're terrified of you, Adolfo. You're getting more violent by the day.

Adolfo Laura came to your office?

Isabel No, it's what Marietta says.

Adolfo   What do those girls have against me?

Isabel   You should have let the intimacy director –

Adolfo   The only director in that room is me!

Isabel   Then accept you're the only one responsible for your actions!

Adolfo   …

Isabel   …

Adolfo   What are you talking about?

Isabel   Do you dislike them … because they're women?

Adolfo   Can you hear yourself? No, this can't be –

Isabel   Is that what it is?

Adolfo   Are you accusing me of – ?

Isabel   Were you ever inappropriate with a male student at the school?

Adolfo   …

Isabel   Did you ever pressure one of the young guys into – ?

Adolfo   Isabel!

Isabel   Answer my question!

Adolfo   Which one? Because suddenly it's like I'm here with a police officer endlessly interrogating me and not with someone who's been my friend for all these years.

Isabel   Please, tell me you've never –

Adolfo   No! Of course I haven't!

Isabel   So why, now, now of all times, does this ghost appear?

She looks for something on her cellphone and shows him. Warily, he reads for a few seconds.

Adolfo   …

Isabel   You understand I find this alarming?

Adolfo   …

Isabel   You and Henry were such good friends.

Adolfo   I swear –

Isabel   Why would he need to invent this now?

Adolfo   …

Isabel   Right now.

Adolfo   Evil … has no explanation. It has no time.

César *enters with his cellphone in his hand.*

César   Have you seen it?

Isabel   What?

César   Henry Méndez …

Adolfo   What about Henry Méndez?

César   He's accused you, Adolfo.

Shows him his cellphone. **Adolfo** *reads.*

César   He's posted it online.

Isabel   Posted what?

César   A link to an interview he just did. Alongside the same photo, Isabel.

Adolfo (*looking up from the phone*)   You'd seen this photo before?

César   I … It was just –

Adolfo (*to* **Isabel**)   You've been showing this photo to people?

Isabel   Henry found my number and asked to talk to me, he wanted to make a deal. And if I didn't, he threatened to –

Adolfo   What deal?

Isabel   He said he'd been in touch with people from the company, he knew how much hostility –

Adolfo   The two things have nothing to do with each other!

César   Well, that's not so clear to this journalist.

Adolfo   How dare they publish these lies?

César   You're sure it's a lie?

Adolfo   What the hell are you insinuating?

Isabel   Please, calm down!

Adolfo   Where's Lorena?

César   She saw that Ana had shared the link to the interview and she went to the green room to ask her to delete it.

Adolfo   She shouldn't be with those people.

He makes to exit when **Lorena** *enters, upset.*

Lorena   Dad!

Isabel   What's happened?

Adolfo   Lore!

Lorena   They're like animals! I had to tell them you'd left the theatre, that I'd seen you leaving … so they'd leave me alone and not follow me here.

Isabel   It can't be …

Lorena   The interview, with all those lies, it's everywhere … It's all they're talking about. Marietta's gotten hysterical, she insulted me … Jaime screamed at me, 'Accomplice! You enabled that abuser!'

César   Jaime?

Lorena   'Are you still going to support your sleazebag father …?'

Adolfo   I have to go there and see them.

Lorena   No, Dad!

Isabel's *phone rings.*

Isabel (*looking at the screen*)   It's the newspaper.

César *receives a message.*

César   Ana's asking me where I am.

Lorena   Why?

César   They've gone downstairs, they're outside the theatre … Talking to the TV people, look. (*Shows her.*)

Isabel   TV people?

Adolfo   …

Isabel (*about her phone, which is still ringing*)   Should I pick up?

Lorena   No!

Isabel   We have to do something! (*Hangs up.*)

César (*to* **Adolfo**)   What you told me about Gauguin … Why did you need to show me that painting by Gauguin?

Adolfo   What are you talking about?

Lorena   What's this about Gauguin?

Isabel   Like at the Opera House … It can't be!

Lorena   Are we losing our minds?

César's *phone starts ringing. He picks up.*

Adolfo   But you do trust me, Lore, right?

Lorena   Don't worry, Dad.

César (*replying*)   No! Don't call me for that bullshit! (*Hangs up.*)

Lorena   What did they say?

César (*to* **Adolfo**)   They're demanding you go on camera and …

Lorena   And what?

César   And resign.

Isabel   I warned you, Adolfo! I warned you!

Isabel*'s cellphone sounds again. The tension outside grows.*

Adolfo   I have to show my face!

Lorena   You won't achieve anything by going out there.

Isabel (*about her phone*)   It's the head of the union.

César   They must have found out, they'll want to –

Adolfo   I have to go explain the truth to them!

Isabel (*picks up*)   Yes …? What?

César   Maybe it is a good idea you go out there and confess.

Lorena   Confess what?

César   Anything! Whatever they want to hear!

Isabel (*on the phone*)   No, I don't know!

Lorena (*to* **Adolfo**)   Explain what? They won't listen!

César (*looking at a photo that has just arrived to his cellphone*)   Even Norma had to stand with them, take their side.

Adolfo   Norma?

Isabel (*on the phone*)   I said I don't know! I didn't know anything! (*Suddenly hangs up.*)

César   They're all standing outside the theatre.

Lorena   Maybe they know you're in here now, that you didn't leave.

Adolfo   It's not fair that we have to go through this, Lore!

Lorena   What do we do?

Isabel (*almost raving*)   Everything that happened at the Opera House …

Adolfo   What is it they want?

César   For you to go out and admit your mistake!

Adolfo   And do you admit yours? Are you giving me lessons on morality, César?!

Lorena Stop it, please!

Isabel (*delirious*) My mistake ... Your mistake ...

Adolfo How could all those people who have been with me, who know me, support this kind of slander? They have not one shred of proof against me!

César What more proof do you want?

Lorena What did you do, Dad?

Adolfo I don't know, I don't know what I did! I'm not even sure what it is they're accusing me of!

Isabel Your carelessness, your pride, Adolfo.

Adolfo What are you saying?

Isabel The photo, the constant complaints from those girls, the interview, the cameras, your rudeness, your belligerence, your delusions of grandeur ... It's all mixed together!

Adolfo It's all smoke and mirrors! There's no proof against me!

Lorena Slander needs no proof!

Suddenly, a ghostly silence. Seven, eight seconds ...

Adolfo 'The dram of evil
Doth all the noble substance of a doubt
To his own scandal.'

The ruckus outside is heard again.

Adolfo Yes.

César ...

Adolfo They're there.

Isabel ...

Adolfo They're waiting for me.

Lorena ...

Adolfo I have to go out there.

The light on the characters grows more and more merciless.

Suddenly, blackout, and silence.

Glossary of Names and References

Antón Arrufat Mrad (1935–2023). Playwright and poet of Cuban and Lebanese heritage, winner in 2000 of the Cuban National Literature Prize. The same year that Padilla won the Writer's Union poetry award (1968), Arrufat won the theatre award with the play *Seven Against Thebes*. The play suffered the same fate as Padilla's book: both were published with a note from the Writers' Union opposing their content, causing Arrufat to be ostracized on the island for a long time. The play finally premiered in Cuba in 2007. *Outside the Game.*

Bad Memory. *La mala memoria*, an autobiographical essay, published in 1989. *Outside the Game.*

Boarding school. During the time when *Nevada* is set, it was extremely difficult for young people wishing to take the *bachillerato* – equivalent to high-school courses – to study in Cuba's towns or cities. While those undertaking vocational training were able to remain in urban environments, students taking 'pre-university' courses were required to attend rural boarding schools where, alongside their studies, they would work on the land. Having left military school, enrolling in such a boarding school is, in Lucía's view, Osmel's only remaining option. *Nevada.*

Bola de Nieve. Ignacio Jacinto Villa Fernández (1911–71), Cuban singer-songwriter, better known by his stage name, literally 'Snowball'. *Outside the Game.*

Caramel curds. *Dulce de leche cortada*, a very popular dessert in Cuba and across the Spanish-speaking Caribbean, is made by heating and curdling milk using citrus, sometimes flavoured with spices or dried fruit. *Nevada.*

Church of the Angel. Built in the seventeenth century, the church's full name is the *Iglesia del Santo Ángel Custodio*, the Church of the Holy Guardian Angel. Cuba's national hero José Martí was baptized there. *Chamaco.*

Commander. Fidel Castro (1926–2016), is frequently referred to in the play as *El Comandante*. Leader of the Cuban Revolution until his death, he is widely considered a dictator. *Outside the Game.*

Corín Tellado (1927–2009). A Spanish romance novelist with a prolific output whose many books (in the hundreds) became bestsellers across the Spanish-speaking world and were also widely translated. *Outside the Game.*

Cuatro Caminos market. Large shopping plaza in Havana, founded in 1920. Today it has fallen into disrepair. *Chamaco.*

Currency. For many years in Cuba, and particularly during the twenty-first century, the Cuban peso (CUP) existed alongside the US dollar. This was part of daily life in the country and as such is referred to by the characters with some frequency. For a long time, the dollar was illegal. In the 1990s, the Cuban state put into circulation an official currency 'equivalent' to the dollar, named the 'convertible peso' (CUC). However, foreign currency continued to circulate on the Island, albeit clandestinely. The evolution of the relationship between the value of the dollar and that of the increasingly devalued peso is a sign of the economic crisis that has permeated Cuba for decades. For example: at the time when *Chamaco* and *Nevada* were written (2004 and 2005, respectively), 1 dollar or 1 CUC was worth 25 Cuban pesos or CUP. The average prostitute could earn around 20 dollars with one or two clients in one night, that is, the same amount that a doctor would make in a month (500 CUP). At the same time, the cost of living was extraordinarily high: 2 dollars for a litre of cooking oil, 1 dollar for a soda, 25 dollars for a pair of shoes and so on. Over the years, inflation has skyrocketed. Currently, 1 dollar is worth around 300 CUP, and the cost of living has increased a great deal more. *Chamaco, Nevada, Weathered.*

El Capitolio. Built in 1929, the Capitol is the former seat of the Cuban Parliament and now a national landmark and symbol of the city. *Nevada.*

El Floridita. A well-known fish restaurant and cocktail bar, opened in 1817 and world famous thanks to Ernest Hemingway, who visited it regularly. *Chamaco.*

Grand Theatre. The magnificent *Gran Teatro de La Habana* is located on the Paseo del Prado, very close to Parque Central, El Capitolio and the Payret Cinema. The current building, in neo-baroque style, was inaugurated in 1915 as the headquarters of the Galician Centre of Havana. During the nineteenth century, the same location was the site of the legendary Teatro Tacón. *Chamaco.*

Granma. Founded in 1965, *Granma* was, and remains, the official news outlet of the central committee of the Communist Party of Cuba. It is named after the yacht that Fidel Castro, leading an expeditionary force of eighty-two fighters, set sail on from Mexico on 25 November 1956, landing on the Cuban coast on 2 December of the same year. The event marked the beginning of a guerrilla war that culminated in the triumph of the Cuban Revolution on 1 January 1959. *Outside the Game.*

Guillermo Cabrera Infante (1929–2005). Cuban writer and diplomat. Having supported the Revolution, he was appointed as Cuba's cultural attaché to Brussels in 1962, but later in the 1960s went into exile in Europe having been accused of counter-revolutionary activities. *Tres tristes tigres* (*Three Trapped Tigers*) was published in 1967. In 1964, it had won Spain's prestigious Seix Barral Biblioteca Breve Award but was banned in Cuba as counter-revolutionary and led to Cabrera being expelled from the Cuban Writers' and Artists' Union and labelled a traitor. *Outside the Game.*

Heroes Are Grazing in My Garden. *En mi jardín pastan los héroes*, a novel by Heberto Padilla, published in 1981. *Outside the Game.*

Glossary of Names and References   329

'I have black tears ...' From the song *Lágrimas negras*, composed by Cuban musician Miguel Matamoros in 1929, and first performed by Trío Matamoros. *Chamaco.*

Jorge Edwards (1931–2023). Novelist and diplomat from Chile. In 1971 he was appointed to the Chilean embassy in Cuba by the then Chilean president Salvador Allende, but was declared *persona non grata* by Fidel Castro shortly thereafter. He wrote a book entitled *Persona non grata*, published in 1973, based on his experiences in Cuba, which critiqued the Cuban regime. It went on to be banned in both Cuba and Chile. *Outside the Game.*

José Lezama Lima (1910–76). Cuban novelist, essayist and poet. His novel *Paradiso* is considered one of the best of all time in the Spanish language. *Outside the Game.*

La Revoltosa. A snack bar, almost a public canteen, one of the many popular shops where clients can buy cheap food, rum and cigarettes, drink coffee or eat pizza. Fictional. *Chamaco.*

'Let me believe in you ...' From the song *Déjame creer en ti*, performed by Olga Guillot, known in Cuba as the 'Queen of bolero'. *Chamaco.*

Letters to Anne Frank. *Cartas a Ana Frank*, a collection of poems by Belkis Cuza Malé, published in 1966. *Outside the Game.*

Louvre Arcade. Under the arcades of the Inglaterra Hotel can be found one of the best-known cafes in Havana, directly opposite Parque Central, just a few steps from the Grand Theatre and El Capitolio. *Chamaco.*

Malecón. The iconic promenade, built between 1901 and 1958, that stretches along the north coast of Havana for eight kilometres. *Chamaco, Nevada, Weathered.*

Manuel Díaz Martínez (1936–2023). Cuban poet, journalist and diplomat, exiled in Spain since the 1990s. *Outside the Game.*

'Martina, little cockroach, prettiest by far. / Knowing I'm not pretty, I thank you even more. / Martina, little cockroach, will you be my wife?' From a children's story entitled *La cucarachita Martina* (*Martina, the Little Cockroach*). *Chamaco.*

Microfraction. *Microfracción* was a term created in the late 1960s by the Cuban government to label a group of Communist party members, who had been members of the Popular Socialist Party, who openly criticized Castro's leadership for being increasingly authoritarian and argued for closer ties with the USSR. After their arrest and summary trials, the members of the microfraction were harshly condemned, in what to this day is one of the darkest and most violent episodes of the Castro dictatorship. *Outside the Game.*

Moving house. From the first years of the Cuban Revolution and until 2012, selling and buying houses was prohibited in the country. There existed, in fact, no legal way to do so. The habitual mechanism that was established was that of *permutas*, or house-swaps, whereby families would live together in a single building, or divide a property into two or more dwellings, depending on their needs. Given the clear inequalities of many of these exchanges in terms of the quality of the properties (owing to their size, state of repair or location), these operations were often accompanied by clandestine payments between the home-owners, as well as bribes to the government workers who would ensure that the transactions appeared legal. *Nevada, Weathered.*

Nicolás Guillén (1902–89). Cuban writer, journalist and communist activist, winner in 1983 of the Cuban National Literature Prize. At the time when *Outside the Game* is set, and up until his death, Guillén was president of the Cuban Writers' Union. *Outside the Game.*

Norberto Fuentes (b. 1943). Cuban writer and journalist. He was one of the writers accused by Padilla in his forced confession. Having been close to Castro for decades, he eventually left Cuba in exile in 1994. *Outside the Game.*

Paradiso. The only novel completed and published during the lifetime of its author, the Cuban writer José Lezama Lima. Although published during the Revolution (1966), it was set before it and contained gay themes, leading to controversy and its eventual banning. It is now widely read throughout the Spanish-speaking world. *Outside the Game.*

Park of Lies. A nickname derived from the fact that this green square is located directly opposite the former Presidential Palace, which today houses the Museum of the Revolution. *Chamaco.*

Parque Central. Not to be confused with its New York namesake, Parque Central is by comparison a relatively small green square on the edges of Habana Vieja (Old Havana). It is lined on all four sides by streets and arcaded buildings comprising mainly hotels, theatres and cinemas. One of its sides is part of the Paseo del Prado. It is also very close to El Capitolio. *Chamaco.*

Paseo del Prado. Also known as the Paseo de Martí, this is a wide, long thoroughfare that slices through central Havana at the edge of the area known as Habana Vieja (Old Havana), from the Fuente de la India (India Fountain) to the Malecón. *Chamaco.*

Payret Cinema. Inaugurated in 1877, the *Cine Payret* owes its name to its promoter and first owner, the Catalan Joaquín Payret. Since then, it has been one of the most iconic cinema theatres in Havana and a symbol of nightlife. Located on the Paseo del Prado, next to Parque Central and El Capitolio, it has suffered years of abandonment and neglect by the authorities. It is currently closed and its demolition has been announced. *Chamaco, Nevada.*

Popular Socialist Party. Founded in 1925, the *Partido Socialista Popular* was a Cuban Communist party that supported the Cuban Revolution in 1959. In 1962 it was integrated into the United Party of the Socialist Revolution of Cuba, itself replaced as the single party in 1965 by the Communist Party of Cuba. *Outside the Game.*

Provocations. *Provocaciones*, a collection of poems by Heberto Padilla, published in 1973. *Outside the Game.*

Santa María beach. One of the most popular beaches on the east coast of Havana. *Weathered.*

Saratoga Hotel. Built in 1880 as a warehouse, remodelled as a hotel in 1933 and reopened in 2005, the Saratoga is an icon of Havana. Its terrace bar, *Aires libres*, was an important cultural space for much of the twentieth century. In 2022, an explosion at the hotel caused severe damage and dozens of deaths. It is now permanently closed. *Nevada.*

Shared cab. During the fuel crisis of the 1990s, cabs shared by several people proliferated in Havana. Known by locals as *taxis* or *boteros*, they followed specific routes along which passengers could board or alight. *Chamaco, Nevada.*

Sławomir Mrożek (1930–2013). Polish dramatist, writer and cartoonist, particularly recognized for exploring human behaviour, alienation and the abuse of power of totalitarian systems. *Outside the Game.*

Sóngoro Cosongo. A classic poetry collection published in 1931 by the Cuban writer and Communist activist Nicolás Guillén. *Sóngoro Cosongo*, like many of Guillén's works, drew on the author's mixed African and Spanish ancestry, fusing Hispanic and West African literary styles. *Outside the Game.*

Square under Siege. *Plaza sitiada*, a novel by Norberto Fuentes, published in 2018. *Outside the Game.*

Statue of the hero. This refers to the hero *par excellence* in Cuba: José Martí (1853–95), poet, writer and politician; one of the protagonists of the movement for national independence. *Chamaco.*

Union of Young Communists. Based on earlier organizations, the *Unión de Jóvenes Comunistas* was founded in 1962. Admission to it is selective for young people between fifteen and thirty years old. *Outside the Game.*

Urbino's Passion. *Pasión de Urbino*, a novel by Cuban writer and Communist diplomat Lisandro Otero (1932–2008), published in 1966. The author won the Cuban National

Literature Prize in 2002. Padilla's article describes the book as 'a leap into banality'. *Outside the Game.*

Villa Marista. A former Catholic seminary on the outskirts of Havana, Villa Marista was taken over by the Revolutionary government in 1963 and converted into a prison and interrogation centre, the headquarters of the Cuban State Security service. It remains in use today. *Outside the Game.*

Writers' Union or ***Writers' and Artists' Union of Cuba.*** Founded in 1961, the purpose of the *Unión de Escritores y Artistas de Cuba* (UNEAC) was to unite intellectuals within the framework of the Cuban Revolution, to maintain, strengthen and expand Cuban culture. *Outside the Game.*

Author and Translator Bios

Abel González Melo was born in Havana in 1980. He is a writer, theatre director and academic.

Since his successful début as a playwright with *Chamaco* (*Kiddo*) at the Teatro Nacional de Cuba, his plays have been produced and published in over twenty countries, translated into twelve languages and the recipient of multiple awards. These include *En busca de La Peregrina* (*In Search of La Peregrina*, BBVA Leonardo Grant, 2022), *Intemperie* (*Weathered*, City of Santa Clara Foundation Award, 2021), *Bayamesa* (Casa de las Américas International Award, 2020), *Epopeya* (Virgilio Piñera National Playwriting Award, 2014), *Mecánica* (*Inner Workings*, Writers' and Artists' Union of Cuba Award, 2014), *Talco* (*Talc*, Goethe Institute Cuba-Germany Play Award, 2009), *Ataraxia* (*Ataraxy*, Calendario Award, 2008), *El hábito y la virtud* (*Habit and Virtue*, Calendario Award, 2005), *Adentro* (*Within*, José Jacinto Milanés Award, 2005) and *Ubú sin cuernos* (*Ubu without Horns*, José Jacinto Milanés Award, 2002). *Chamaco* was the recipient of the 2005 Spanish Embassy in Cuba Award.

He has on three occasions won the Cuban Literary Critics' Award and is the five-time recipient of the Villanueva Theatre Critics' Award. His volume of essays *Festín de los patíbulos: poéticas teatrales y tensión social* (*Feast of the Gallows: Theatre Poetics and Social Tension*) won the 2009 Alejo Carpentier Award, and in Madrid he received the 2012 Cultura Viva Award for his collected literary works, including short stories and poetry.

He holds a PhD in Literary Studies and an MA in Theatre and Performing Arts from the Complutense University of Madrid and a BA in Theatre Arts from ISA, the University of the Arts, Havana. He was a participant in the 2005 Royal Court Theatre international playwrights residency in London (where he wrote *Nevada*) and studied with Panorama Sur in Buenos Aires and at the Maxim Gorki Theatre in Berlin. Since 2010 he has been director of the Carlos III University theatre company in Madrid.

Since 2006 he has been a member of the Cuban theatre company Argos Teatro, where seven of his plays have premiered – including *Protocolo* (*Protocol*, 2016) and *Sistema* (*System*, 2017) – and where he has directed works by Juan Mayorga, Josep Maria Miró and Sergio Blanco. In 2015–16 he was playwright in residence at HOME, Manchester (where he wrote *Weathered*), and since 2018 he has been playwright in residence at Teatro Avante in the United States, where his works including *Disonancia* (*Dissonance*, 2024), *Mejor me callo* (*I'd Better Shut Up*, 2022), *Ubú Pandemia* (*Pandemic Ubu*, 2021), *Bayamesa* (2019) and *En ningún lugar del mundo* (*Nowhere in the World*, 2018) have been premiered at the prestigious Miami International Hispanic Theatre Festival. Other plays include *Fuera del juego* (*Outside the Game*, Grec Festival of Barcelona, 2021), *Cádiz en José Martí* (*Cadiz in José Martí*, Cadiz Ibero-American Theatre Festival, 2020), *Abismo* (*Abyss*, 2022) and *Vuelve a contármelo todo* (*Tell Me the Whole Thing Again*, 2021), the latter two premiering at the Miami-Dade County Auditorium. His screenwriting credits include the screenplay *La partida* (*The Last Match*, 2013) and the film adaptation of *Chamaco* (2010).

Since 2022 he has been artistic associate at the Teatro de La Abadía, Madrid, incorporating his role as artistic coordinator of the Alcalá de Henares Corral de Comedias, an iconic, original Spanish Golden Age theatre, first opened in 1602, where he has himself directed classic works by Miguel de Cervantes and Pedro Calderón de la Barca.

William Gregory is a translator, theatre practitioner, educator and, at the time of writing (February 2024), Interim Literary Associate at the Royal Court Theatre, London. His translations of plays for the Royal Court have included *A Fight Against…* by Pablo Manzi, *B* by Guillermo Calderón, *Villa* and *Speech* by Guillermo Calderón (later produced by Prime Cut, Belfast, and Play Company, New York), *The Concert* by Ulises Rodríguez Febles (later produced by BBC Radio Drama), numerous plays for the Royal Court *New Plays from Chile, Cuba Real, Arena Mexico* and *The Big Idea: PIIGS* seasons and multiple works in development with Royal Court playwriting workshops throughout the Spanish-speaking world.

Other productions of his translations have included *The Bit-Players* by José Sanchis Sinisterra (Southwark Playhouse, London), *I'd Rather Goya Robbed Me of My Sleep than Some Other Arsehole* by Rodrigo García (Gate, London; Théâtre Excentrique, Sydney), *Chamaco (Kiddo)* and *Weathered* by Abel González Melo (HOME, Manchester), *Cuzco* by Víctor Sánchez Rodríguez (Theatre503, London), *An American Life* by Lucía Carballal (Cervantes Theatre, London) and numerous works as staged readings for festivals including Out of the Wings and CASA (London), the International Voices Project (Chicago) and the Columbia International Playwriting Festival (New York).

His published translations include *The Oberon Anthology of Contemporary Spanish Plays* (finalist, Valle-Inclán Award for literary translation from Spanish, 2019), *Poor Men's Poetry* by Juan Ignacio Fernández and *Nou Fiuter (No Future)* by Franco Calluso (both in *The Oberon Anthology of Contemporary Argentinian Plays*), *The Children of Taltal* by Bosco Israel Cayo Álvarez (Laertes Press), *The Widow of Apablaza* by Germán Luco Cruchaga (Inti Press), *The Peasants Walk the Pathways* by Pablo Antonio Cuadra (Inti Press), *An Isolated Incident* by Antonio M. López (Perpetuum), *A Young Swallowman* by Laura Santos (Policarpo Q.), *The Bread and the Salt* by Raúl Quirós (Performance Books) and *The Uncapturable*, a collection of essays by the Argentinian theatre director Rubén Szuchmacher (Methuen).

As an educator he has designed and facilitated theatre translation workshops for the London-based theatre company Foreign Affairs, the University of Kent *Performing International Plays* project, *Bristol Translates* at the University of Bristol and the Royal Court, where he led the theatre's first-ever *Introduction to Translation* programme in 2022. He has facilitated the theatre strand at the long-running British Centre for Literary Translation (BCLT, University of East Anglia) summer school since its first appearance there in 2020.

He is a visiting research associate at King's College London and a former committee member of the Translators' Association of Great Britain. In 2020–21 he was joint inaugural BCLT Translator in Residence and in 2018 was inaugural Translator in Residence at the Arniches Theatre, Alicante, Spain. Since 2015 he has been a member of Out of the Wings, a theatre collective promoting and platforming the playwriting of the Spanish- and Portuguese-speaking worlds and its translation into English.

Originally from Grimsby in the north of England, he now lives in London.